Pedagogy in Practice is quite a masterful guidepost to more active and engaging media studies/governance courses, programmes and activities that will sharpen your project-based learning competencies, confidences and communications. If you're a media studies educator, simply immerse yourself in any page and walk away with a whole new vision of what transformative learning in the twenty-first century can really look like.

Professor Curtis J. Bonk, Professor of Instructional Systems Technology, Indiana University, USA

Pedagogy in Practice fills an important gap in the current pedagogical literature. Media literacy, together with media policy and governance, has emerged as one of the most salient issues of our time, critical to understanding the formation of public opinion and to the survival of democracy itself. Meanwhile, project-based learning is recognised as one of the best pedagogical tools available for engaging students. These are combined effectively in this book, which provides the perfect tool for teachers to understand and educate others about media-related issues. I would like to offer my congratulations to the authors on the creation of this practical, clear and helpful guide.

Professor Sung Kyum Cho, Former President, Korean Society for Journalism and Communication Studies, South Korea

Pedagogy in Practice is a smartly edited and indispensable volume for those studying Indian media analysis, news mapping, market structure of cultural industries, regulatory policy shifts and media governance. The different chapters have a wealth of hands-on pedagogic advice for teaching at the MA and PhD levels. Faculty will find it innovative, practical, comprehensive and stimulating. For serious students, the world of contemporary mass media is a place for big ideas and controversies about citizen activism, diversity and individual rights. The authors have done a first-rate job in providing a roadmap to this complex policy universe and the latest in innovative teaching methods. One of its best features is that it provides the tools for students and policy experts to acquire a critical view of the far-ranging impact of media studies in contemporary times.

Professor Daniel Drache, Professor Emeritus, Department of Politics, York University, Toronto, Canada

This is an interesting and timely publication and provides valuable insights on evidence-based teaching and active learning strategies. It will help strengthen, standardise and innovate pedagogical practices in media studies and can be used and adapted in any classroom setting including higher education and professional studies. I see this book as being of great value to educational leaders and pedagogues across the world.

Dr Sheila Jagannathan, Global Head, Open Learning Campus, World Bank, Washington, DC, USA

Rarely one finds a book that combines the best of pedagogy in a disciplinary context. *Pedagogy in Practice* is one such publication that presents reflective practitioners' documentation of adopting project-based learning in media education. Set in the context of media policy and governance in India, and a larger project on developing conceptual framework and pedagogic analysis on the subject, the book provides lived-in experiences of the authors supported with sound theoretical perspectives on designing and implementing hands-on projects and workshops to prepare media professionals and researchers. The editors of the book bring together their extensive experiences of teaching and research on education and media to provide a balanced contribution on theory and practice of teaching and learning in media education.

Dr Sanjaya Mishra, Director (Education), Commonwealth of Learning, Vancouver, Canada

Timely, comprehensive, rigorous and practically engaged, this volume should be read by students, educators and media policy analysts, both in classrooms and beyond, across Asia and the Global South.

Professor Jack Linchuan Qiu, Research Director, Department of Communications and New Media, National University of Singapore, Singapore

Pedagogy in Practice

Pedagogy in Practice

Project-Based Learning in Media Policy and Governance

Biswajit Das, Santosh Panda
and Vibodh Parthasarathi

BLOOMSBURY
NEW DELHI • LONDON • OXFORD • NEW YORK • SYDNEY

BLOOMSBURY INDIA
Bloomsbury Publishing India Pvt. Ltd
Second Floor, LSC Building No. 4, DDA Complex, Pocket C – 6 & 7,
Vasant Kunj, New Delhi, 110070

BLOOMSBURY, BLOOMSBURY ACADEMIC INDIA and the Diana logo
are trademarks of Bloomsbury Publishing Plc

First published in India 2022
This edition published 2022

Bloomsbury Academic
An imprint of Bloomsbury Publishing Plc

ISBN: HB: 978-93-54358-47-0; eBook: 978-93-54359-68-2

2 4 6 8 10 9 7 5 3 1

Typeset in Minion pro by Manipal Technologies Limited
Printed and bound in India by Replika Press Pvt. Ltd

Contents

List of Tables

List of Figures

Foreword

Media education is an important topic, and this book will contribute significantly to its improvement. Not long ago, academics in traditional disciplines, not only in humanities and sciences but also in the social sciences, regarded media studies as a trivial subject—something of a joke. Media and communications were 'soft' subjects for students who lacked the brain or the motivation to engage with a 'real' discipline.

Yet today, our rapidly evolving media environment has a massive impact on daily life, from the behaviour of individuals to the decisions of governments. Even in this fast-changing world, the speed of developments in media and communications technologies and their applications is breathtaking. In their lifetimes, the authors have seen the arrival of the 24/7 news cycle, the multiplication of television channels, the rise and decline of national and local newspapers, the explosion of social media (and a growing appreciation of their anti-social impact), the emergence of the platform-based economy, mobile telephony and the advances of digitisation.

These developments have upended cultural, economic and political assumptions about how media should be organised and regulated, leading to extensive fragmentation in the structure of policymaking in the media and communications industry. Policymaking is being conducted with little objective input from independent sources outside government and industry.

This book aims to enhance such sources by improving media education. It is focussed particularly on India but draws on global scholarship and research conclusions that have worldwide relevance. The study was made possible by a Ford Foundation grant to Jamia Millia Islamia, which is renowned for its Centre for Culture, Media and Governance. The development and offering of a master's degree in media and governance provided much of the material for this book. Designing this programme gave the authors the chance to bridge the gap between practice-based and theoretically informed courses, neither of which alone provides appropriate training for professionals in today's complex media environment. It also allowed them to highlight the centrality of governance in understanding the present media environment and ensure that the relationship between media and governance is understood in both instrumental and transactional terms.

Against this background, the introductory chapter of the book explores the field of media policy and governance and gives a rounded account of the design and application of the strategy of project-based learning for media policy analysis in media studies and governance. It is followed by two chapters presenting the foundation for the book and describing the field of media education and pedagogies in practice. Four chapters then use the understanding of these basic concepts to engage with four cases of media policy and governance analysis. The two final chapters look to the future, making recommendations for the professional development of media educators and exploring pedagogy and technology in the future of media education.

The four cases of media policy and governance analysis are described in admirable detail. Each of them ends with a hands-on project to make the bridge between theory and practice, which is the overriding aim of the book. The first course, Media and Politics, enumerates media diversity. The second, Introduction to Media Economics, explores the market structure, ownership and industry to deepen the understanding of the working and organisation of media markets. A course on Policy Research and Evaluation follows, which gives students tools for document analysis in media policy research and enhances their understanding of the process of policy formulation and analysis. The fourth case, Regulation and Theory in Practice, maps shifts in policy regulation. In all four cases, the course objectives, the curriculum and the hands-on projects are described in sufficient detail to be very helpful to those developing similar courses elsewhere.

This book is a powerful antidote to the view that media and communications are marginal topics for academic study. I write this foreword at a moment when, in many parts of the world, our shared reality is under assault. The authors insist throughout that democracy relies on evidence-based information. However, bad-faith actors and misguided believers of their lies have broken that societal norm. A major military conflict in Europe was initiated by Russia after continued distortions of history, and disinformation had misled a population whose access to independent media is savagely controlled.

In my own country, Canada, blockades of vehicles besieged the capital city, Ottawa, for three weeks, allegedly to protest the requirements in both Canada and the US for truck drivers crossing the border between the two countries to be vaccinated against Covid-19. But, as columnist Andrew Coyne has argued in 'Our Shared Reality is Under Threat' (*Globe and Mail* 2022, 11), the blockades were merely the symptom. The disease is disinformation. Large numbers of citizens can be made to believe almost anything, which is a huge challenge to our democracy—a challenge all the greater because we are reluctant to acknowledge it. If lots of people are upset about something, we assume they must have reasons. We are taught that there are usually two sides to every question, which is mostly a good rule to follow. We should, however, avoid the mistake of thinking that any belief is worth discussing just because many hold it. There are not two sides to whether the earth is flat, even though millions think it is.

The Ottawa blockade movement and similar campaigns around the world bring together various counterfactual ideas. They are opposed to science, authority and expertise of all kinds—in a word, knowledge. This is not, for Coyne, simply a set of individual deficiencies but rather a collective failure of socialisation. People have detached themselves not only from the behavioural norms of civil society but also from the whole transmission chain by which knowledge is spread among the population. Knowledge is a social process. We form our beliefs with the help of those around us, often through the communications media, thus absorbing the accumulated wisdom of society. We cannot individually relitigate every elementary fact of human knowledge every day.

But this process is now breaking down. Instead of being transmitted vertically, knowledge is moving horizontally. Some protest movements are described as class wars, but today they are class wars of a particular kind, where the dividing line is not money or birth but knowledge. This means that today's class warriors are not out to smash physical and financial capital assets as their predecessors once did. Since capital now resides in knowledge, they seek to undermine knowledge itself and its repositories: the universities, the courts and the media. All these are not merely fallible but hostile enemies of the people, filled with lies—with facts they refuse to believe.

Such class warriors must then try to make sense of the world unaided, doing their own 'research' on the internet and sharing their findings with each other on social media. This makes them defenceless and vulnerable to bad actors seeking to manipulate them. This, writes Coyne, is the other and more disturbing discovery that we are making. Not merely how easily part of the population can be made to believe the most egregious lies, but how willing certain people are to tell those lies. These people know exactly what they are doing. They know that they are spreading falsehoods and validating lunacy, crossing lines previously considered uncrossable, but they no longer care.

How do we protect democracies against the widespread assault on our shared reality that Coyne describes? We cannot expect the media to wage the fight alone. But by showing the way to train media practitioners, owners and scholars by blending theory and practice effectively in real-world projects, this book gives us better defences. A generation ago, media studies was often considered a 'breeze' subject. Today, thanks to books like this, it can take centre stage in the vital project of constructing humane knowledge societies and bring evidence-based pedagogy to the centre stage of curriculum and teaching.

Sir John Daniel
Chancellor, Acsenda School of Management, Canada;
Former Vice Chancellor, Laurentian University, Canada; The Open University, UK; Assistant Director General, UNESCO, Paris; and President, Commonwealth of Learning, Canada

Acknowledgements

The editors would like to thank the following persons and acknowledge their contributions therein:

1. Dr Raveena Aggarwal, programme officer of the Ford Foundation, Delhi, for funding this innovative research project Mapping Media Policy and Law (2010–2013), the outcomes of which form the basis of Chapters 4 to 7 in this book.
2. Project officials (Nahid, Sushrita and Jitha) of the Ford Foundation project at the Centre for Culture, Media and Governance, Jamia Millia Islamia (JMI), New Delhi.
3. Professor Saima Saeed, honorary director and faculty member at the Centre for Culture, Media and Governance, JMI, for extending support as well as active participation during the project.
4. Athikho Kaisii, Pradosh Nath and Debolina Mukherjee for conducting the workshops.
5. Sincere thanks to the Ford Foundation fellows at the Centre for Culture, Media and Governance: Professor Santosh Panda, director, STRIDE, IGNOU, New Delhi; Professor K.D. Rao, vice chancellor, National Law University, New Delhi; Anindya Choudhary, fellow, NISTADAT, for their active engagement and contribution towards the deliverables of this project.
6. Students and research scholars of CCMG (JMI) for their creative ideas and participation.
7. Ridhi Kakkar, research scholar, CCMG, for preparing tables, charts, diagrams and formatting the chapters of the manuscript.
8. Shayeree Ghosh for preparing the references and Ghulam Hussain for redrawing figures, tables and diagrams.
9. Guneet Kaur for meticulously copy-editing the manuscript.
10. The CPEPA project staff for supporting the progress and following up on the manuscript.
11. The librarians and staff members of the Centre for Culture, Media and Governance and Nehru Memorial and Museum Library, Teen Murti House, New Delhi, for their generous support.

Section 1

Media Education and Media Pedagogy

1

Introduction: Designing Media Policy and Governance

Santosh Panda, Biswajit Das and Vibodh Parthasarathi

The objective of this book is to showcase the application of evidence-based teaching and learning strategies in the discipline of media and communication studies with specific reference to project-based learning (i.e., hands-on projects) on media policy analysis. This is in line with India's National Education Policy (NEP) 2020 that significantly emphasises activity-based, application-oriented and constructivist learning over the often-practised traditional concept-based rote learning. The book intends to translate theoretical ideas and knowledge in the light of new pedagogic developments and effective learning and teaching designs that can be taken up in any classroom setting and applied to any curriculum in higher and further education. Precise but comprehensive reviews have been undertaken in Chapters 2 and 3 on 'pedagogy and teaching-learning strategies' and 'media education', respectively, as a basis to re-examine innovative instructional and learning designs for disciplinary teachings. Accordingly, practising educators of media education and new media studies will authentically report on work-based projects as pedagogy as well as teaching and learning practices for transacting curriculum at the master's level. They also demonstrate how pedagogic interventions can ease learners and instructors to make teaching and learning convenient and engaging. The book underscores project-based learning (PBL) as one of the best practices for teaching media policy and delivering a practical experience to students to learn policy formulations, foundations, shifts and challenges. In short, it may be called a reference book for hands-on projects on media policy analysis. It is also envisioned as a resource book for similar academic initiatives. It will be useful in curricula across the disciplines of media studies, law and other social sciences.

Studying Media Policy and Governance

Policy studies, as a subdiscipline, has received critical acclaim and has become, as a concept, an instrument in the organisation of contemporary societies. One needs to problematise policy not only as a concept but also as a set of associated practices (Shore and Wright 1997; Wedel et al. 2005). Policies impinge on all aspects of our lives. They are difficult to ignore as it is impossible to escape their influence. Studying policies allows us to move beyond regarding them as being a given to the question of meaning or ontological status as a category (Shore 2012).

The study of the impact and art of policymaking helps us clarify problems and gives us an incentive to resolve, manage and regulate institutions and individuals in general (Wedel et al. 2005). As Greenhalgh (2008) highlights, the problematisation of policies helps us to explore social relationships, identities and practices through institutional intervention.

Policies are viewed by governments as an instrument for regulating society through the mechanism of reward and sanction. They become a purely technical, rational and action-oriented instrument used by policymakers to address problems. But the instrumentalist notion of *policy* has shortcomings in understanding policies that may have a variable impact on individuals and societies in myriads of ways. The advent of globalisation has made the policy space a level playing field where 'the loss of the nation-state's autonomy happens in relation to the expansion of regional and local governance structures, as national governments decentralize governance of local networks that serve as links to a larger global economy' (Chakravartty and Sarikakis 2006, 37).

The term *governance* here provides a better way of engaging with the complex dimension of policy that addresses the intent of policymaking and implementation and the beneficiary's interest and involvement in policymaking. 'Indian media sector too witnessed significant changes as a result of government policies during the last four decades with the rise of 24/7 news cycle, television channels, newspapers (both English and regional), social media, the emergence of platform-based economy, mobile telephony and advancement in digitisation processes; thereby, transforming into a more competitive and more vulnerable economy of media production and delivery that subsequently have changed the landscape of media in India' (Das and

Kakkar 2020, 28). However, Parthasarathi talks about 'the need to recognise the regulatory, organisational, and cultural conditions under but not the least governance processes. At present, we only have some scattered accounts of bureaucratic strategies in hands to depicting the influence of communication-media over behaviours of actors/experts in governance' (2018, 28–29). This confusion arises because the shifts in media policies engulfing India since 1991 have been guided neither by creating the necessary knowledge nor market-related institutions. Instead, they are guided by a policy framework on the state that can best be described as strategic neglect. Consequently, there is extensive fragmentation at all levels in the structure of policymaking in the media and communication industry. Media policymaking has thus been conducted without adequate input from independent quarters outside government and industry (Das and Parthasarathi 2011).

While engaging with media policy, we notice that it deals exclusively with news and cultural production, content curation and distribution, and information services to individuals. Conventionally, media policy was defined within the rubrics of legacy media: print, television, radio and cinema; it did not include telecommunication policy into account (Pool 1983). But the recent digitisation process has rendered the division obsolete, thanks to technological convergence. Price, Puppis and Verhulst (2013) rightly point out that the margins separating other policy-related fields, such as communications policy, telecommunications policy, information technology (IT) policy as well as cultural policy, are readily getting porous because of constant digitisation and converging as well as how the globalisation of new communications technologies overshadow conventional technological and regulatory distinctions. Similarly, Napoli writes, '[I]n the communications field there are a large number of somewhat indistinct policy arenas that overlap with the media policy field, each employing distinctive terminologies and each reflecting somewhat different areas of emphasis' (2007, 2).

Besides, it is equally important to engage and understand media policy within the larger context of a media milieu that could grapple with issues of regulation, infrastructures, access and culture (McQuail 1992).

Even though there are disagreements among scholars on the nomenclature—whether to name it communication policy or information policy—according to Puppis, the term *media policy* has a better purchase to address and understand media organisations, mediated interactions and questions of technology and infrastructure. Although terms such as *media policy* and *media regulation* are used interchangeably, there is a substantial difference between the two. The former refers to the paradigms that inform policy and the latter to the implementation process and governance (Van den Bulck 2018). While reflecting upon wider concerns within the framework of media policy, what probably can be expected is that this particular field has tremendous diversity in terms of methodological approaches. For instance, historical research has examined the relationships between stakeholders across diverse media policy-related issues with updated contemporary policy discussions (McChesney 1993; Horwitz 1989).

On the one hand, effective research focuses on older policy deliberations, such as the concern related to the regulation of indecent content and issues related to the development of learning content for kids. On the other, research on audience behaviour highlights media consumption dynamics in ways that envisioned informing policymaking associated with both conventional and new technologies (Webster 2005; Hindman 2007). Content studies have attempted to explore the correlations between media markets, larger media establishments and contents offered by such institutions for informing policymakers about the regulation of ownerships, contents and allocations of licenses (Hamilton 2000).

All these diverse methodological approaches construct economic and legal analyses that provide an analytical core towards media policymaking despite constant criticisms that policymakers tend to neglect cultural and political concerns that form the basis of media policy (Stucke and Grunes 2001; Baker 2001). One persistent trend about the collaboration between media policy and the communication field is that the field in itself is largely discontented with the extent to which policy debates have been shaping up. This shift reflects a much larger tension between the cultural or political policy objectives and the economic, which has characterised policymaking in the media. The cultural or political policy objectives may include a diversity of viewpoints and the media system that supports local communities' needs, while the economic policy objectives may include goals like competition and consumer satisfaction (Entman and Wildman 1992). Interestingly, in the last three decades, the extent of economic policy objectives has been found to gain substantive priority among media policymakers (Van Cuilenburg and McQuail 2003). The discipline of communication has experienced some level of marginalisation in policymaking, although the discipline's proficiency lies in the cultural and political realms rather than in the economic. When the media policy field and its theoretical foundations are explored, the significance of cultural and political policy objectives clarify the questions on the relevance of contemporary policies (Napoli 2001).

The association between the media, society and the state is a fundamental part of any deliberation on media policy. Such discussions contribute to diverse sets of ideas or paradigms, which vary in their perspectives and orientations (Hall 1992; Künzler 2012; Napoli 2001). Napoli (2007) highlights that the scope and boundary of media policy may not be addressed through technology or its dynamics; instead, it should be addressed with the help of substantive communicative issues. This is further endorsed by Braman (2004), who defines the field in terms of issues related to freedom of expression. Further, McQuail (1992) states that the media policy field is founded on the cultural and political dimensions of communicative practices.

Accordingly, scholars highlight that the liberal paradigm encourages the principles of free market and commercialisation of the media system whereas the social responsibility paradigm gives prominence to the role of the state and emphasises public service media organisations and grants for the press. Hence, it becomes quite clear that media policy is a challenging field of inquiry, where ideas, norms, assumptions, conduct and structure inform the media that is in operation. Moreover, it also helps frame and applies rules as a collective step for giving a dimension and shape to media institutions (Freedman 2008; Puppis et al. 2016). Thus, a media policy is concerned with the productivity of policymaking and involves framing and enacting rules for various stakeholders involved in making and managing policies (Freedman 2008). Furthermore, the participation of multistakeholders confirms the need for restructuring state functions from a consolidated view of government to a diversification of its interest. Such an arrangement requires a strong partnership among several agencies and institutions, governmental and non-governmental (Jessop 1999). Other research asserts that the concept of media regulation has a narrow focus, especially when media policymaking becomes an overarching concept (Freedman 2008; Puppis et al. 2016).

Media policies are framed by several normative theoretical constructs that are open to interpretation. Interestingly, such theories provide the foundations for assessing the performance of media organisations and shaping policies for enhancing the overall performance of the media system (McQuail 1992). The criteria for assessing media performance vary in different contexts; however, the core principles may be seen as the central building block for framing effective media policy and guiding media policy research. As Napoli (2007) underscores, three strands govern the discussions on media policy, which are as follows:

Free Speech

Free speech can be described as one of the principal definitional constituents of media policy. In the global context, the right to speak freely might not always be as clearly articulated as observed in some of the recent free speech movements. For instance, the First Amendment to the US Constitution guarantees freedom of speech; the analogues can be found in several international contexts (Youm 2002). The centrality of free speech as the basis of media policy principles develops from the fundamental function wherein mediated communication aids in democratic procedures. Free speech guarantees free flow and widespread dissemination of opinions and ideas necessary for creating a well-informed community (Fiss 1996). All these show the significant role of free speech in media policymaking, which is firmly entwined with the role of the media in any democratic system (Sunstein 1995).

Media policymaking is both enabled and controlled, at the same time, by the principle of free speech. This idea of empowerment is taken from the concept that media policies are committed to enhancing communication opportunities for the larger citizenry. Policy efforts aimed at maximising broadband utilisation and efforts for diversifying media ownership are premised mostly on maintaining a vast distribution of equal communication opportunities (Baker 2007). Such constraints exist because media policies are mostly directed towards improving speech opportunities for the larger community but, possibly, invade individual speech rights. For example, efforts at diversifying media ownership for augmenting free speech might also end up imposing individual rights to free speech, including those of media owners (Napoli 2001; Parthasarathi 2021).

This paradoxical situation explains the central tension in the role of free speech in media policymaking and free-speech rights on policymakers. This tension is specifically illustrated by the present state of the US broadcasting directive, which is based on the idea that the speech rights of audiences are as important as the rights of the speakers in the technological and institutional frameworks in which the media functions (Barron 1967). It is on these grounds that a wide range of content is being regulated.

Public Interest

Public interest as an idea has a very long and argumentative history in the context of media policymaking (Napoli 2001). The relative uncertainty of the term is undoubtedly the chief reason why the concept has such an argumentative history. This idea of public interest serves as the fundamental benchmark for the assessment of media policies. This normative principle has become the standard that many policymakers expect to adhere to while making decisions. Generally, policy decisions should not just imitate the interests of individual communities but reflect awareness about the outcomes of the policies that will eventually serve the larger populace.

According to McQuail (1992), the notion of public interest is rooted within a vast array of normative criteria extending from competition, diversity, objectivity to access. This concept is well invested across nations (Hitchens 2006; McQuail 1992) and has acquired variations over time as technological conditions and regulatory principles changed (Aufderheide 1999; Van Cuilenburg and McQuail 2003). Variations can also occur at any time across diverse stakeholders who contribute to the concept becoming argumentative within policy debates. It is imperative to note that the concept of public interest has served conventionally as a normative guide for policymakers and media establishments in decision-making to a certain extent. The contribution has been to the extent that cultural and political dimensions of the media's institutional performance have been beyond the concerns of revenues and profits (Napoli 2001). Hence, the concept of public interest signifies a direct mechanism through which researchers, media critics and policymakers can aptly assess and give judgement regarding the performance of an individual or collective media market.

Marketplace of Ideas

The concept of the *marketplace of ideas* and the importance of media policy in promoting and safeguarding it are where the pressures between political or cultural and economic foundations for media policymaking have been noticed. The metaphor signifies the comprehensive conceptualisation of media policy as both a field of academic analysis and professional practice. It is also considered the guiding metaphor from which various analytical perspectives for developing media policies have mostly originated. Hence, the notion of the marketplace of ideas, like the other theoretical constructs discussed, is subjected to multiple yet potentially conflicting interpretations.

Interestingly, policy scholars from the economic discipline perceive the marketplace of ideas in a way that highlights the dependence on marketplace incentives over state interventions to achieve desired social results (Owen 1975). It is indeed worth noting that such an analytical outlook leads to strong opposition to state regulation of media markets and is in favour of significant deregulation for growth. However, in recent years, there has been a withdrawal from such extreme analytical perspectives and conventional outlooks adopted from the economic aspect towards policy issues (Stucke and Grunes 2001). Such deregulatory opinions are embedded in the First Amendment theory or assessments related to the media marketplace, emphasising the rising significance of 'new media technologies' and the reduced importance of conventionally regulated media (Baker 2007).

Another significant point from the perspective of media policy is applying a marketplace of ideas in the democratic process. Cultural or political ways towards the metaphor associated with a marketplace of ideas reflect a very different grounding theoretically that draws out of the democratic theory and not the economic theory per se. It could be observed in the works of John Stuart Mill and John Milton, as their works specifically articulated the concepts of truth achieved through free competition of ideas serving the larger good by way of vast distribution of viewpoints and ideas (Schwarzlose 1989). An emphasis will be placed on the centrality of competition between opposing standpoints for an informed society and effective self-governance (Meiklejohn 1948). From this standpoint, media policy needs to prioritise serving people's informational needs and enhancing the effective democratic process. So, what is observed here is that the interpretative approach puts more emphasis on the ideas of localism, diversity and pluralism as the fundamental elements for a healthy marketplace of ideas (Van der Wurff 2005; Hitchens 2006).

Challenges Ahead for Media Policy

There are several challenges associated with the idea of media policymaking. First, media policymaking must go through a highly complex technological milieu, where new media technologies present new sources and forms of content creation into the media mix and provide new platforms for the delivery of conventional media content. Thus, in such a situation, defining the media market becomes extremely difficult, so is accurately maintaining the roles and responsibilities of different kinds of media towards society. The policymakers need to come to grips with how such increased migration of users to interactive media platforms and the importance of user-generated content may impact the media policy lines (Benkler 2006).

Today, we are witnessing a complete technology-led 'de-institutionalisation' of the media. The question arises as to how this ongoing change be reflected in media policies that are conventionally directed and formulated by large media institutions. Lastly, it needs to be understood here that media policy generally varies from other fields of policy because the subject and the role the media plays in the policymaking process affect the power dynamics of the politics of media policymaking. Media institutions are not merely unbiased intermediaries; they are also affected by the directive that raises significant questions regarding media policy coverage (Ali and Puppis 2018). The media possesses the power to control public perceptions with regard to regulation and media structure (McChesney 2008). This might lead to 'media policy silence' and 'media policy bias', eventually changing the power dynamics between different actors involved in media policy politics (Freedman 2010).

Hands-on Project on Media Policy

The work reported in this book is the outcome of a Ford Foundation project at the Centre for Culture, Media and Governance, Jamia Millia Islamia, New

Delhi. Besides its ongoing postgraduate teaching programme, the centre initiated the idea of developing a conceptual framework in the area of media policy and governance—an interdisciplinary postgraduate programme—and its pedagogic analysis for teachers and students of media governance. While this book could be used as a self-learning tool for various hands-on project workshops in four areas of policy analyses—mapping news diversity, market structure and industry, mapping policy shifts and document analysis—we also visualise the possibility that teachers who teach and guide students in organising and presenting similar project workshops may also use this book to facilitate more effective and productive learning.

The master's programme, on which the hands-on projects on media policy were designed, engages students with a creative mix of conceptual issues, theoretical debates and methodological views and calls for a serious appraisal of media in contemporary times. It uses a variety of pedagogical tools within the ambit of classroom teaching and self-learning. One of the tools used by the teachers was a hands-on project focused on the workshop method used across four projects through four semesters, equipping students to obtain the practical application of theoretical knowledge imparted in courses. The postgraduation course is a two-year programme, and each year constitutes two semesters; in each semester, there are five courses (including one choice-based course) with four credits each—I Media and Politics (first semester), II Introduction to Media Economics (first semester), XII Policy Research and Evaluation (third semester) and XIII Regulation in Theory and Practice (fourth semester)—and each one has workshop components for internal evaluation of students. Each workshop is designed to assess the theoretical aspects that students have learnt in each of the corresponding courses, leading to a project on policy analysis.

The present book exemplifies the prototypes of such workshop modules that highlight, in a self-learning mode, how to undertake and conduct similar exercises in the media or related disciplines (presented in Chapters 4 to 7). The very idea of this book emanated from a realisation of the lack of a standardised format for teaching and learning media studies, particularly policy analysis, in an integrated manner, in South Asia.

The hands-on project design provided instructional objectives and assessment for different policy-analysis modules to aid teachers on how to conduct a student exercise for academic evaluation of theoretical understanding in a workshop model. The book has been presented in a user-friendly manner for students; teachers will also find it handy as a complement to their classroom teaching. It will be a guiding source for students in accomplishing workshop modules as part of an academic endeavour towards developing competencies in media policy analysis. It can also be used by students and teachers of other disciplines, media advocacy groups and trainers as a model for conducting workshops for academic or other general training purposes.

Keeping in view the lack of standardised pedagogical practices in media studies, the purpose and rationale of this book is also to advance a format that can be adopted, adapted or modified for conducting hands-on, project-based workshops in different academic institutions, including in media studies, media practice, law and even management programmes. Such exercises will also enable the learners to understand the multiple contexts of the genesis and practice of media governance and its policymaking mechanisms and empower them in advancing and facilitating critical academic interrogations whereby one can advocate and practice a more participatory venture with the involvement of varied stakeholders of diverse interests. This, in a way, will augment the employability of graduates in the emerging field of media policy and media governance.

How to Use This Book

The curriculum for the master's programme in media policy and governance included practical projects on media policy analysis designed to give students a practical experience to discern policy formulation, its foundation, shifts and challenges. Four out of twenty courses were designed partly to impart a practical understanding of theoretical learning through workshop-oriented hands-on projects. Chapters 4–7 detail the pedagogic and academic engagements of all the four hands-on workshops. This is done to assist students in applying or relating theoretical knowledge with the ability to critically analyse the undercurrents and underlying processes of policy formulation, chiefly on media, and the challenges thereof in the Indian subcontinent. And, this is done keeping in view the emerging scenario of unbounded geography and abundant growth of information, which in turn resulted in policymaking at multiple locations by a plethora of stakeholders who primarily attempted to safeguard their own interests. The cases reported in the four chapters are designed to guide students and teachers to maximise their engagement with the curricular goals and demands of the project workshops. It is also envisioned as a pedagogy resource workbook for similar academic initiatives and is useful across curriculums that focus on media studies, law and social sciences.

A brief highlight of the four hands-on projects on various aspects of media policy analysis are as follows. Given hereinafter, in four subsections, is a brief on the usability of this book, that is, how best this can be used in preparing for and presenting various hands-on projects on media policy analysis (and also in any other discipline).

Enumerating Media Diversity

This course is taught in the first semester of the master's programme. The hands-on project workshop is designed to analyse television news and its approaches towards pluralism in India. It is intended to give students hands-on training with critical insights to be able to analyse television news, and understand media pluralism through television news analysis in a classroom scenario. The project focuses on the presence of different elements in a news story and how students can study those elements through quantitative and qualitative techniques to analyse the extent of plurality in news broadcasting, such as the themes of news stories, the geography of news, the voices of actors in news stories, the demography of actors in news themes, the treatment of news stories, the sources advertisements and the types of advertisements within a news bulletin. Students are encouraged to dissect news based on news value and explore the tone and fine distinction within different news organisations. This also creates an enabling environment to understand the concept of media and democracy in India.

Market Structure, Ownership and Industry

This workshop is designed to give students practical training in data analysis, to make them understand media ownership, to present various aspects of economic data and to collate data to feed into the larger goal of policy analysis. As part of the course within the first semester, the project workshop aims to make students competent in using qualitative and quantitative methodological tools to identify and critically analyse various aspects of media economics discussed in the classroom. The aim is to train and practically locate various media companies that make up the media market, analyse elements of media ownership measurement and look into its various parameters. One of the central focuses of the course and the project workshop is to equip students with analytical tools, such as Microsoft Excel and basic economic formulas, for a critical understanding of ownership and market, as these tools/skills are required for analysing the data collected towards fulfilling basic requirements for undertaking the workshop.

Document Analysis for Media Policy Research

In the third semester of the master's programme, the course focuses on the principal stage of learning: to analyse policy formulation processes. It introduces an organised way of interpreting government documents, such as inquiry commission reports and various other reports on the media before the 1990s. During the course, students learn to recognise key actors in the media space, analytically reflect on quantitative and qualitative evidence provided and unravel opinions on policy options. Structured in a hands-on workshop mode, it provides a thorough grounding in a select set of techniques that are commonly used in understanding the process of policy formulation. The hands-on project identifies document analysis as one such technique for media policy analysis.

Mapping Shifts in Media Regulation

The course is taught in the fourth semester and focuses on the most effervescent sectors in the media industry. The sectors that witness increased regulatory activities are picked as case examples. It constructs on the understanding of policy arrangements in several media sectors and institutional arrangements of media regulation. It explores deeper into issues of access, impartiality and the public good, which are vital for both deliberations on governance and methodologies for policy analysis. It is identified that unravelling successive policy provisions requires drawing on numerous sources and not just reading into obvious 'policy' announcements. The module aims to help students acquire a thorough understanding of re-regulation.

Pattern of Presentation

The speciality of this hands-on project book on media policy analysis is that modes of teaching and learning are both built into it without the need for any external agency to demonstrate or explain the subject. Creating instructional material for a self-learning mode is an art in itself. The aim is to make it user-friendly so that the user—a teacher, a student or a trainer—can use it without any external help. It is presented in such a flow that any of the categories of users can use it without any difficulty.

Special Features

As presented in this book, each case in the hands-on project on media policy stand out vis-à-vis their special integrated features, making them pedagogically more enriching for both students and teachers.

Presentation of cases: The book is presented in a manner that addresses the needs and requirements of different categories of users such as students, teachers and trainers. However, the primary focus has been to facilitate students to learn to organise, work on and present policy analysis project workshops. The concept maps on each project and the hands-on project on policy analysis shall introduce to users the course and its projects and the underlying themes and interlinkages within themselves and the larger theme.

Illustrative case examples: Each workshop module provides one illustrative case example of students presenting their analysis of news items, media market structure or document or policy analysis. Each workshop culminates in PowerPoint presentations by students on the practical exercise that they have chosen to undertake as a part of it.

Training in Microsoft Excel, PowerPoint presentation and report writing: Some of the hands-on project modules, especially news mapping and media structure and economics, demand a thorough knowledge in handling Microsoft Excel sheets for data analysis. Since all the students may not have the skill to handle Microsoft Excel, an elaborate description of how to use the software is provided with supporting visuals and diagrams, so that students can learn it without any external help. Further, students are also given training in PowerPoint presentations with a coherent storyline on the conceived aspect of media policy analysis; they are required to make PowerPoint presentations at the end of the course. Students complete the course only after they have submitted their final narrative reports based on what they had presented. Hence, the course includes a segment on how to write a report.

Standard referencing style: Different styles of referencing are practised by different sources. To standardise it, the book provides a recommended referencing style, for instance, on how to make a list, specifically, of the reading materials that students have referred to for developing the narrative reports and presentations.

Evaluation/assessment: In any academic exercise, the evaluation and assessment criteria should be both explicit and transparent. This hands-on project is no exception. The book elaborates on how this exercise will be achieved based on a uniform evaluation pattern evolved through our past experiences of conducting such exercises in classrooms. The evaluation is done based on skills the course instructor has set out, which students need to learn during the process of this hands-on project.

Student feedback: Students are also trained to assess the hands-on project exercises carried out by fellow students and to undertake a peer review.

Keywords: The book lists key concepts that repeatedly appear in the text generally and with reference to a particular hands-on project.

Glossary: Besides key concepts, the book also has a glossary section that sets down difficult words, jargon and concepts, with brief explanations.

Additional readings and references: Each project module gives a list of additional readings, which will aid students in carrying out workshop exercises. Also, it gives a list of references in a separate section.

Curriculum Design: Media Governance

The present book is the outcome of a major research project on pedagogic applications in interdisciplinary media studies, particularly media policy analysis taught in the master's programme in media governance. The master's programme is designed to provide a critical and interdisciplinary academic engagement with the evolution, functioning and dynamics of media policies in the contemporary media environment. The master's programme in media governance is an attempt to address the incongruity of the present-day academic field of media studies. Media studies, so far, has been blind in bridging the gap between professional training and critical social engagement in the field of communication. Moreover, it also neglected the crucial field of media policy, which deeply connects the institutions of state, market, civil society and a constantly evolving communication milieu and the mediascape, specifically those relating to the configurations of communication and the processes creating them. The mediascape, in general, witnessed unmatched transformations that resulted from tremendous technological proliferations that percolated into the field, coupled with the abundant growth of information with all its dynamism and the influx of multiplicity of avenues, platforms, sites as well as actors. This emerging situation, with all its complexities, poses challenges to the communication field of media at least on two fronts:

First, the governance of these multiple avenues and platforms through the instruments of appropriate mechanisms, such as regulations and policy formulations, to satisfy divergent stakeholders, including the public, becomes very tricky.

Second, in order to generate a more meaningful interface, it becomes extremely important to develop a systematic, creative yet critical engagement of the academia to address emerging questions posed by multiple sites and actors of media avenues, especially its process and institutions of governance. Such an exercise requires an engagement with every sphere of our life: social, cultural, political, historical and, least of all, economic. This exercise becomes even more crucial considering the multicultural and multiethnic population within which we operate.

A scrutiny of these challenges and investigating possible ways to tackle them will be equally rewarding towards redefining the disciplinary contours of media/communication studies. Moreover, under the circumstances, it becomes significant to interrogate the sphere of media and the nature and form of its academic disciplinarity within the centrality of governance both at operational and theoretical grounds. The curriculum of this programme has been structured to provide students with a policy-oriented understanding of the media setting. It imparts key theoretical and methodological perspectives from interrelated disciplines to engage with larger issues of relevance and function of the media, understand shifts in media industries and how these are consequential to the process of governance.

At different historical periods, due to the diversity of interests of the stakeholders involved, the process of policymaking has been a site for bargaining, if not contestation, between:

- the colonial government and the nationalists during the pre-Independence period, witnessing an environment of proscriptions.
- the centralised state and plural voices after Independence till the early 1990s.
- the state, market (corporate groups) and civil society after the post-liberalisation period (post-1990s), witnessing market-centred de-regularisation.

Policies were formulated and research and other studies were invariably promoted, resources were allocated, laws and legislations were conceptualised and, notably, academic courses were designed following this line. Thus, as discussed in Chapter 3, the academic discipline of media education went through its formative period in pre-Independence India, consolidated its base and grew further with horizontal expansion after Independence. It was firmly established by meeting the requirements of the market in the post-liberalisation era. Throughout these different phases of birth, growth and expansion of media studies, it fed policy formulations and orientations of dominant actors. This is because, more than any other discipline, research studies and disciplinary growth in media education were promoted, facilitated and guided by policies and orientations of the state at different historical periods, as communication was always viewed as instrumental in governing the masses. Moving in line with the national development initiatives and regulations, most of the communication studies in the post-Independence period were attempts to legitimise state-sponsored projects and justify technocratic solutions for social change. Precisely due to the instrumental role of the media in the wider project of nation-building, the teaching programmes of the period were conceptualised as 'professional' courses, that is, those imparting training in relevant technological medium towards producing manpower to be deployed in government's development-oriented communication initiatives. Despite the pronounced expansion of foreign and Indian electronic media and the shift in media ownership from the state to the market, the approach towards teaching communication and media hasn't changed much in India, except for the redesigning of media education to meet the requirements of the market.

In short, the media courses across the country are geared more towards addressing the marketing requirements instead of having disciplinary orientation. Thus, media studies remained a neglected field of inquiry. It lacked theoretical and methodological engagements built into it. Media studies, therefore, is yet to evolve to achieve a distinctive disciplinary status. Also, with the immense transformation that occurred in the socio-cultural, economic, political as well as technological terrains, especially in the beginning of the 1990s, the field witnessed transformations emanating from two fronts:

- Transformations in their traditional, literal conception are expanded to entail various forms (numbers and data, text and hypertext, symbols and cultural commodities), all of which may variedly exist in tangible and intangible forms. These forms have legal implications since their production and circulation is shaped by legal and regulatory frameworks existing at the formal level.
- Transformations in perceiving the foundational social science concepts, such as culture, nation, state, democracy and community, in general, and within the media sphere.

These aspects, in combination, became crucial in shaping the communication process in the contemporary period. Moreover, during the post-liberalisation phase, when its singularity was challenged, the centrality of the state itself became a point of contestation. What became a challenge during this phase was to address issues that traversed time, space and territorial sovereignty, though paradoxically the nation state remained a central location for deliberating communication policy. Under the circumstances:

- policies were no longer made at a definable location but across various sites and amidst debates among actors of diverse interests and institutional dynamics.
- the process of policymaking became a forum to display power.
- the new variables involved in policymaking posed critical questions relating to the specificities of socio-cultural, historical and political contexts in the interests of individuals both as consumers and citizens.

- the state had very little or no role to play in policymaking, which gave way to transnational corporate media with no accountability towards citizenry.
- there emerged a renewed thinking on the need for democratising the media and searching for alternatives to the dominant way of media making.

Thus, the changes that occurred in the post-liberalised media arena made policymaking multidimensional. With the supplanting of the era of media scarcity and geographical boundedness by information abundance and the opening of transnational communication channels, it became essential to know more about the details of each policy-related question. Very little is known about the fundamental forces that influenced the meanings of these questions and the actual course of policy outcomes. And the academic field of media and communication, the way it has grown and expanded over the decades, was ill-equipped to engage with the emergent scenario.

This is precisely because it lacked critical academic engagement to dissect the media and its policy instruments from a multidimensional and multicontextual perspective, resulting in a lopsided growth of an academic discipline, specifically in scrutinising and exploring the policy avenue from an interdisciplinary perspective. Policy formulations continue to remain outside the terrain of academic analysis and academia in general, mostly found conforming rather than engaging creatively with regulation and regulatory institutions in the governance of the media economy. This means communication requires both a systemic engagement and multiple levels of analysis, especially from a governance perspective. Such an understanding of media governance ensures that the relationship between media and governance is understood in both instrumental (i.e., the role of media systems in governance) and transactional terms (i.e., governance of media systems).

Given the emergent situation, the two-year master's programme in media governance has been designed to provide a policy-oriented understanding of the evolving media environment. It emerged from a recognition that global media governance could only achieve from conceiving and operationalising an intense dialogue between research, higher education and policymaking. The objective is to study the interlinkage between media and governance in their innumerable forms at different sites and their grounding in broader political, historical and economic processes. The aim is to discover the increasing complexity in the governance of media institutions, that is, regulatory reform, best practices and legal instruments that outline media justice and access and equity. Therefore, the focus is on developing pedagogic advances in both academia and professional training.

Throughout the master's programme, the objective is to explore the level to which the media, new or old, is shaped by changes in the understanding and process of modern democracy. Exploring conventional institutions and practices, the course will inspect the media's inner workings and outer structures. The curriculum is spread over a two-year teaching programme of four semesters drawn out in twenty courses. Each course comprises three modules for students to build perspectives, theoretical debates and methodological standpoints to engage with the evolving media milieu. The core component of this programme aims to familiarise students with media policy from an institutional perspective. However, different perspectives from media studies and social sciences form a part of the training to appraise and critique media policies.

The programme is, therefore, structured to familiarise students with different practices and institutions of governance, stakeholder groups, organisations, mediations by corporate, citizen and social networks to foster a broader understanding of their interrelationships in the working of media, media market, policies and their interface with consumers, citizens, state and market. The crux of the programme is to engage with media technologies and how evolving policy frameworks shape and are shaped by contemporary democracy, questions of advocacy, media rights and responsibilities. To this extent, the curriculum is designed to introduce students to the need to discern and appraise different facets of state–media dynamics, commercial and technological structures, (re)regulations, ownership and the media market structures and their engagement with instruments of polity and economy. The approach is interdisciplinary, intended to engage with technology studies, politics, law, sociology and economics, even as communication is retained as its fulcrum. The curriculum is arranged to gradually impart theoretical and methodological orientations towards media policy debates and the interplay of media and governance in key spheres of state, market and law.

Concept Map

Mapping the Master's Programme

The following were the considerations we had kept in mind while designing the master's programme reflected in Figure 1.1.

- As an interdisciplinary centre, the first consideration of the teachers was to utilise the creative resources of the faculty drawn from diverse disciplines of social sciences, humanities, law, media studies with a common objective and goal. It was realised that the faculty had a common frame of reference, which is engagement with communication studies. Although communication studies is a relatively new field of enquiry both in India

Figure 1.1: Concept Map: Master in Media Governance

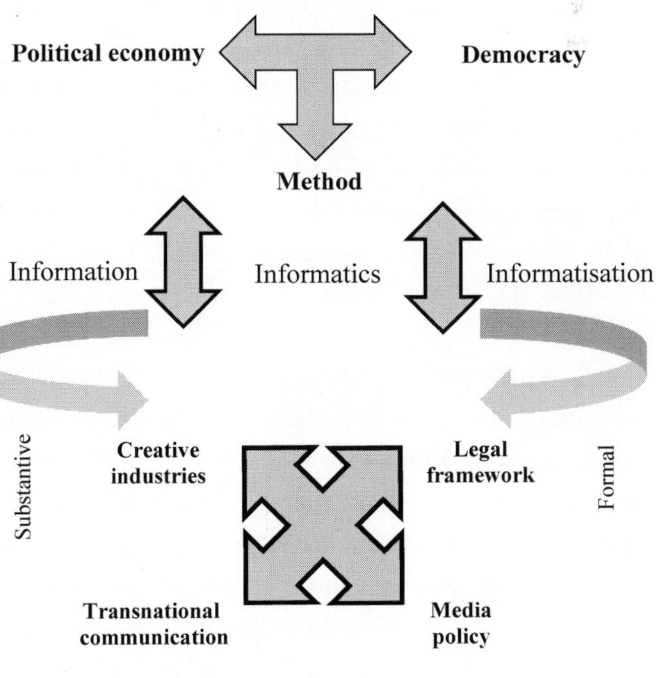

Source: Authors

and abroad, the teachers did not want to miss the opportunity to engage in nurturing interdisciplinarity in the field. The conventional reading of media courses emphasised 'medium' and its use and applications. However, such emphasis has a purchase and purpose subject to the 'materiality' of the practice and architecture of the medium under scrutiny. Mere examination of the medium as a conduit for communication does not provide sufficient ground for theorisation, analysis and understanding. The idea of technology or technology-mediated communication is very new and dates back to the industrial revolution. Though communication is used in all forms of interaction, rarely has it been theorised and analysed. At best, it remained a meta concept. Hence, the faculty were engaged in situating wider intellectual roots and traditions of communication. Such an exercise transcends the medium-centric view of communication and situates communication within the larger epistemological and ontological traditions of communication.

- While reviewing the existing syllabi and curriculum across the world, and more specifically in India, we realised that there is a gap between Media Studies and media studies. While the former pertains to professional skills and production-oriented courses in mass communication, the latter refers to media taught in various social sciences and humanities courses. The production-oriented courses have evolved for a while and now emerged as practitioner-based research; however, it has a severe knowledge problem. Rarely, these practices are documented and added to the knowledge about the field. This resulted in a broad divide between practice-based courses and theoretically informed courses. Both the courses had shortcomings. While in the former case, we witness the courses are untheorised, in the latter case, we observe a case of under theorisation, keeping aloof from the debates and discussions in social theory. There is neglect in both cases.
- Along with the institutionalisation of Media Studies, courses and departments mushroomed across universities in India. These developments were at best in the sphere of transformation in technology, thereby undermining the role and relationship between media and society. Similarly, courses taught in media studies across social sciences and humanities could not grow and at best remained a sub-field or optional courses within their established disciplines. Thus, the disciplinary concern

of communication remained fuzzy and amorphous; at best, it was treated as a field of inquiry rather than a discipline.

- Before such polemical issues were settled, the questions posed by various actors and agencies, such as the state, civil society and the market, in everyday life, and their engagement with communication, remained unaddressed and lacked attention within academia. Hence the need to survey these agencies, their specific concerns and growing challenges, and explore common ground for conversations and future engagements.
- Reviewing the trends and debates posed by various actors and agencies over the last two decades, we notice the inability of communication to engage and address the changing media milieu. The present media milieu has transformed from a provision of scarcity to abundance and transcended from territorially bounded geography to transnational sites of jurisdiction. The rising civil society aspirations and engagement in policymaking have enriched the scope and meaning of communication, the sites of jurisprudence and the profile of macro and micro actors engaged in making and managing communication. The transformations also intensely impinged on the notion of work, leisure and labour practices in communication. These issues cannot be addressed within the confines of conventional courses such as mass communication, social sciences or humanities.
- The growing civil society engagement also interrogates the conventional wisdom of the relationship between the state and civil society. It is no more the state's prerogative to inform people; instead, civil society interrogates the assumptions, highlighting the importance and shift from 'media reform' to 'media justice' and 'media democracy' to 'media rights'. Further, digitisation has thrown new challenges to the conventional notion of politics and decision-making. As a result, the shift from government to governance requires a renewed engagement with changing models of governance and communication.

Why This Schema?

- The foundation of this programme (see Figure 1.1) was shaped by two principles: one looks at the trajectory of democracy and its institutions, and the other, the political economy within which such trajectories of democracy have evolved. Together they contribute to developing a method to understand the larger developments within the communication and information sector.

- Currently, the information sector has undergone many transformations, resulting in its traditional, literal conception being expanded to entail various forms (numbers and data, text and hypertext, symbols and cultural commodities) all of which may variedly exist in tangible and intangible forms.
- These forms have legal implications since their production and circulation is shaped by legal and regulatory frameworks existing at the formal level. Moreover, at the substantive level, these forms have contributed immensely to and engaged with the foundational social science concepts such as culture, nation, state and democracy.
- Communication processes are shaped by transformations both at formal and substantive levels, equally within and beyond national boundaries. Any engagement with communication today requires an interrogation of the very dynamics of transnationalism and its influence on the national media policy. The above explanation shows that communication requires a systemic engagement and multiple levels of analysis, especially from a governance perspective.
- This then brings us to the centrality of governance in understanding our present media environment and extending the scope of communication and information to other spheres of governance. Such an understanding of media governance ensures that the relationship between media and governance is understood in both instrumental and transactional terms.

Graduate Attributes

The master's programme is planned for graduates interested in the extensive areas of media policy. Its main focus is on the growth of media environments, their legal-administrative systems and their exposure to concepts and tools needed to grasp the interaction of media and governance. This was pertinent to students looking for prospects in public institutions, national/local governmental organisations, non-governmental and multilateral organisations, and apex industry bodies. The programme provides the students hands-on experiences in research and analysis. It equips them with the intricacies of collecting and handling data, their analysis to meet the goals of many media research, advocacy and market research organisations.

It enables them to analyse policy documents with a critical eye, keeping in view the stakeholders, whether governmental, non-governmental or corporate. The practical classes of various courses also enhance the skills of the students. The theoretical and practical grounding in the course offers an interesting basis for those motivated towards further study and for contributing towards policy research in different settings.

The graduates of this master's programme can find prospects in various media and interdisciplinary fields, such as academic and teaching opportunities in media studies, media wings of research institutions in the development sector or corporate houses, policy research institutions operating at governmental, non-governmental or international levels, et cetera.

The knowledge gained can be quite handy in journalistic and report writings as well.

The programme quite adequately aids a larger or macro level, facilitating the citizenry towards an informed community life, making them aware of the process of globalisation, adjusting and influencing its course of action and enabling a global view.

Courses and Modules

Over the two years, the teaching engages with theoretical architectures, academic discussions and methodological stances needed for a critical assessment of trends in the media setting.

- The master's programme consists of twenty papers of four credits each (each credit equivalent to twelve hours of teaching) taught over four semesters.
- Each paper constitutes three taught modules (1 credit each) and submission of the term paper or student project (1 credit).
- For the two semesters in a year, a student semester is evaluated with written exams in December and May.

Instructional Objectives

This master's programme intends to develop the competence of students to help them:

- comprehend, critique and appreciate the interrelationship among media technologies, media environment, structures, evolving policy frameworks and contemporary democracy.
- develop an ability to comprehend, intercept and apply different theoretical and methodological tools to discern trends and shifts in media policy, evolution, formulation and its processual influences in the contemporary media milieu.
- distinguish, appraise and relate to the implications of various actors—state, market or civil society—in the domain of media policy and the dynamics of evolving communication environment.
- foster an ability to critique media policy and substantially debate the role of governance in the media industry.
- explain, define, relate, describe, correlate and demonstrate different facets of key concepts in media policy studies, media industry and governance.
- develop skills to gather information from the public domain, explore, collate and analyse data related to media industries and their different elements to build a critical and comprehensive understanding of conflicting and competing elements that nurture policies and their interrelated domains of governance law and law culture.
- develop competency to engage with underrepresented media policy, advocacy and research to boost interventions or mediate among various stakeholders in a dense media scenario.

Learning Outcomes

After going through the master's programme, students should be able to:

- describe, infer, distinguish and interpret various media legislations and policies concerning our media environment.
- analyse key theoretical and methodological tools from social sciences and media studies to discern trends and shifts in evolving media policy frameworks, industry and democratic practices.
- appraise and articulate analytical links between policy evolutions, policy formulation, inputs (collective demands and preferences) and outputs (the actual measures adopted).

- debate trends in global and national media systems and markets and their influence on the formulation and interventions of public policies and their relationship to media, regulatory and legislative systems.
- explain, define, give examples of, correlate and describe different facets of the key concepts in media policy studies, media industry and governance.
- differentiate and critically debate policy shifts in media, market and state, and explore their consequences to democratic processes, market structures, public interest and communication.
- demonstrate interdisciplinary competence and practical skills by critiquing and explaining convergences and divergences of media technologies and products, economic liberalisation, shifting engagements of state and non-state actors, media policy legislation and advocacy.
- apply theoretical concepts and raw data in coherent formats like reports to illuminate key arguments that explicate policies, elements and strategies.
- appreciate the theories and methods for a career in media and policy institutions, non-governmental and multilateral organisations, advocacy and training groups and related industries.

The hands-on projects on media policy derive their learning outcomes, as presented in Chapters 4–7, from these broad learning objectives of the master's programme based on appropriate instructional design and application of the pedagogy of PBL.

Key Concepts

Several keywords/concepts have been repeatedly used in this book. The important and often used terms are explained here. The following concepts have been explained and presented in an interrelated manner so that students can get a holistic picture while comprehending the meaning of each key concept.

Institutionalism is the process of institutionalising the underlying principles and values of an action, activity or practice according to which various social and cultural practices in society are organised or coordinated.

Or say, institutionalism is the process wherein the major social sources of codes, rules and relations are put in place, which ensures regulatory and organising constructions of any society that controls individuals and individuality. Institutionalism is a standardising process that includes or excludes certain organised actions, activities or practices and so on as a part of some category or other based on certain institutional constraints or limitations. Constraining the power of organisations is one of the chief functions of the process of institutionalising them. But how should this take the pace and who should implement the constraints?

Here comes the role of *regulations*. Historically, the European model of controlling media activities that followed the social-democratic line in the public sector and the state's role in overseeing or regulating, particularly broadcasting, became significant. Thus, broadcasting in a public sector is normally regulated by a set of necessities laid down in a founding license or charter and then scrutinised for performance. Outside of broadcasting, other media like cinema, press and advertising came up with systems of self-regulation as part of their institutionalisation in the twentieth century. Self-regulation implies that institutions appoint panels or a committee of individuals from the industry (and independent persons from outside the industry) who are responsible for administering a code of behaviour. With the advent of economic *reforms* towards the close of the 1980s and the end of the Keynesian regulatory-economic era moving to free-market capitalism, the state's intervention in the economy got restricted to the flow of money in the economy only. Investment decisions were made based only on prevailing money market conditions and profit potentials of investments.

The economic restructuring also filtered into the media market around the world, moving to a phase called *deregulation* and *liberalisation*. This phase is marked by the loosening of regulatory controls, particularly in the broadcasting sector, which allowed formerly tightly regulated media practices to lose some of their public service obligations.

The liberalisation of the media market was made possible by gradually removing cross-media *ownership* and giving new licenses for the functioning of many (both old and new) media sectors, thus making way for shifting dynamics of media ownership or controlling any media sector through increased shareholding.

Thus removing the grip of public sector monopolies in broadcasting and telecommunications, the channel was thrown open for *privatisation*, encouraging a shift in media ownership from state-owned to privately owned. The state-led planned development path that the Indian state followed since Independence was marked by public ownership of enterprises in important economic sectors.

The era of privatisation witnessed media companies taking advantage of changing media technologies, mergers, takeovers, buyouts, et cetera.

As a result of the size of companies that now function, they can expand into more than one media area, promoting *cross-media ownership*.

The liberalisation era and the deregulated environment also witnessed many shifts in *media and communications policy*, that is, the general principles that guide the decisions of the authorities, usually governments, about the function of the media in general. The objects of media policy are assumed to be content, ownership of media industries, matters of technical set-up and technological development, the relationship between the media and the public, and matters regulating the association of the media with authorities and the market.

The media market is a region where the population can receive the same media content and offerings of different media such as television, radio, newspaper, the internet and so on. In the contemporary period, with the possibility of media reaching across geographical boundaries, the scope of the media market has grown to a global level. Different types of market structures also mark a market. The basic types are:

- appropriate competition: numerous buyers and sellers, where none can impact prices;
- oligopoly: numerous large sellers who have some regulation over prices;
- monopoly: a sole seller with substantial control over supply and prices; and
- monopsony: a sole buyer with substantial control over demand and prices.

The introduction to the book provides a precise but comprehensive explanation of the design and application of a new pedagogic strategy, that is, PBL for media policy analysis, in the field of 'media studies' and 'media policy and governance'. The next two chapters provide a foundation to such an exercise: a brief account of pedagogies in practice and the field of media education. Based on the understanding of these foundational concepts, one can easily engage with the four cases on media policy analysis presented from Chapters 4 to 7.

References

Ali, Christopher and Manuel Puppis. 'When the Watchdog Neither Barks nor Bites: Communication as a Power Resource in Media Policy and Regulation.' *Communication Theory* 28, no. 3 (2018): 270–291.

Aufderheide, Patricia. *Communications Policy and the Public Interest: The Telecommunications Act of 1996*. New York: Guilford Press, 1999.

Baker, C. Edwin. *Media, Markets, and Democracy*. Cambridge, UK: Cambridge University Press, 2001.

———. *Media Concentration and Democracy: Why Ownership Matters*. Cambridge, UK: Cambridge University Press, 2007.

Barron, Jerome A. 'Access to the Press. A New First Amendment Right.' *Harvard Law Review* 80 (1967): 1641–1678.

Benkler, Yochai. *Markets and Freedom*. New Haven: Yale University Press, 2006.

Braman, S. 'Where Has Media Policy Gone? Defining the Field in the Twenty-first Century'. *Communication Law and Policy* 9, no. 2 (2004): 153–182.

Chakravartty, Paula and Katharine Sarikakis. *Media Policy and Globalisation*. Edinburgh, UK: Edinburgh University Press, 2006.

Das, Biswajit and Ridhi Kakkar. 'Media Governance: Ethos, Values and Integrity.' *Yojana* September (2020): 28–31.

Das, Biswajit and Vibodh Parthasarathi. 'Media Research and Public Policy: Tiding Over the Rupture.' In *The Handbook of Global Media and Communication Policy*, edited by R. Minsell and M. Raboy, 245. London: Wiley-Blackwell, 2011.

Entman, Robert M. and Steven S. Wildman. 'Reconciling Economic and Non-economic Perspectives on Media Policy: Transcending the "Marketplace of Ideas".' *Journal of Communication* 42, no. 1 (1992): 5–19.

Fiss, Owen. *The Irony of Free Speech*. Cambridge, MA: Harvard University Press, 1996.

Fowler, Mark S. and Daniel L. Brenner. 'A Marketplace Approach to Broadcast Regulation.' *Texas Law Review* 60 (1982): 207.

Freedman, Des. *The Politics of Media Policy*. Cambridge, UK: Polity, 2008.

———. 'Media Policy Silences: The Hidden Face of Communications Decision Making.' *The International Journal of Press/Politics* 15, no. 3 (2010): 344–361.

Greenhalgh, Susan. *Just One Child: Science and Policy in Deng's China*. Berkeley: University of California Press, 2008.

Hall, Peter A. 'The Movement from Keynesianism to Monetarism: Institutional Analysis and British Economic Policy in the 1970s.' In *Structuring Politics: Historical Institutionalism in Comparative Analysis*, edited by Sven Steinmo, Kathleen Thelen and Frank Longstreth, 90–114. Cambridge, UK: Cambridge University Press, 1992.

Hamilton, J.T. (Ed.). *Television Violence and Public Policy*. Ann Arbor: University of Michigan Press, 2000.

Hindman, Matthew. 'A Mile Wide and an Inch Deep: Measuring Media Diversity Online and Offline.' *Media Diversity and Localism: Meaning and Metrics* 40, no. 2 (2007): 327–348.

Hitchens, Lesley. *Broadcasting Pluralism and Diversity: A Comparative Study of Policy and Regulation*. London: Hart Publishing, 2006.

Howlett, Michael. 'Policy Analytical Capacity and Evidence-based Policy-Making: Lessons from Canada.' *Canadian Public Administration* 52, no. 2 (2009): 153–175.

Horwitz, R.B. *The Irony of Regulatory Reform: The Deregulation of American Telecommunications*. New York: Oxford University Press, 1989.

Jessop, Bob. 'The Changing Governance of Welfare: Recent Trends in its Primary Functions, Scale, and Modes of Coordination'. *Social Policy and Administration* 33, no. 4 (1999): 348–359.

Künzler, Matthias, Natascha Just, and Manuel Puppis. 'It's the Idea Stupid! How Ideas Challenge Broadcasting Liberalisation.' In *Trends in Communication Policy Research: New Theories, Methods and Subjects*, edited by N. Just and M. Puppis, 55–74. Bristol, Chicago: Intellect, 2012.

McChesney, Robert W. *Telecommunications, Mass Media, and Democracy: The Battle for the Control of US Broadcasting, 1928–1935*. New York: Oxford University Press, 1993.

———. *The Political Economy of Media: Enduring Issues, Emerging Dilemmas*. New York: Monthly Review Press, 2008.

McQuail, Denis. *Media Performance: Mass Communication and the Public Interest*, vol. 144. London: SAGE, 1992.

Meiklejohn, Alexander. *Free Speech and Its Relation to Self-Government*. New York: Harper & Brothers, 1948.

Napoli, Philip M. *Foundations of Communications Policy: Principles and Process in the Regulation of Electronic Media*. New York: Hampton Press, 2001.

———. *Media Policy: An Overview of the Field*. The Donald McGannon Communication Research Centre Working Paper Series 19, New York: Fordham University Press, 2007.

Owen, Bruce. *Economics and Freedom of Expression: Media Structure and the First Amendment*. Cambridge, MA: Ballinger, 1975.

Parthasarathi, Vibodh. 'Between Strategic Intent and Considered Silence: Regulatory Contours of the TV Business.' *The Indian Media Economy* 1 (2018): 144–166.

———. 'Dismembering Media Diversity'. *Media, Culture & Society* 43, no. 4 (2021): 764–765.

Pool, Ithiel de Sola. *Technologies of Freedom: On Free Speech in an Electronic Age*. Cambridge, MA: Harvard University Press, 1983.

Price, Monroe E., Manuel Puppis, and Stefaan G. Verhulst. *Media Policy and Governance*. Oxford Bibliographies (Online), 2013.

Puppis, Manuel, Seamus Simpson, and Hilde Van den Bulck. 'Contextualising European Media Policy in the Twenty-First Century.' In *European Media Policy for the Twenty-First Century: Assessing the Past, Setting Agendas for the Future*, edited by Seamus Simpson, Manuel Puppis, and Hilde van den Bulck, 1–20. London: Routledge, 2016.

Puppis, Manuel. 'Media Governance: A New Concept for the Analysis of Media Policy and Regulation.' *Communication, Culture & Critique* 3, no. 2 (2010): 134–149.

Schwarzlose, Richard A. 'The Marketplace of Ideas: A Measure of Free Expression.' *Journalism and Communication Monographs* 118 (1989).

Shore, Cris and Susan Wright (Eds.). *Anthropology of Policy: Critical Perspectives on Governance and Power*. London: Routledge, 1997.

Shore, Cris. 'Anthropology and Public Policy: Why Policy Matters.' In *The Sage Handbook of Social Anthropology*, edited by Richard Fardon and Olivia Harris, 89–104. Auckland: SAGE, 2012.

Stucke, Maurice E. and Allen P. Grunes. 'Antitrust and the Marketplace of Ideas.' *Antitrust Law Journal* 69 (2001): 249.

Sunstein, C. *Democracy and the Problem of Free Speech*. New York: Simon & Schuster, 1995

Van Cuilenburg, Jan and Denis McQuail. 'Media Policy Paradigm Shifts: Towards a New Communications Policy Paradigm.' *European Journal of Communication* 18, no. 2 (2003): 181–207.

Van den Bulck, H. Mediabeleid. *Media Policy*. Antwerp: University of Antwerp, 2018.

Van der Wurff, Richard. 'Competition, Concentration and Diversity in European Television Markets.' *Journal of Cultural Economics* (2005): 249–275.

Webster, James G. 'Beneath the Veneer of Fragmentation: Television Audience Polarization in a Multichannel World.' *Journal of Communication* 55, no. 2 (2005): 366–382.

Wedel, J.R., Cris Shore, Greg Feldman, and Stacy Lathrop. 'The Use and Usefulness of the Social Sciences: Achievements, Disappointments, and Promise.' *Annals of the American Academy of Political and Social Science* 600 (2005): 30–51.

Youm, Kyu Ho. 'Freedom of Expression and the Law: Rights and Responsibilities in South Korea.' *Stanford Journal of International Law* 38 (2002): 123.

2

Pedagogy and Teaching-Learning Strategies

Santosh Panda

Introduction

In Chapter 1, we introduced the field of media policy and governance, including the curriculum and learning design issues. In the next chapter, we shall present a critical analysis of media education and pedagogy in India. Though a growing discipline, the field of media education, including media studies and media policy and governance, is well established and institutionalised in Indian higher education. What needs critical scrutiny, vis-à-vis curriculum design and development, is the pedagogy and teaching-learning strategies for the discipline, or area of study, to facilitate both teachers and students to critically and meaningfully engage in translating theory into practice in the context of media policy and governance, specifically in policy discourse and policy analysis. In this chapter, we examine the discourse and practice of pedagogy, and also its translation into teaching-learning strategies in general, specifically focusing on project-based learning (PBL) as one of the significant methods to combining theory and practice in learning. Based on the background provided in the first three chapters, PBL in practice has been worked out in detail across four cases—enumerating news diversity, media structure and industry, document analysis and mapping shifts in media regulation—in terms of detailed learning design and pedagogy-based practices in the subsequent four chapters (Chapters 4 to 7).

Over centuries, teachers, researchers and educationists have often been concerned with finding out what learning is all about, how it happens and how this can be facilitated better. Pedagogy, or simply teaching-learning, across all disciplines, is directly concerned with these issues. Within the emerging context of the twenty-first–century learners and learning, methods such as portfolio-based, project-based and problem-based learning are being emphasised more in the process of teaching and learning, especially in higher education. While we delve into pedagogy in little more detail subsequently in this chapter, the above issues have been addressed in more generic ways, irrespective of subject or discipline pedagogies, though in the chapters that follow, we delineate PBL in the context of the discipline of media policy/governance or even media studies.

The twenty-first–century learners face more complex and networked information and knowledge structures; and learning, therefore, necessitates more collaborative and interdisciplinary engagements and navigation through diversified but related fields (Panda and Mishra 2020). Autonomy in learning and critical thinking skills are becoming more prominent than before. Engagement in this complex and networked knowledge society demands more inquiry-based, reflective and meaningful learning. The concurrent constructivist and other related formulations of learning necessitate real-world engagements and practical experiences in context; individual construction and social negotiation of meaning have become more prominent. In recent work at UNESCO, Scott (2015) underlines that distinctive and special forms of pedagogy are required to facilitate students acquire twenty-first–century skills. A strong need is felt to embed pedagogies and learner competencies into disciplinary studies. Therefore, teachers are required to develop competencies of discipline pedagogies, besides their well-established intellectual discipline discourses. Learning through projects throughout the educational (i.e., teaching-learning) process is of prime importance in learning through authentic real-world contexts and problem-solving. This chapter articulates both pedagogy and pedagogy for project-based learning in a specific disciplinary context that could equally be applicable across other disciplines.

Pedagogy or Epistemology?

In our explanation of the discourse on pedagogy, a preliminary question comes to mind: Could pedagogy and epistemology mean the same thing? Epistemology is essentially all about knowledge—its nature, origin, the process of acquisition, among others. To exercise epistemology, one must apply at least a single method or even a host of methods. For instance, a scientist may follow a positivist method, a social scientist may follow a constructivist or phenomenological method, a philosopher may apply the method of dialogue and so on. Each one pursues knowledge, and so, each one follows an epistemological method.

On the other hand, pedagogy is all about the science or art of teaching or instruction. This science could either be related to a discipline or subject domain or be concerned with specific approaches irrespective of disciplines, such as problem-based learning, project-based learning, behaviourist/constructivist/connectivist view of learning, et cetera. What could be the difference between 'how knowledge is acquired' (epistemology) and 'how to impart or facilitate the acquisition of knowledge' (pedagogy)?

It may not be construed that an adult is a larger version of a child (or, in other words, a child is a miniature adult) and, therefore, an epistemology for the child is a smaller version of the same epistemology for an adult. That may not be the case. First, a child is different from an adult and has a distinct identity from an adult with a distinct cognitive structure, certainly not a smaller version of an adult. Therefore, how knowledge is acquired is distinct from, though related to, how teaching or instruction should take place, which is separate for children and adults. Second, in social-constructivist learning formulations, say, for instance, in the case of Lev Vygotsky's learning pathways from novices to becoming experts in learning skills (i.e., zonal of proximal development), the conditions and learning processes for a novice are different from those of an expert in the community of practice. Therefore, how both novices and experts acquire knowledge cannot be the same as how teaching-learning or instruction and mentoring should be organised. In other words, how children and adults learn cannot be the same as how they will be taught. When the construct of pedagogy (i.e., the science of teaching children) is extended to that of andragogy (i.e., the art of facilitating adult learning), the important variable of experience and more diversified skills come to play. While the acquisition of knowledge needs to be distinguished from teaching to learn, the latter needs an extension to a larger canvas of facilitating learning.

We shall delve into the distinction between pedagogy and andragogy in a later section once we appreciate the nature of pedagogy itself.

Nature of Pedagogy

What are the formulations of pedagogy across various periods of human history? Let's talk about ancient India where the traditional wisdom lies. Instances of teaching-learning in ancient India come to the fore through various Upanishads that were written about 5,000 years back. For instance, the *Kenopanishad* talks about 'knowledge leading to immortal state', and that '*sā vidyā yā vimuktaye*' (true education liberates). In such a formulation, the teachers and students engaged in a process that took them to a higher state of 'consciousness'. And today, traversing through pathways leading to higher 'consciousness' is considered the right direction to discovering the truth. Both science and philosophy converge on this formulation. In another instance, a story from *Brihadāranyaka Upanishad* on the three sons of Prajāpati talks about divergent perceptual filters of students, where the teacher had to work through an individualised perceptual filter to teach each student (NCTE 2016). It was believed that every student had the potential to achieve success and that everything in the universe could contribute to that success and, more so, in harmony with the universe. A student was intended to achieve four attributes: *viveka* (wisdom), *vairagya* (dispassion), *shama* (calmness) and *mumukshutva* (liberation). The teacher was to facilitate both livelihood and self-knowledge, establish a link between *para* (direct vision) and *aparā* (secular knowledge) and move from the former to the latter. The methodology, in other words, the pedagogy, included *sushrusha* (knowing), *shravana* (listening), *grahana* (grasping), *dhārana* (retaining), *uhā* (guessing), *apoha* (dismissing illogicality) and *tattvajnāna* (understanding the truth). The teacher was the person who had attained self-realisation and guided the student to ascend from *para* to *aparā*. In a way, that involved involution, that is, in this case, teaching from self-practice, going beyond the intellect to achieve imperishable self-realisation by simply lighting the fire within and travelling together. The process was highly dominated by dialogue. In this context, the Indian philosopher Swami Vivekananda talked about 'drawing out the best already in the man/woman'.

In the examination of the ancient Greek society, we find that education was understood in terms of *educere*, that is, drawing out learning in students. As Pestalozzi, the great educator, believed, each one can learn, education is ingrained in human nature and all the three aspects of human personality (hand, head and heart) join together to make it complete. In the early twentieth century, two prominent educational thinkers—John Dewey (American) and Lev Vygotsky (Russian)—provided the much-needed foundation to the educational processes, Dewey through his *Democracy and Education* (1916) and *Experience and Education* (1938) and Vygotsky through his *Mind in Society* (1936, translated in 1978).

Pedagogy, as is understood today, connotes the art and science of teaching children (we shall compare this with andragogy in a section further). This understanding underwent several noteworthy developments, which, put together, relate to the meaning that we interpret today.

In ancient Greece, almost about the fourth to fifth century BC, there was the use of two distinctive terms: *paidagogus* (caretaker of a child's personality) and *didaskalos* (teachers who teach in a class or a school) (Smith 2012). The former was supposed to be slaves in the house of their masters, tasked with carrying the schoolboy and accompanying the child to school and back home. This practice was invariably present in the Greek, Romanian and Jews societies. The slaves, in the process, were to be identified with the caretaker of the child; they shape the morality, values and personality of the child. Known as the 'pedagogue', the duty involved the twin tasks of being the custodian (*paidagogus*) of the child, teaching them to be good men and leaders (*hegemonas*), and ensuring the safe movement of the child from home to school and back. While the *didaskalos* (the school teachers) were responsible for instruction in the class, the *paidagogus* (the slave mentors) were much above the former in the sense that they were permanent members of their masters' families and were responsible for shaping the morality and personality of the child. Here lies the distinction between teaching and pedagogy.

Before some more discourse on pedagogy, a few words about didactics are in order here. It may be underlined that both didactics and pedagogy had a strong foundation in continental Europe than in the English-speaking countries of England and the United States. Even if much research has taken place in the English-speaking countries in the twentieth century, the curriculum still dominates over pedagogy, for instance, in Great Britain (Alexander 2001). It is, therefore, not surprising that pedagogy is a weaker practice than curriculum in educational institutions in India (a British influence!).

Pedagogy could be distinguished from, but in a way to be read in conjunction with, didactics in the sense that both had origin in the non-English speaking part of the globe, and in most instances, both meant the same thing. When John Comenius published the book *Didactica Magna* in Czech in 1648—which got translated into Latin in 1657 and English in 1896—didactics came to the fore, which was interpreted as teaching everything (*omnis*) to everybody (*omnia*) in the best possible manner (*omnino*). The principles that Comenius underlined included teaching as per the child's level, teaching from known to unknown and teaching step by step. This may be distinguished from what Immanuel Kant said in the early nineteenth century in his book *Uber Padagogik*, published in 1803: that education, going beyond the discipline aspects to include instruction and mentoring, should be as per the nature of each child, that this leads to the development of a child's culture and that (private) instruction was lower than (personal) mentoring and guidance. The European concerns in the sixteenth and seventeenth centuries distinguished between curriculum and teaching, where the latter was referred to as didactics, that is, providing guidance, exemplifying the content and its application and building interdisciplinary and knowledge hierarchy pathways.

There were contemporary developments in pedagogy in the form of Johann Herbart's publication of *Allgemeine Padagogik* (General Pedagogies) in 1806, in which he distinguished between teaching and education: teaching (*instructio* in Latin) referred to imparting of knowledge and skills and developing aptitudes, and education (*educatio* in Latin) referred to holistic development through character building. The latter got prominence over the former for many decades.

In the English tradition, as noted earlier, pedagogy or teaching would mean art, craft as well as the science of teaching. 'Art' because teaching is a creative and intuitive process of responding to the needs of the learners, 'craft' because it requires certain skills and their practice/training and 'science' because of the theoretical underpinnings of the design and its execution based on research. This formulation will align more with didactics since it is concerned with the content of teaching (what), the process of the transaction (how) and the goals it aims at (intention). It has also been pointed out that since 'gy' (meaning 'logic') is added to the original Greek formulation, pedagogy may be referred to as the 'logic of leading children' instead of the 'science of leading children' (Hamilton 2009).

Pedagogy versus Andragogy

Andragogy became a very popular framework for adult learning, especially in the UK and the United States after the publication of the works of Malcolm

Knowles, an American educator, though the notion has existed for almost two centuries now. The formulation by Alexander Kapp, a German teacher, in 1833, through his use of the terms *andr* (man) and *agogos* (leading), suggested 'leading man/adult' as against 'paid' (child) and *agogos* (leading), which suggested 'leading child/children'. However, since the education of children was the prime concern of the day and there was hardly any attempt to educate adults or older people, the above interpretation was obliterated for a long time till Rosenstock reintroduced it in 1921 (Nottingham Andragogy Group 1983), underlining that there is a need for special teachers and methods for educating adults. Though we shall examine the works of Malcolm Knowles in some detail later, it was, in fact, the central European countries of France, Holland and Yugoslavia where the term was used extensively to refer to the 'science of adult education'.

The distinction between pedagogy and andragogy lay in how children and adults are distinguished. In terms of social engagement and social behaviour, a child is engaged largely with the social role of a full-time student, especially in schools. In contrast, an adult is one who has crossed the above stage and is engaged in the social role of a member of the world of work and, maybe, in the role of a parent. The distinction is teaching children, who are yet to enter the world of socially productive work, and teaching adults, who have already taken up the responsibility of their own lives. It may also be interpreted that while pedagogy was concerned with more conceptual understanding and applications, andragogy was dealt more with the application of knowledge to real-life situations.

The term was revived by the American educator Malcolm Knowles, who published his first book on this subject towards the end of the 1960s (Knowles 1968a). The work of Knowles is respected all over the world by contemporary and subsequent educationalists. He had been propagating the distinction since the 1950s when he was the executive director of the Adult Education Association of the USA, that adult education needs a different approach, away from 'educating people' to 'helping people learn'. The principles of andragogy were founded on the notion of self-direction in learning. The distinction between pedagogy and andragogy as articulated by Knowles (1980) is given in Table 2.1.

Table 2.1: Pedagogy versus Andragogy

Regarding	Pedagogy	Andragogy
Concept of the learner	The learner is dependent on the teacher, and society expects that the teacher takes full responsibility and determines what, when, how to learn, as also if the learning has actually taken place.	In the due process of maturation, an adult naturally moves from dependency to self-directedness, though the rate of self-directedness varies from person to person, and any dependency depends on particular situations. The role of the teacher is to take responsibility for encouraging and nurturing this adult characteristic.
Role of learners' experience	The teacher, the textbook writer, the audiovisual aid producer, and other experts contribute to learning by the learner, and the transmittal techniques include lecture, assigned reading, AV presentations. In this context of primacy of transmission, the experience that learners bring with them is of less value.	Instead of transmission of knowledge, the accumulated experiences of adults become an increasingly rich resource for learning, and adults learn most from experiences. The experiential techniques include laboratory experiments, discussion, problem-solving cases, simulation exercises, field experience, and the like.
Readiness to learn	Readiness to learn depends on what the school and society prescribe what is to be learnt, and people of the same age are ready to learn the same things. In this context, a standardised curriculum is followed, where there is a uniform step-by-step progression for all learners.	Learning depends on problems faced in life and the need to learn to solve the problems. Therefore, teachers and educators need to create conditions and facilitate learners to discover their learning needs; and organise learning around learners' life applications and readiness to learn.
Orientation to learning	Education is seen as the acquisition of subject-matter content that may be useful at later stages of life. Therefore, the curriculum follows a subject-centred approach with courses sequenced in subject-matter units, and teaching follows the method of simple to complex, known to unknown, etc.	Education is seen as the process of developing competencies (knowledge and skills) toward achieving full potentialities in life, and to apply in current and future life situations. Therefore, the curriculum is built around life experiences and competency development and is performance-based.

Source: Knowles (1980)

Interest in andragogy grew not as much as credit-based formal education but more as informal adult learning organised in workplaces, community centres, trade unions, religious places, et cetera, in which open, flexible and experiential learning programmes were carried out for the larger interest of the community and society. Such formulation of learning was influenced by many, including the humanitarian approach of Carl Rogers and various works on democracy. Conversely, this influenced the works of multinational agencies such as UNESCO through the works of Philip Coombs on non-formal education. Since informal adult learning/education is the backbone of democracy, it needed to inculcate the skills of human relations and learning to undertake cooperative living. For this, adults need to understand themselves, develop the attitude to respect others, develop the attitude to life changes, appreciate the causes of, rather than the symptoms of, problems and human behaviour, develop multi-skills to achieve full human potentiality, respect human values and varied human experiences, appreciate social dynamics and social order and intelligently engage with them. Knowles extended these notions of informal adult education to andragogy (the science or art of facilitating adult learning) based on four foundational assumptions (see also Table 2.1):

- Self-concept: More maturing (ageing) and experience leads one to be less dependent and more self-directed.
- Experience: Growing and maturing leads to the acquisition of diversified experiences, which are rich sources of learning.
- Readiness: Growing in age leads to engaging in developmental tasks related to one's social role and education, which ensure greater readiness to learn.
- Orientation: As one matures and gets experience, the orientation to learning shifts from the earlier subject/content-centred learning to more problem-centred learning. Problem-based learning and project-based learning address this aspect more closely than other strategies and methods.

Knowles added two more assumptions: 'motivation to learn', indicating internal, rather than external, locus of control, and 'finding meaning in learning'. Knowles was influenced by both the behaviourists, such as Thorndike and Skinner, and humanists, such as Carl Rogers. Critical works on andragogy followed, and some researchers succinctly labelled this as a description of adult characteristics and how adults should be taught rather than as a theory of adult learning. However, today, the notion of 'self-directed learning', preferably in a non-linear fashion, and contextually problematic learning projects assume significance even in cases of organised and formal credit-based (classroom) learning. Subsequently, Knowles (1980) revised his notion of the relationship between pedagogy and andragogy, that is, a spectrum that ranged from subject-centred pedagogy to learner-centred andragogy. He wrote:

> Originally, I defined andragogy as the art and science of helping adults learn. I am at the point now of seeing that andragogy is simply another model of assumptions about learners to be used alongside the pedagogical model of assumptions, thereby providing two alternative models for testing out the assumptions as to their 'fit' with particular situations. (1980, 43)

In the present context of teaching-learning in higher and further education institutions, there is simultaneous and need-based use of both pedagogic and andragogic principles and methods all over the world, and Peterson and Ray (2013) refer to this as 'metagogy'. Young (2020) analyses his experience in teaching clinical neurology to suggest the futility of both the terminologies; he prefers the Latin word *itinere* to refer to teachers-students journeying together.

Since the discourse and practice of pedagogy have been researched and debated over the past seven decades, alternative interpretations have emerged and have influenced the discourse and practice in the last three decades or so. A significant few are in order.

Critical Pedagogy

In a democracy, it has been argued that (higher) education must provide conditions and mechanisms and engage in such pedagogy that provides for free debate and reflection on the linkage between education and democracy on the one hand and human knowledge and public service on the other. Such a pedagogy develops in learners' critical capacities as social agents. Giroux (2012) writes:

> [P]ublic intellectuals within and outside of the university defend higher education as a democratic public sphere, connect academic work to public

> life, and advance a notion of pedagogy that provides students with modes of individual and social agency that enable them to be both engaged citizens and active participants in the struggle for global democracy. (329–330)

Of late, education has been treated as a tradable commodity, preparing students to compete in the global marketplace instead of encouraging critical engagements for democratic values and social needs. In an earlier critical work, the authors argued:

> Most specifically, democracy necessitates forms of education and critical pedagogical practices that provide a new ethic of freedom and a reassertion of collective identity as central preoccupations of a vibrant democratic culture and society. (Giroux and Giroux 2006, 31)

Critical pedagogy argues that learning as social interaction is a political act to serve political purposes and that 'pedagogy' itself is a political, moral and critical practice. This pedagogy balances between critique and imagination, finds space in voice and agency and challenges inequitable practices. Learning in schools and colleges must, therefore, engage students in social spheres that are both creative and transformative. As against serving economic interests, the role of education is more emancipatory in its pursuit of social justice related to prominent social-learning theories like that of Communities of Practice (CoP) of Lave and Wenger (1991). If we go beyond this, the premise is that all social interactions are political, and such a pedagogy should work towards justice and a more inclusive democracy.

The most prominent discourse is American (Giroux 1997), though there are critical works in Great Britain (Walker 2006) and elsewhere. Henry Giroux argued that disciplinary study is limiting and elitist; disciplinarity and interdisciplinarity are alternatives; and disciplines perpetuate hierarchically ordered forms of knowledge, authority and exclusion. And, this stifles critical inquiry. However, there are counter-arguments in favour of disciplinary study: that such critical inquiry, in relation to and within social contexts, is possible, rather desirably possible, within the disciplinary discourse of 'retaining complex and diverse forms of knowledge in any public space' (McArthur 2010, 312). Inclusive and authentic higher education is desirable and possible within disciplinary discourses that can be open to critical changes and with 'myriad of links into interdisciplinary hedgerows' (ibid.).

Feminist Pedagogy

The feminist movement, especially in the 1970s, raised concerns about women's socialisation and professional engagement, especially in American society. To start with, there exists a strong relationship between art education and feminism through the works of women historians, artists, art critics, especially non-sexist approaches to art within teacher education vis-à-vis gender imbalance. The patriarchal aspects of schooling, curriculum and teaching-learning methods were questioned and revisited to discover a hidden curriculum favouring men over women. Alternative instructional models emerged in which social prescriptions of being men or women were examined within gendered human experiences, a new scholarship on women. The study of gender justice and genderedness in social relations with social structures and institutions both paved the way for a new pedagogy that fosters community, empowerment and leadership. Shrewsbury (1993) writes:

> Feminist pedagogy is engaged teaching/learning—engaged with self in a continuing reflective process; engaged actively with the material being studied; engaged with others in a struggle to get beyond our sexism and racism and classism and homophobia and other destructive hatreds and to work together to enhance our knowledge; engaged with the community, with traditional organizations, and with movements for social change. (8)

Influenced by the works of Paulo Friere (*Pedagogy of the Oppressed*) and John Dewey (*Democracy and Education*), among others, feminist pedagogy will stress critical thinking that fosters respect for others and working *with* others and working towards enhancing the wholeness of others. Sandell (1991) writes, 'Critical to the education of oppressed, be they women, minorities, or others, feminist pedagogy attempts to foster a confirmation of self-knowledge for the knower that is not provided by teaching in the traditional academic style' (181).

This is also related to the model of connected teaching and women's ways of knowing (Belenky et al. 1986).

Pedagogy of Capabilities

Based on the capability approach of Amartya Sen (1992; 1999) and the works of Nussbaum (1997; 2000), Walker (2006) developed the approach of the 'pedagogy of capabilities' that views higher education contributing to social well-being and public life through individual development based on engagement, transformation and change. The author writes, '[P]edagogy as structurally and contextually located but also as a matter of micro-processes of capability development, agency and learning in which we make futures' (Walker 2006, 5).

Sen's approach to development centres around human capabilities; through the process of development, educational endeavours focus on human freedom, the actual ability to be and to do. As against the human capital approach, the capability approach fosters individual-informed and reflective choices in ways of living and self-determination for ends and values of life dominated by considerations of justice and equality.

The central idea behind 'pedagogy of capabilities' is that education must develop individual capabilities to value freedom and dignity and ensure rights—the right to the enhancement of new possibilities, the right to inclusion and the right to participation—as also questioning and reflecting on educational development: for whom and what? Capability and freedom to pursue development through capacitation are crucial, and justice is central to teaching-learning and assessment. In a way, educational developments in higher education (colleges and universities) get a normative framework to deal with what, who and for whom; they also deal with equality and justice *on* and *in* higher education and *through* higher education policy and practice. It is about pedagogic freedom in developing capabilities as well as putting capabilities to practice (towards justice, equality and inclusiveness). This also entails teachers' reflective professional learning and a kind of professionalism that foregrounds pedagogic questions of why and for whose benefit.

Twenty-First–Century Pedagogy

Based on past experiences, and also on research and development on human development, human learning, workplace requirements and social learning in community of practice, new and revised formulations in integrating comfortable 'job and learning' as well as 'balanced happy life' have emerged in the twenty-first century, which are based on both pragmatism and humanitarianism of the networked world. New formulations and interpretations of pedagogy have emerged. The twenty-first–century learning and twenty-first–century competencies for learners require teachers to adopt newer and specific pedagogies to facilitate learners engage in meaningful learning. Scott (2015), under the aegis of UNESCO, underlined the following pedagogies in which PBL finds equal prominence.

- Focusing on quality
- Fostering participation
- Customising and personalising learning
- Employing project-based and problem-based learning
- Encouraging collaboration and communication
- Engaging and motivating learners
- Cultivating creativity and innovation
- Employing appropriate learning tools
- Designing real-world learning activities
- Teaching metacognitive skills
- Promoting learning without borders, lifelong learning and non-traditional learning.

Any higher education curriculum is required to engage with the listed prerequisite competencies. The choice-based credit system of the University Grants Commission of India has, of late, made outcome-based learning compulsory, which the National Education Policy 2020 has upheld as foundational.

Curriculum, Pedagogy and Teaching-Learning

In the English tradition, the curriculum is considered broad (for instance, whatever a school or an institution does), within which pedagogy forms a part (and denotes teaching methods). This interpretation of pedagogy is closer to what is understood in the European tradition of didactics: knowledge of the subject and how it is imparted. The curriculum that is more contested in the Anglo-American tradition is an umbrella term. All other variables, including pedagogy, are involved in it, while in the European tradition, pedagogy largely includes curriculum and didactics (Alexander 2001). The author further underlines pedagogy to be much broader, and that this connotes discourse while teaching is an act. Pedagogy includes theories of teaching-learning as also the act of teaching. According to Alexander, 'Pedagogy is the discourse with which one needs to engage in order both to teach intelligently and make sense of teaching—for discourse and act are interdependent, and there can be no teaching without pedagogy or pedagogy without teaching' (2009, 4). Besides the related discourse of educational theories, which is discussed in the next section, pedagogy also involves the personal values and beliefs of the teacher as well as the teaching-learning environment or context.

Curriculum today is considered to encompass the larger umbrella of the entire teaching-learning experiences, including the learning resources and how teaching-learning and assessment take place. In that case, the very curriculum is translated into instructional design or learning design for teaching-learning and learning resources, informed by various teaching and learning theories. While a curriculum is an organisation of what to teach, pedagogy is concerned with how that teaching-learning or leading, guiding, facilitating and educating practically takes place and with what intentions or conceptions.

From the English perspective, curriculum, which sets out goals of student learning, represents pedagogies and teaching-learning strategies and mapping of instructional design and learning-resources design, and the various teaching-learning theories guide the teacher on how to address curriculum and teaching (Figure 2.1).

Figure 2.1: Relation between Curriculum, Pedagogy and Learning Theory (Excluding Technology)

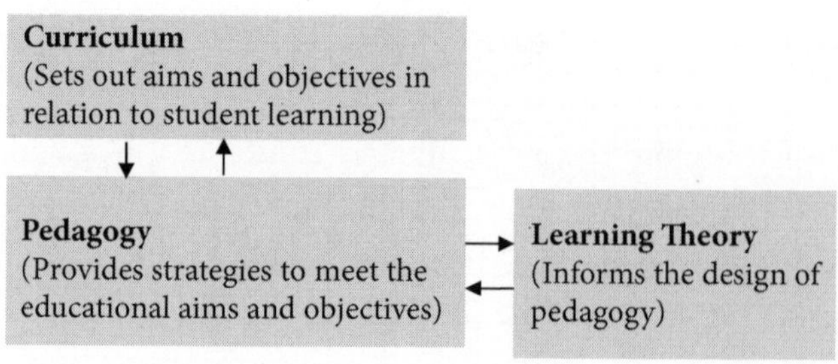

Source: Taber (2016)

As teachers, instructors and trainers, we may have wondered many times why does one teacher organise teaching or curriculum in one particular way and why the other teacher does it differently; why does one teacher prescribe certain learning activities for the same concept while the other teacher prescribes quite different learning activities. Though no two teachers are the same, just as no two learners, including twins, are the same, and that all teachers have full autonomy to design and organise their teaching-learning, what becomes essential is dialogue and negotiation of meaning across the board such that we could objectively communicate what is being done and why that is done the way it is being done. Further, for dialogue, we need a common frame of reference to which each could relate to, contribute to and derive from; we require a formal representation of the teaching-learning processes or sequences or what may be called an explicit design for teaching-learning or instruction (Eckel 1993). Bruner (1966), one of the founders of constructivist theories of learning, proposed an objective and scientific process of specifying the rules of instruction (a theory of instruction) so that the quality of instruction and, therefore, that of learning can be tracked and improved.

The learning design may be preceded by or may form a part of the curriculum. Today curriculum is viewed in a much broader way than what its origin suggests. Derived from the Latin word *currere*, it suggests running in a track, which is a pre-determined and systematically planned study cycle within which the syllabus forms a part. It is identified as inclusive of learning goals, contents, pedagogy (teaching-learning), learning activities, assessment rubric and extracurricular experiences. The academic use of the term goes back to 1633 and was subsequently broadened to include all aspects of teaching and learning (Kemmis and Fitzclarence 1991). In the context of the current discourse on globalisation and/or internationalisation, Leask (2015) distinguished between three curriculum areas: (a) formal curriculum, which included the orderly syllabus and all planned curricular activities, (b) informal curriculum, which included various support services that are not part of the syllabus but contribute to supporting learning and (c) hidden curriculum, which included all kinds of unintended informal guidance provided to the students: all sorts of pre-course completion of course-entry requirements, in-course volunteering activities, gender awareness and human rights awareness, among others, though the hidden curriculum, as the term was articulated at the time of its original use, suggested much deeper connotations to include sometimes implicit ideological stances, among others.

Put simply, pedagogy is concerned with the following questions:

1. What is intended to be good teaching and what is the goal of that activity?
2. What is being done (and how and why) to teach and facilitate students' learning?
3. What ideology and perspective influence the teacher in viewing, organising and evidencing that teaching?
4. Does the teacher consider conceptions (theories) of teaching or learning in organising teaching and ensuring student learning?
5. Why and how does a teacher engage students in collaboration, cooperation, contextualisation and creativity? Undertaking such activities through projects—either individual or group projects—engages students in translating theory into practice and in the individual and collective reflection within the community of practice. (This is where PBL comes into the picture. A section on PBL is offered later in this chapter, and Chapters 4 to 7 detail PBL pedagogy in practice in the context of media policy and governance.)

While teaching styles of teachers influence their perception about and practice of pedagogy, this is also influenced by the context of educational organisation. These managerial and contextual activities conversely depend on the goals of teaching activities: the role of teachers and students, time and pacing, resources, tasks and social structure (Watkins and Mortimore 1999), though the broader goals could remain subservient to the learning objectives and learning outcomes. Further, teachers' conception about their subject matter, which differs across teachers, and the organisational climate affect their pedagogy. More experienced teachers handle all of these in totality, while novice teachers undertake a differentiated dealing with context, subject knowledge and pedagogy.

For quite some time now, the context and learning and the role of self-regulated learning (SRL) and metacognition in achieving higher-order learning have come into focus, especially due to the constructivist interpretations of learners. Based on cognitive-constructivist formulations, Jerome Bruner (1966; 1996) said such higher-order learning that teachers could focus on could treat students in two different ways: (a) facilitate them through collaboration and knowledge sharing to build on their own experiences and understand their thinking and the process of arriving at that and (b) help students to examine and test knowledge through hypothesising and evidence building. In both contexts, teachers are required to make their own understanding or knowledge, vis-à-vis that of students', explicit. Brown et al. (1989) talked of the situatedness of cognition (i.e., learning is sharing and experiencing in the context of community discourse explained through their cognitive apprenticeship approach), that learning is embedded in in-context activity. (Note: A long time ago, John Dewey underlined project-based learning for such contextual as well as activity-based understanding.) Moreover, such experiencing needs to occur in a variety of diversified contexts or situations. We can relate this to Kolb's (1984) experiential learning and Knowles's (1975) self-directed learning. In this context, Watkins and Mortimore (1999) write, 'An explicitly pedagogical focus on the learning process advances the learner's conceptions of learning, improves what they learn and increases the likelihood that they will see themselves as active agents in learning' (8).

There have been varied interpretations of what learning means. The works of authoritative researchers, such as Marton et al. (1993) and Saljo (1979), could be summarised as follows:

- Acquisition of (more) *information/knowledge*
- Memorisation and *reproduction* of information/knowledge
- Acquisition and application of *procedures*
- Making sense of *meaning*/construction of meaning
- Resultant *personal change* (in cognitive structure, personality, identity)

Recent research studies point out the learning conditions that influence pedagogy, as also curriculum design, instructional design and design of assessment (Osher et al. 2017, 15):

- Student background and knowledge
- Cognitive load and the limits of working memory
- Metacognition
- Social, emotional and cognitive development
- Motivation
- Interpersonal factors that affect learning
- Social and emotional conditions of learning
- Cultural responsiveness and competence

Besides the conditions of learning, Ireson et al. (1999) point out that while in any effective teaching-learning there should be an alignment between teaching methods, learners' needs and learning outcomes, there are also conditions that determine a pedagogy to be effective:

- Pedagogy must have clear goals.
- Pedagogy must induce high expectations and higher levels of motivation. In other words, it should align with learners' orientations to learning and the development of deep approaches to learning and the development of self-regulation and metacognition as an integral part of the curriculum and learning environment. Further, motivation is generated in contexts where both students and teachers develop strong beliefs in their abilities to succeed.
- Pedagogy should be technically competent to align itself with learners' needs effectively, the desired learning outcomes and activities designed to achieve learning outcomes. Besides this, there should also be an alignment between teachers' teaching methods (lectures, presentations, group work, discussions, critical review, field applications through projects, etc.) and learning outcomes. This also depends on the quality of tasks designed and assigned by the teachers. The more challenging the tasks are, the more interested and motivated the students will be. However, given the time limit within which the syllabus needs to be completed or transacted, a balance needs to be maintained between knowledge transmission and critical task engagement or deep learning.
- Pedagogy should be theoretically sophisticated. That means both teachers and students need to be aware of their learning; the former need to employ pedagogic strategies that encourage the latter. To do this, they need to raise awareness of their learning. Therefore, it is essential that teachers openly discuss among themselves their perceptions and strategies in an environment of mutual respect and high professional integrity. There can be more informed discussion and updating of knowledge, provided teachers are aware of the theories behind their pedagogic strategies or initiatives and, especially, apply them to their teaching-learning contexts. This shall inform them why they are doing what they are doing, or not, and how the quality of student learning can be enhanced or enabled.

This, further, means that learners can apply their conceptual knowledge to an authentic context, especially to diversified contexts, so that real-life situations can be dealt with in a connected way. This is how higher-order learning, which is theoretically enriched and practically experienced in diversified contexts, can be facilitated.

Pedagogy: Instructional Design, Teaching-Learning Strategies, Pedagogic Methods

As can be seen in Figure 2.2, pedagogy, which is holistic, operates through teaching-learning strategies (acting as conceptual frameworks), instructional design (guiding organisation of content and designing learning activities) and pedagogic methods (teaching-centred or content-centred or learner-centred teaching). While these are briefly enumerated as follows, the figure also locates PBL within learning based on constructivist conceptual framework of inquiry.

Theories of Teaching-Learning

Learning is as much an individual activity as a collaborative exercise. One learns for oneself and does not learn for others. But one's learning is influenced or negotiated, besides teachers, by peers and learning contexts and activities with which one is engaged through the process of learning. As we can see the historical development of various learning theories in Table 2.2, although they are distinct from each other, the distinction is only thin, as also overlapping across all the theories inasmuch as there is a thin line between pedagogy and andragogy. Insofar as learning design is concerned, three types of learning are crucial (and could be derived from the theories of learning) (Hong and Sullivan 2009): (a) learning as acquisition and appropriation of knowledge, (b) learning as participation in learning community and its activities and (c) learning as a creation of knowledge through innovations and disruptive problem-solving.

The various teaching-learning or pedagogical paradigms summarised in Table 2.2 (Conole et al. 2004, 19–21; Kivunja 2014, 83) are self-explanatory.

Figure 2.2: Schema of Pedagogy

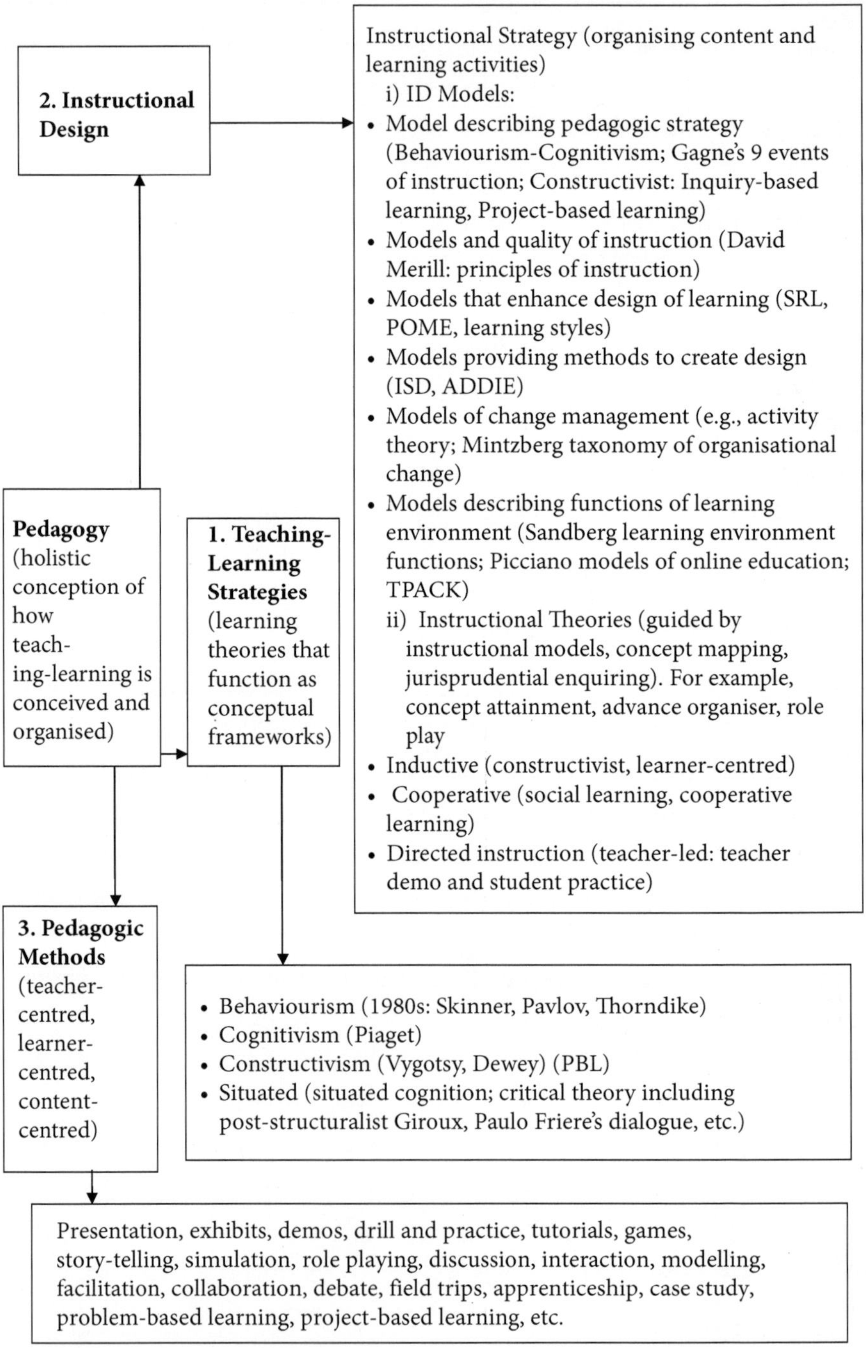

Source: Author

Table 2.2: Teaching-Learning or Pedagogical Paradigms[1]

Paradigms (and key figures)	Nature of learning	How does learning happen	How can learning be facilitated
Transmission (Aristotle, Plato)	▪ Direct transmission ▪ Blank slate, tabula rasa ▪ Passive absorption ▪ Behaviour modification	▪ Teacher transmission ▪ Rote learning ▪ Memorisation and recall ▪ Factual knowledge ▪ Observable outcomes	▪ Direct delivery ▪ Lecturing ▪ Instruction ▪ Dictation ▪ Assessment and feedback
Behaviourists (Skinner, Pavlov, Thorndike)	▪ Stimulus-response (stimuli from the environment) ▪ Learning of basic concepts	▪ Memorising and responding to stimuli ▪ Change in external behaviour ▪ Operant conditioning	▪ Presentation of stimuli ▪ Observing response ▪ Feedback: reward and punishment ▪ Reinforcement
Cognitivist/ Individual Constructivist (Piaget, Anderson, Salomon, Wenger)	▪ Active discovery ▪ Strategies, rules, patterns ▪ Complex and intellectual storage ▪ Subject construction of reality	▪ Individual interaction with the environment. ▪ Personal discovery and experimentation ▪ Assimilation and accommodation of knowledge ▪ Adaptation ▪ Reframing of mental models	▪ Activation of current individual knowledge schema ▪ Application of cognitive learning strategies ▪ Contextual/ problem/project engagement, application, analysis
Social Constructivist, Activity-based (Vygotsky)	▪ Active discovery ▪ Active construction of knowledge	▪ Authentic socio-cultural relationships ▪ Cooperative learning ▪ Problem-solving ▪ Sharing and negotiation of meaning ▪ Zone of Proximal Development (ZPD)	▪ Collaborative work and scaffolding ▪ Collaboration opportunities ▪ Discussion and argument ▪ Extension of ZPD

1 We have not included the Connectivism of George Siemens (Bell 2011) since that framework deals more with web-based, connected and networked learning.

Paradigms (and key figures)	Nature of learning	How does learning happen	How can learning be facilitated
Socially-Situated (Lave and Wenger, Vygotsky)	▪ Social participation ▪ Imitation and modelling	▪ Use of language for communication and psychological organisation	▪ Promoting dialogue and interaction ▪ Organisation of communities of practice
Experiential (Dewey, Kolb, Jarvis)	▪ Experience as learning ▪ Reflection to transform the experience	▪ Engagement in problem and context, and reflection in and on action	▪ Organising situations and activities for engagement and reflection
Systems Theory (Laurillad, Senge)	▪ Organisational learning ▪ Modelling the development of learners based on feedback	▪ Learning situations in organisations	▪ Discussion ▪ Feedback, mentoring, modelling development

Source: Author

Instructional Design

Instructional design models suggest how best teachers could design the organisation of content and learning activities to achieve the best learning outcomes. They suggest pedagogic strategies to improve the quality of instruction to enhance the quality of learning. Therefore, the design of the quality of the learning environment assumes significance. There are a host of instructional design models and frameworks to facilitate teachers, including the ADDIE model, Principles of Instruction by Merrill, Nine Events of Instruction by Gagne, Bloom's Taxonomy (Figure 2.2). A teacher has to make decisions, especially in respect of the following frameworks (Pellegrino 2004):

- Knowledge-centred: The teacher organises instruction around appropriate goals and meaningful problems.
- Learning-centred: The instructional strategies focus on scaffolding for the solution of meaningful problems.
- Assessment-centred: Instruction is organised around provision for practice, followed by feedback, revision and reflection.

- Community-centred: Instruction is designed for collaborative learning in social contexts for both independent learning and distributed expertise.

New research findings suggest that while instructional design and instructional objectives are still in vogue, there is, instead, formulation of learning design and learning objectives or outcomes in the past decades. Teachers select various pedagogic methods (Figure 2.2) to organise teaching-learning based on any or a combination of the aforementioned frameworks.

Pedagogic Methods

Any curriculum design, across disciplines, could be either teacher-centred, content-centred or learner-centred, or any combination of the aforementioned three designs across the entire curriculum or a part of it. There is an educational purpose behind each curriculum design, with specific intention to improve student learning. Each of the three curricular designs has a defined purpose of how to contribute to student learning.

Subject-centred: A subject-centred curriculum keeps the discipline knowledge in focus: what is to be studied and how it is to be studied. There is a greater degree of standardisation without due consideration to student learning styles and approaches, though teachers have the freedom to organise teaching-learning with limited flexibility.

Learner-centred: Such curriculum, besides the discipline knowledge base, keeps students' needs and goals in focus, as also individual differences in student's perception and ability. Students have a choice in choosing the learning pace, learning activities, assignments, et cetera. Institutions, though, may find it difficult to spare time and resources for this learner-centredness.

Problem-centred: This follows an inquiry-based approach in which students have the freedom to select problems for investigation and locate problems in real-life contexts. Problem-based learning and project-based learning fall under this kind of curricular design.

Insofar as the pedagogic orientation of teachers is concerned, two fundamental contrasting paradigms could be explained (Knowlton 2000; Table 2.3). Teachers use various pedagogic methods (listed in Figure 2.2) depending on their pedagogic orientation and beliefs.

Table 2.3: Pedagogic Orientation and Two Contrasting Teaching Methods

	Teacher-centred	**Student-centred**
Pedagogic orientation	**Positivism**	**Constructivism**
Things (i.e., new perspectives in courses)	Introduction of the things to students and their implications.	Teachers and students together undertake the tasks of introduction, interpretation and implications.
People (i.e., teachers and students)	Largely one-way; teachers disseminate and students take note and reflect on the transmission.	As a community of learners, both teachers and students explore together through teacher-mentoring and active student participation.
Processes (i.e., of teaching-learning)	Generally, it involves teacher presentation by modelling and mapping, and students taking notes, with occasional question-answer and discussion.	Generally, it involves dialogue and collaborative learning (inquiry-based, problem-based, project-based) by students, with teachers acting as mentors for students' individual construction/ understanding and group negotiation of the meaning of content.

Source: Author

Project-Based Learning

Towards the end of the 1990s, there was a visible shift from traditional behaviourist and objectivism-based teaching to teaching approaches that encouraged constructivist and active learning (Palmer 1998). PBL is one such approach that underlines social constructivism as its epistemological paradigm and is derived from process-oriented models associated with critical theory (of enquiry, reflection, negotiation, collaboration and self-directed learning). PBL encourages students to be independent learners with critical thinking and lifelong learning abilities (so required from twenty-first–century learners and citizens). It goes beyond just a way of learning to more of working together and working on context-based, authentic, process-oriented projects and tasks. In simple words, it is an inquiry-based, learner-centred in-depth investigation of real-world problems through student use of disciplinary concepts, processes, instruments and experiences (Krajcik and Blumenfield 2006).

PBL is situated in the epistemological paradigm of individual and social constructivism, though a teacher can judiciously mix the positivist and constructivist frameworks for PBL. In teacher professional development programmes, Roessingh and Chambers (2011) designed PBL based on both the Skinnerian behaviourism of empirical knowledge as well as the critical theory that draws on the humanistic and clinical psychology of Rogers (1969) and Freire (1985) and took a mid-position under social constructivism. The teacher-centred behaviourist principles included planned stimuli, practice, reinforcement, feedback and reward, and the learner-centred post-structuralist critical theory included situating processes in a social context, individual and group meaning-making and giving credence to voice and identity. The constructivist paradigm emphasised active learning and personal development of knowledge, with personalised mentoring from a competent mentor (Vygotsky 1978). Constructivist learning underlines that primarily subjective knowledge is constructed and negotiated by individuals in the social context, through their perceptions and experiences and through learning as a culturally embedded, socially constructed process. Both academic and social dialogue contributes to individual development and transformation through differing cultural and linguistic backgrounds, worldviews and experiences. Learners discover connections in the individual and collective experiences through interaction and dialogue, thereby questioning and reorganising their subjective knowledge and interpretations, resolving contradictions and transforming individual cognitive structure.

Based on the contemporary articulations on constructivist learning and learning by doing, Kilpatrick (1918; 1921), supposedly the earliest pioneer of project method, developed PBL through working on any project that is 'any unit of experience dominated by such a purpose sets an aim for the experience, guides its process, and furnishes the drive for its vigorous prosecution' (1918, 287–288). Inquiry is the hallmark of the project, carried out through (a) formulation of appropriate goals of learning, (b) providing for strategies of individual/group work and scaffolding, (c) provision for formative assessment, feedback and reflection and (d) participatory engagement (Barron et al. 1998).

Based on the review of literature and research evidence, Condliffe et al. (2017) suggest the following that PBL can do to develop new knowledge and skills in students, which the teachers should facilitate:

- Promote the construction of knowledge, including in-depth inquiry, problem-solving and critical thinking.
- Cultivate student engagement by kindling the desire to need to know.
- Use learning scaffolds to guide students to accomplish tasks through project templates, interactions, practice workshops and peer counselling.
- Provide greater choice and autonomy to students to be self-directed, though eventually both students and teachers join in together to formulate project questions and project design.
- Support collaborative learning towards inquiry-based expert problem solving and meaningful learning in a fast-changing knowledge-based and networked society.

Research evidence suggests that PBL significantly contributed to teaching-learning in many disciplines and interdisciplinary settings:

- In the case of preservice teaching education, PBL contributed to student learning in terms of interdisciplinary knowledge, increasing motivation and responsibility and critical reflection through formative assessment (Frank and Barzilai 2004). In the case of educational website design for preservice teacher education, PBL enhanced motivation as well as engagement (Papastergiou 2005). There has also been evidence that preservice teachers' understanding of mathematics improved after the completion of a science-based project (Wilhelm et al. 2008).
- While teaching geometry in architectural design, Thomas (2000) observed that PBL students have greater accuracy in their design projects, which were further improved by consulting additional resources.
- In the case of engineering education, it has been reported that PBL enhanced the skills of students in multidisciplinary problem solving as also working in teams (Lipson et al. 2007). However, significant challenges faced by students have also been underlined (Henry et al. 2012).

It has been argued that the philosophy and theoretical foundations of PBL are not at fault; what is essential for PBL to succeed is implementing it in any discipline. Six criteria have been suggested by Markham et al. (2003, quoted in Lee et al. 2014), which could be considered in designing effective PBL:

1. The project should deal with an authentic and real-world problem.
2. There should be academic rigour in designing and implementing PBL.
3. There should be an application for/of learning through teamwork, effective communication and information analysis.
4. A variety of resources should be gathered through active exploration by learners.
5. Connection and interaction are important in the process.
6. As much as possible, there should be a variety of formative assessment methods integrated into the process of PBL; it is, in fact, desirable.

Some of the best practices in PBL suggest some guiding principles for effective instructional design for PBL (Roessingh and Chambers 2011):

- The project guide and mentor must have expertise in both project areas as well as the pedagogy of PBL.
- The adopted instructional design should be learner-centred and also flexible.
- There must be a question or problem that should guide project exploration.
- There should be explicit statements about both instructional objectives as well as learning objectives or outcomes.
- Both teachers and students select and engage with learning tasks that are authentic as well as engaging.
- There should be effective mediation and integration of instruction, as in the case of Vygotskian actual and proximal levels of development.
- PBL should be so designed that the entire or part of the process promotes critical reflection and higher-order thinking skills.
- There should be provision for continuous assessment and monitoring.

In the study on teacher professional development (Roessingh and Chambers (2011), the linkage for essential design elements for PBL involved: project overview and rationale → learning objectives → materials and resources → enabling tasks → assessment strategies.

In the design of PBL for media policy and governance, which is the theme of this book, and further enumerated in subsequent chapters, the essential design elements included: programme concept map and graduate attributes

→ course concepts map and learning outcomes → course instructional objectives → learning outcomes → key concepts → projects concept map → pre-project workshop exercises → template parameters and guidelines → learning resources → illustrative case and case presentation → student self-evaluation → evaluation and assessment rubric and methods (components, contents, presentation) and criteria for grading.

While the rationale has been underlined in Chapter 1, PBL-in-action is articulated by practitioner teachers, with a contextualised application within the field of media policy and governance, in Chapters 4 to 7.

References

Alexander, R.J. *Culture and Pedagogy: International Comparisons in Primary Education.* London: Wiley Blackwell, 2001.

———. 'Towards a Comparative Pedagogy.' In *International Handbook of Comparative Education*, edited by R. Cowen and A.M. Kazamias, 923–942. Switzerland: Springer, 2009.

Barron, B., et al. 'Doing with Understanding: Lessons from Research on Problem and Project-Based Learning.' *Journal of the Learning Sciences* 7, no. 3 and 4 (1998): 271–311.

Belenky, M., B. Clinchy, N. Goldberger, and J. Tarule. *Women's Ways of Knowing: The Development of Self, Voice, and Mind.* New York: Basic Books, 1986.

Bell, F. 'Connectivism: Its Place in Theory-Informed Research and Innovation in Technology-Enabled Learning.' *International Review of Research in Open and Distance Learning* 12, no. 3 (2011): 98–118.

Brown, J., A. Collins, and P. Duguid. 'Situated Cognition and the Culture of Learning.' *Educational Researcher* 18, no. 1 (1989): 32–42.

Bruner, J.S. *Towards a Theory of Instruction.* Massachusetts: Belknap Press, 1966.

———. *The Culture of Education.* Cambridge, MA: Harvard University Press, 1996.

Condliffe, B., et al. *Project-Based Learning: A Literature Review.* New York: MDRC, 2017.

Conole, G., et al. 'Mapping Pedagogy and Tools for Effective Learning Design.' *Computers and Education* 43 (2004): 17–33.

Cook-Sather, A. 'Lessons in Higher Education: Five Pedagogical Practices that Promote Active Learning for Faculty and Students.' *Journal of Faculty Development* 26, no. 1 (2012): 1–7.

Dewey, J. *Democracy and Education.* New York: Macmillan, 2016.

Eckel, K. *Instruction Language: Foundations of a Strict Science of Instruction.* Englewood Cliffs: Educational Technology Publications, 1993.

Frank, M. and A. Barzilai. 'Integrating Alternative Assessment in a Project-Based Learning Course for Preservice Science and Technology Teachers.' *Assessment and Evaluation in Higher Education* 29, no. 1 (2004): 41–61.

Freire, P. *Pedagogy of the Oppressed.* Harmondsworth: Penguin, 1972.

———. *The politics of Education: Culture, Power and Liberation.* Connecticut: Bergin and Garvey, Westport, 1985.

Giroux, H.A. *Pedagogy and the Politics of Hope.* Boulder: Westview, 1997.

———. 'Higher Education Under Siege: Rethinking the Politics of Critical Pedagogy.' *Counterpoints* 422 (2012): 327–341.

Giroux, H.A. and S.S. Giroux. 'Challenging Neoliberalism's New World Order: The Promise of Critical Pedagogy.' *Cultural Studies: Critical Methodologies* 6, no. 1 (2006): 21–32.

Hamilton, D. 'The Pedagogic Paradox (or why no didactics in England?).' *Pedagogy, Culture and Society* 7, no. 1 (1999): 135–152.

———. 'Blurred in Translation: Reflections on Pedagogy in Public Education.' *Pedagogy, Culture and Society* 17, no. 1 (2009): 5–16.

Henry, H., et al. 'I Know this is Supposed to be More like the Real World, but…: Student Perceptions of PBL Implementation of an Undergraduate Materials Science Course.' *Interdisciplinary Journal of Problem-Based Learning* 6, no. 1 (2012): 43–81.

Henschke, J.A. 'A Perspective on the History and Philosophy of Andragogy: An International Sketch.' In *Proceedings of the Commission on International Adult Education Pre-Conference*, edited by M. Boucouvalas, 54–122. Cleveland, Ohio: AAACE, 2009.

Hong, H.Y. and F.R. Sullivan. 'Towards an Idea-Centered, Principle-Based Design Approach to Support Learning as Knowledge Creation.' *Educational Technology Research and Development* 57, no. 5 (2009): 613–627.

Ireson, J., P. Mortime, and S. Hallant. 'The Common Strands of Pedagogy and their Implications.' In *Understanding Pedagogy and its Impact on Learning*, edited by P. Mortimore. London: Paul Chapman, 1999.

Kemmis, S. and L. Fitzclarence. *Curriculum Theorising: Beyond Reproduction Theory*. Victoria: Deakin University Press, 1991.

Kilpatrick, W.H. 'The Project Method.' *Teachers College Record* 19 (1918): 319–335.

———. 'Designers and Difficulties of the Project Methods and How to Overcome Them: A Symposium.' *Teachers College Record* 22, no. 4 (1921): 283–288.

Kivunja, C. 'Do You Want Your Students to be Job-Ready with 21st-Century Skills? Change Pedagogies: A Pedagogical Paradigm Shift from Vygotskyian Social Constructivism to Critical Thinking, Problem-Solving and Siemens' Digital Connectivism.' *International Journal of Higher Education* 3, no. 3 (2014): 81–91.

Knowles, M. *Andragogy in Action: Applying Modern Principles of Adult Learning*. San Francisco: Jossey Bass, 1968a.

———. 'Andragogy, not Pedagogy.' *Adult Leadership* 16, no. 10 (1968b): 350–352, 386.

———. *The Modern Practice of Adult Education: Andragogy versus Pedagogy*. New York: Association Press, 1970.

———. *The Adult Learner: A Neglected Species*. Houston: Gulf Publishing, 1973.

———. *Self-Directed Learning: A Guide for Learners and Teachers*. Englewood Cliffs, NJ: Cambridge Book, 1975.

———. *The Modern Practice of Adult Education: From Pedagogy to Andragogy* (revised edition). New Jersey: Cambridge Book, 1980.

Knowlton, D.S. 'A Theoretical Framework for the Online Classroom: A Defense and Delineation of a Student-Centred Pedagogy.' *New Directions for Teaching and Learning* 84 (2000): 5–14.

Kolb, D.A. *Experiential Learning: Experience as a Source of Learning and Development.* New Jersey: Prentice-Hall, 1984.

Krajcik, J.S. and P. Blumenfield. 'Project-Based Learning.' In *The Cambridge Handbook of the Learning Science*, 317–333. New York: Cambridge University Press, 2006.

Lave, J. and E. Wenger. *Situated Learning.* Cambridge: Cambridge University Press, 1991.

Leask, B. *Internationalising the Curriculum.* London: Routledge, 2015.

Lee, J.S., S. Blackwell, J. Drake, and K.A. Moran. 'Taking a Leap of Faith: Redefining Teaching and Learning in Higher Education through Project-Based Learning.' *Interdisciplinary Journal of Problem-Based Learning* 8, no. 2 (2014): 18–34.

Lipson, A., A. Epstein, R. Bras, and K. Hodges. 'Students' Perceptions of Terrascope: A Project-Based Freshmen Learning Community.' *Journal of Science Education and Technology* 16, no. 4 (2007): 349–364.

Lotz-Sisitka, H., A.E.J. Wals, D. Kronlid, and D. McGarry. 'Transformative, Transgressive Social Learning: Rethinking Higher Education Pedagogy in terms of Systemic Global Dysfunction.' *Current Opinion in Environmental Sustainability* 16 (2015): 73–80.

Markham, T., J. Larmer, and J. Ravitz. *Project-Based Learning Handbook: A Guide to Standards Focused Project-Based Learning for Middle and High School Teachers.* Novato, CA: Buck Institute for Education, 2003.

Marton, F., G. Dall Alba, and E. Beaty. 'Conceptions of Learning.' *International Journal of Educational Research* 19, no. 3 (1993): 277–300.

McArthur, J. 'Time to Look Anew: Critical Pedagogy and Disciplines within Higher Education.' *Studies in Higher Education* 35, no. 3 (2010): 301–315.

Moore, A. *Teaching and Learning: Pedagogy, Curriculum and Culture.* London and New York: Routledge Falmer, 2000.

NCTE. *Upanishads: Messages for Teachers and Teacher Educations.* New Delhi: National Council for Teacher Education (Government of India), 2016.

Nottingham Andragogy Group. *Towards a Developmental Theory of Andragogy.* Nottingham: Nottingham Department of Adult Education, 1983.

Nussbaum, M. *Cultivating Humanity: A Critical Defence of Reform in Liberal Education.* Cambridge: Harvard University Press, 1997.

———. *Women and Human Development.* Cambridge: Cambridge University Press, 2000.

Osher, D., et al. *Science of Learning and Development: A Synthesis.* Arlington, VA: American Institutes for Research, 2017.

Palmer, P. *The Courage of Teach.* San Francisco: Jossey-Bass, 1998.

Panda, S. and S. Mishra. 'Epilogue: Towards Mainstreaming Technology-Enabled Learning.' In *Technology Enabled Learning: Policy, Pedagogy, Practice*, edited by S. Mishra and S. Panda, 225–244. Vancouver: The Commonwealth of Learning, 2020.

Papastergiou, M. 'Learning to Design and Implement Educational Websites within Preserve Teacher Training: A Project-Based Learning Environment and its Impact on Student Teachers.' *Learning, Media and Technology* 30, no. 3 (2005): 263–279.

Pellegrino, J.W. 'Complex Learning Environments: Connecting Learning Theory, Instructional Design, and Technology.' In *Curriculum, Plans, and Processes in Instructional Design: International Perspectives*, edited by N.M. Seel and S. Dijkstra. New Jersey: Lawrence Erlbaum, 2004.

Peterson, C. and C. Ray. 'Angragogy and Metagogy: The Evolution of Neologisms.' *Journal of Adult Education* 42, no. 2 (2013): 80–85.

Piaget, J. *The Child's Conception of the World.* London: Routledge, 1929 (reprinted 1997).

Roessingh, H. and W. Chambers. 'Project-Based Learning and Pedagogy in Teacher Preparation: Staking Out the Theoretical Mid-Ground.' *International Journal of Teaching and Learning in Higher Education* 23, no. 1 (2011): 60–71.

Rogers, C.R. *Freedom to Learn* (2nd edition). Michigan: C.E. Merrill, 1969.

Saljo, R. *Learning in the Learner's Perspective I: Some Common-Sense Perceptions.* Gothenburg, Sweden: University of Gothenburg, 1979.

Sandell, R. 'The Liberating Relevance of Feminist Pedagogy.' *Studies in Art Education* 32, no. 3 (1991): 178–187.

Scott, C.L. *The Futures of Learning 3: What Kind of Pedagogies for the 21st Century?* Working Paper 15. Paris: UNESCO, 2015.

Sen, A. *Inequality Re-examined.* Oxford, UK: Oxford University Press, 1992.

———. *Development as Freedom*. New York: Knopf, 1999.

Shrewsbury, C.M. 'What is Feminist Pedagogy?' *Women's Studies Quarterly* 21, no. 3 and 4 (1993): 8–16.

Smith, M.K. 'Social Pedagogy.' In *Encyclopaedia of Informal Education*, 2009. http://infed.org/biblio/b-socped.htm (Retrieved March 2020).

———. 'What is Pedagogy?' In *Encyclopaedia of Informal Education*, 2012. http:infed.org/mobi/what-is-pedagogy/ (Retrieved March 2020).

Taber, K. 'The Role of New Educational Technology in Teaching and Learning: A Constructivist Perspective on Digital Learning.' In *Handbook on Digital Learning for K-12 Schools,* edited by A. Marcus-Quinn and T. Hourigan, 397–412. Switzerland AG: Springer, 2016.

Thomas, J.W. 'A Review of Research on PBL.' 2000. http://www.bobpearlman.org/BestPractices/PBL_Research.pdf

Trigwell, K., E. Martin, J. Benjamin, and M. Prosser. 'Scholarship of Teaching: A Model.' *Higher Education Research and Development* 19, no. 2 (2000): 155–168.

Vygotsky, L.S. *Mind in Society: The Development of Higher Psychological Processes*, translated by M. Cole, J. Scribner, V. John-Steiner, and E. Souberman. Cambridge, MA: Harvard University Press, 1978.

Walker, M. *Higher Education Pedagogies*. Maidenhead: Open University Press, 2006.

Watkins, C. and P. Martimore. 'Pedagogy: What Do We Know.' In *Understanding Pedagogy and Its Impact on Learning*, edited by P. Martimore. London: SAGE, 1999.

Wilhelm, J., et al. 'Project-Based Learning Environments: Challenging Preservice Teachers to Act in the Moment.' *Journal of Educational Research* 101, no. 4 (2008): 220–233.

Young, T. 'Pedagogy-walk the Talk, Don't Talk the Walk. An Opinion Piece.' *Higher Education Pedagogies* 5, no. 1 (2020): 53–57.

3

Media Education and Media Pedagogy in India

Biswajit Das

> Media education is a very neglected and underdeveloped field in most developing countries including India. While a good deal of attention has been given to planning the technological side of communication and media, not much attention has been given towards creating the human agents who will use this technology in a socially purposeful and creative manner. (Joshi 2002)

The epigraph highlights the state of media education in India. However, much has changed and still needs to be changed. This chapter deals with a discussion on media education in India. It provides a historical account of the development of the field and the institutions involved in promoting curriculum and research in the field. Besides, the evolution and pedagogical contours of the field have been studied and the need for studying policy has been advocated in media education.

The idea of media education has gained currency in recent years in Indian academia. Although it has been already in place in some form or the other, the recent usage of the term, especially within media academia, is quite intriguing. The question arises, why such nomenclature? Given the fact that historically media courses have been taught in Indian academia almost for a century, they initially started with print journalism courses, followed by mass communication, broadcast journalism, convergence journalism, communication studies, media studies and, now, new media. A sufficient amount of literature on the institutions and mediums studied by scholars is available in India (Desai 2017; Das et al. 2005). Most of these refer either to journalism education and needs (Sanjay 2002, 2006; Eapen 1982; Desai 2008, 2017; Belavadi 2002; Tere 2012; Ranganathan 2006), approaches to journalism education (Kumar 1995, 1999; Vilanilam 1993; Rao 2009; Banerjee 2009) and development and direction (Joshi 2002; Ukeri 2015; Yadav 2003).

These contributions are extremely useful as they discuss various issues pertaining to the study of journalism, institutions, approaches in medium-specific cases and trajectories. However, these studies do not provide sufficient insights into the field's knowledge dimension (Das 2005, 2009). The question remains unanswered whether the idea of media education is an internal compulsion to provide a direction to the fragmented and horizontal expansion in the field or an external influence to streamline, keeping in view the global requirements in the field (Das 2014).

Institutionalising Media Education

India completed hundred years of teaching media education. The past hundred years have witnessed an exponential growth of media education in distinct geographies in the country. Scholars have mapped the early institutional history of media education in the country (Madras, Mysore, Calcutta, Aligarh and Lahore). Much has been written about the early institutional history of media education and the pioneers; however, much needs to be explored about the intellectual, cultural and pedagogical dimensions of these institutions. For instance, the journey of media education from Madras to Lahore is a long shift in terms of the paradigm of media education. This shift equally reflects from an Anglo-Saxon to an Anglo-American perspective of media education in India. Media courses were located under various disciplines and schools within humanities, social sciences, commerce departments and journalism schools. It rose to prominence with a strong interdisciplinary orientation from the beginning. The pioneers came from diverse disciplinary backgrounds and brought their disciplinary baggage in shaping the interdisciplinarity of the discipline. But the demise of interdisciplinarity occurred along with the conscious creation of the discipline with endless re-creations across the country. The identity of the discipline through compartmentalisation may have helped in the expansion of the discipline and disciplinarians across the country, but this resulted in isolation from other disciplines as well.

Thus, the growth of Indian media and communication studies was ushered in after Independence in 1947. Its main attributes were: professionalisation of media and communication studies, emphasis on teaching and research and specialisation in select thematic thrust areas with suitable themes and methods. Although media courses were introduced before Independence in a few cases, the institutionalisation of media education was very much a product of the setting up of the University Grants Commission (UGC) in the country.

Indian political leadership, intellectuals and citizenry were acutely conscious of the challenges of development and nation-building. To this objective, the constitution reflecting the future vision of India as a republic was adopted, and alongside, the Planning Commission was set up to formulate priorities and plans for national development. As new universities and colleges were established, the teaching of media education also began to expand, contributing thus to the growth in numbers of teachers and researchers in the discipline. The UGC was established to provide funds for teaching and research in universities and colleges and regulate its standards. Funds for researching policy-related problems were also made available by the Planning Commission. As a result, the motivation among communication scholars and social scientists to conduct research in the areas of greater social and economic relevance is augmented. The Planning Commission sponsored a series of studies in the areas of urban communication, rural and agricultural development, the nature of poverty, social and economic conditions of the weaker sections, et cetera. Most of these areas were prioritised keeping in view the development agenda and planning in the country. The information gathered helped in generating bench mark information for further intervention in development projects in the country (Das 2012).

These processes, together with other developments in the field, contributed to the professionalisation of communication. Communication is now taught in various educational institutions as an independent subject, and full-fledged communication departments have been set up across central, regional and private universities in India. The UGC constantly supports the professional growth of the field. As a part of its subject-wise national panels of professors, the UGC periodically reviews and revises the syllabi. The UGC also set up an Inter-Ministerial Taskforce on Education in Media Related Courses (2012). Since then, it has regularly undertaken and sponsored research projects, organised seminars and workshops to evaluate the state of the discipline and formulate policies for the modernisation and standardisation of the curricular structure in communication. Due to a high degree of regional diversity in terms of institutional standards and linguistic practices in teaching, efforts have been made with the participation of teachers of communication from all regions of the country to evolve a consensus on the modernisation of curricula. Empirical research on the state of teaching and research of communication and its profession in the country has also helped formulate issues that both deserve discussion at the national level and require a comparative international level upgrade. So far, the suggestions and recommendations made by the national panels have been widely appreciated and incorporated in the syllabi of communication in universities and colleges (Desai 2017).

An impetus was further added to the field of communication in the 1960s with generous contributions from the Indian Council of Social Science Research (ICSSR) through research grants and funds to improve and promote the quality of research in communication in the country. The ICSSR has been responsible for setting up research institutes of social sciences and communication in the Indian states and providing funds to undertake research. It is also responsible for making available fellowships and grants to teachers and students of communication to conduct their research. The ICSSR brings out decennial survey reports highlighting emerging trends of research on communication in India. These surveys reveal both micro and macro dimensions of research undertaken by scholars and are published in/by reputed journals and publishing houses. These contributions are immense and handy for young researchers who want to know about the field and the nature of research undertaken by scholars.

Both UGC and ICSSR have thus been involved in the structuring and evaluation of pedagogy and research in communication. The focus on relevance has been a common value framework promoted by the two bodies, although, while the former seeks it in the curricula and the choice of research projects, the latter focuses primarily on the selection of research themes and methods. In defining relevance, most members of the profession show unanimity about the indigenisation of concepts and theories. It is realised that without erecting walls of separation between communication in India and abroad, Indian communication scholars and social scientists should both creatively adapt concepts, methods and substantive contributions alongside aiming towards evolving concepts and methods grounded in Indian historicity and social and cultural specificity for social and economic development.

Overall, both institutions have greatly impacted the professional and disciplinary growth of communication in India. However, institutions alone cannot create an impact; they may, at best, facilitate it.

It is the scholars and their academic and intellectual pursuits that contribute to the growth of the discipline. New nomenclatures, such as mass communication, communication, media studies, et cetera, were added in the mid-1970s, which have continued to exist today alongside the existing ones, such as convergence journalism, new media, media governance, et cetera. Departments and schools of communication rechristened their academic programmes accordingly. These programmes may have introduced new nomenclatures but did not encourage faculties from other fields; the administrative provision also did not allow such migration. There have been contributions in these diverse areas but may not be considered sufficient enough to create a body of knowledge that may help to understand the field of media studies and education. The 1990s witnessed a sea change not only in media technology but also the geopolitical alignment and information order and disorder. It interrogated the concept of territory, news flows, monopoly of news, news as a public good. The neoliberal agenda opened up news not only to a marketplace of ideas but also allowed voices in civil society and the market to engage with media. Media institutions, too, could not remain as silent spectators to the emerging opportunities. Hence, media institutions expanded along with the expansion of the market, as media education became a prized possession.

This is visible in the proliferation of postgraduate programmes in mass communication, which focused on technical expertise and neglected theoretical, methodological and research skills. Theoretically, the discipline relied on models from the West rather than evolving indigenous perspectives on communication in the Indian context. Media teaching was also used as a ground to train professionals for the media industry within the broader framework of nation-building. The general syllabi proposed by UGC mostly reflected an industry orientation. It is not mandatory as each institution is an autonomous entity to fashion its own syllabus. However, the UGC syllabi reflect the orientation of the senior faculties, who are engaged in formulating the curriculum, and their conviction about the future of the discipline. A cursory glance at the syllabi framed by UGC reveals an industry orientation and training in media education. This emphasis resulted in segregation and distanced the discipline from humanities and social sciences, thus making the field more of a technical enterprise. Media education courses were geared towards medium-specific issues such as editing, reporting and production in print, radio, television and cinema rather than exploring communication–society relationships. This hampered knowledge production in and disciplinary engagement with the field. The lack of engagement with research revealed the poverty of scholarship in the discipline of communication in India. Even though initial contributions in the field reached the social science departments, these contributions were limited in scope. Media technology was treated as an instrument of change, providing a technocratic solution for development. Be it in the health sector, education, rural development, agriculture and family planning, the initial contributions had a clear agenda of communication for development (Gupta 1985; Agarwal 2000).

This utilitarian perspective is shared by Das and Parthasarathi (2011):

> [M]ost research in communication by anthropologists and other social scientists during 1950–1960 reflected this perspective. Such studies used empirical designs of research premised upon the rational-utilitarian paradigm of social action and the shaping of choices in decision-making. This empirical tradition of communication research in India gradually began to establish the relevance of communication in policy formulation and development planning. It also sensitized the need for interdisciplinary perspectives to generate a fuller understanding of social structure and processes. The significance of communication in the analysis of political behaviours, institutions and processes, such as through political parties, leadership, voting behaviour, political mobilization and modernization, among other related issues, is widely reflected in these studies. Support for conducting research on policy-related problems—notably, health and family planning, productivity and innovations in agriculture and community development was initiated by the Planning Commission of the Government of India. It is intriguing that while communication research was conducted in agricultural universities and social science faculties in various universities, courses on media were introduced in some universities without any research orientation. (247)

Besides social science departments, specialised institutions were created by the government to study and evaluate planned intervention through communication technologies. Few institutions also studied press, public opinion and audiences for the media. The idea behind the research was to promote readership for the press, listeners for radio, government programmes through the media, et cetera. In a way, such research emphasised the legitimation of state policies. (Das and Parthasarathi 2011).

As Das, Parthasarathi and Poitevin (2005) write:

> [T]he essential character of communication processes does not reside merely in the advent of a technology or the creation of textual, sonic or visual phenomenon alone. Rather, it concerns the varied set of altered, both re-defined and fresh, social activities incorporating such processes. More specifically, it concerns different ways in which knowledge—as information, cultural forms, ideologies or commodities—came to be socially, and indeed industrially, produced and circulated; the manners in which these processes further shaped how individuals relate with forms of knowledge and through that, to each other and to society as a whole. (85)

The past three decades have witnessed significant expansion and growth of media institutions in the country. New courses were added to the existing ones in the newly created central, state, deemed and private universities and specialised institutes to meet the demands of media education. While there was a phenomenal expansion of institutions across sectors, there is no consensus regarding the subject matter and method. Media and communication courses are placed in different disciplines such as humanities, social sciences, journalism and mass communication and, finally, information technology and science. These different disciplines reflect an interdisciplinary character that informs the theory, method and practice of media education in India (Singh 2010).

Media Studies in India

The processes of institutional recognition and professionalisation of communication contributed to the expansion of the range of research interests of media scholars in India. Its linkage with policy planning and social and economic development reinforced this process. Das and Parthasarathi (2011) comment that the US had a hegemonic influence in the world of social sciences and communication than the UK after the Second World War. In the US, social sciences and communication had made unprecedented strides in the applied areas of media research and brought about myriad innovations in research methodology. This process of growth in American communication logically resulted in differentiation and specialisation in the discipline. We witness a convergence of two types of influences of American communication on Indian media studies soon after Independence. The first relates to the emergence of American communication as a domineering influence on European, even global, communication following the Second World War, and second, its rich and unparalleled advances in policy-oriented research methodologies and techniques accorded it a leadership role in media and social sciences. As a consequence of these developments, and also because in India the process of planned development had just begun, the influence of American communication and social anthropology began to grow. Indian media studies increasingly came under the influence of American communication and social anthropological, conceptual and theoretical orientations. The research contributions during this period bear testimony to it. Most of these contributions attempted to link communication with Indian processes of development and modernisation. Indeed, Everett Roger's (1995) model of 'diffusion of innovation' became the conceptual edifice for theoretical engagement and methodological inputs for most of these studies.

Evidently, we witness here the influence of the American traditions of communication research, which soon came under criticism for being deeply anchored in methodological individualism and abstracted empiricism. The debates on critical issues in communication studies and its discourses, such as how it was grounded in a specific and narrow domain of epistemological and cultural perspective on communication and view on social sciences, was overlooked during this period. Despite its limitation, it had some positive consequences for policy formulation, development planning and sensitisation for interdisciplinary engagement in media education.

These research contributions draw inspiration from the theoretical contributions made by the American behavioural school of political theory. The new concerns in communication studies led to research interests in the areas of information economics, group dynamics and psychometry in both substantive and theoretical terms. However, by the beginning of the 1970s, slowly the impact of positivist theory and methodology on social sciences and communication began to face challenges in the West. Its effects were also felt across Asia and Latin America, including in India. A resurgence began to take place in the grounding of social sciences to their philosophical roots in phenomenology, neo-Marxism and neo- structuralism, which impacted the operationalisation of substantive studies in communication. The disenchantment in Indian communication with Western positivism was, however, located not only in the limitations of its premises or philosophical groundings, but it was also because such theories overlooked the specificities of Indian cultural, social and historical processes in the formulations of conceptual categories. Its premise was derived from the functionalist theory, which was implicit in Roger's model of communication. It showed success only in areas that were selective in a structural sense, such as rich peasants in India benefiting by adopting green-revolution technology to the exclusion of smaller landholders. The model, however, failed to achieve the goals of population control, universal healthcare and eradication of illiteracy. In these sectors, the target groups comprised the poor and very poor. It showed the theoretical limitations of diffusion theory, which relied heavily on manipulating 'motivations' and neglected the role of structural differentiations and inequities, which also governed people making choices on acceptance or otherwise of the innovations sponsored for development and change. As a consequence, most communication research undertaken in the 1970s began to focus on the variability of social structure and culture and their internal dialectics in evaluating the role of communication in bringing about social change.

The process of differentiation in Indian communication today is growing in two directions: first, in the expansion and diversification of the nature of the social, cultural and developmental problems, which communication scholars began to study, and second, in the diversification and differentiation of methodologies and tools of research, which are now available and increasingly being used by media scholars and social anthropologists. It may also be pointed out that the national concern for planned development of the Indian economy and society, which ranged from rural development and urban planning to the empowerment of scheduled tribes, scheduled castes, weaker sections and minorities to the industrialisation of the economy, et cetera, had opened up a vast vista of researchable problems for media scholars and social scientists.

Indian communication came in close contact during the 1950s with the researchers from the West, more specifically with American scholars that not only helped the growth of the field but also borrowed the mainstream model or the so-called dominant paradigm in communication. The focus on method and technique in communication studies, identified singularly with the American influence in communication, came increasingly under criticism for its emphasis on the premise that social systems are essentially consensual and self-integrative or self-maintaining. Functional theory in communication, a counterpart of such methods, began to be treated as inadequate in diagnosing or analysing the significant processes within social systems, for it neglected the role of conflict and contradictions in the structure and process of social realities.

In recent times, we see further division in the field of communication and culture. Consequently, not only in Europe or the developing world but also in America, many alternate theoretical paradigms, particularly those related to conflict theory, Marxist historical materialism or dialectical materialism, phenomenology, ethnomethodology and critical theory, began to gain acceptance. These developments were not sui generis but the product of the emerging global social situation; they exemplify the close relationship that has always existed between theory and social conditions that influence its orientation and growth. These trends have a definite impact on media studies in India. As Das (2012) writes, '[C]ommunications systems—industries, cultural formations and sites of everyday social practice—are now seen as central to the reorganization of economic and imaginative life. This new-found prominence presents fresh insights in understanding theory, method and history that inform communication in India' (158). Studies in India in the past years have shown much interest to analyse the media through newspapers (Israel 1994; Joseph 1994; Rao 2010; Udupa 2015; Rangnathan 2006; Rao 2009), radio (Chatterji 1987; Pinkerton 2008; Das 2005), television (Brosius and Butcher 1999; Farmer 1996, 2000; Johnson 2000; Butcher 2003; Gupta 1998; Krishnan and Dighe 1990; Rajagopal 1993, 2001; Narayan 2014; Verghese 1977; Saeed 2013; Mitra 1993; Mehta 2008; Ninan 1995), films (Pandian 1992; Prasad 1998; Nandy 1998; Bhaskaran 1981; Chakravarty 1993), audiovisual media (Parthasarathi 2005, 2010a, 2010b; Hughes 2002; Manuel 1993). These contributions are immense. Not only do they reflect the internal dynamics of the media and its application to larger society but also the method used to study such phenomena. These contributions reflect the interdisciplinary orientation as well as the interest among scholars from social sciences, humanities and media studies to collectively engage and contribute in making the field of media education vibrant in India (Singh 2010, 2014; Sinha 2010). By analysing the factors that made different audiences respond in contrasting ways to various media texts, these contributions show how various audiences interpret and use media culture differently. These studies insist that culture must be studied within the social relations and system through which culture is produced and consumed and that the study of culture is intimately bound with the study of society, politics and economics. These studies show how media culture articulates dominant values, political ideologies and social developments; they also show how it communicates novelties of the era and conceives Indian culture and society as a contested terrain with various groups and ideologies struggling for dominance. The neoliberal policies of globalisation have transformed media sources into largely market-driven enterprises, scarcely in touch with social ideals. The market-driven reform provides substantive media choices to its consumers. These choices are analysed with the help of borrowed concepts and methodologies from various disciplines. Thus, media education has been growing as an interdisciplinary field of inquiry, addressing diverse issues from social structure, culture, diversity of content, choices, audience and policy dimension of media in India.

Pedagogical Implication of Media Education

The contributions in media studies in India are diverse, ranging from issues of development to journalism, culture, content, mass media, public opinion and so on. This may be broadly classified under three scholarly traditions, namely journalism, humanities and social sciences. These three traditions are not necessarily exclusive but overlapping as well. While the contributions in humanities and social sciences are used in select academic institutions in the country, the remaining institutions in the country follow journalism courses with specific emphasis on industry. Thus, these courses are industry-driven, hence uniformly implemented with little variations across the country. This uniformity with little variations across the region caters to the local needs, such as the employability of students, of media industries. Thus, media education courses in India serve two masters: the media industry and the university system. Both of them have different orientations and purposes. The following pedagogical traditions may be observed:

Journalistic Tradition

This is the dominant tradition that has found much acceptance across regions due to its potential contribution to the media industry. While the more equipped central university departments have kept pace with the developments and introduced courses on electronic media, regional institutions continue to focus on print media. In both cases, the industry is the main supplier of teachers. Practising correspondents and editors provide an experiential overview of the everyday life and challenges of the profession. They are the role models of success that the students emulate, which sustains the demand and supply chain of the field. However, practice-based journalism teaching is seldom accompanied by critical reflections on the philosophical foundations, socio-political context and development in the field and its interlinkages with democracy. Often, these courses elude the academic frame altogether. An under-theorised field, journalism education is, therefore, a long way from qualifying as journalism studies.

Cultural Studies and Humanities Tradition

This came into prominence in the 1990s within the rubric of postmodern and post-structuralist thinking. Drawing heavily from semiotics and literary theories, the cultural studies departments opened up new vistas of research on everyday consumption and social and cultural practices around the media. They continued the sociological and anthropological traditions of enquiry of the impact of media on culture and society, which were a favoured research domain in the early decades of Indian communication studies. However, on many occasions, the texts of cultural studies fetishise more than deconstruct and have been severely critiqued for neglecting matters of political economy, especially when media, markets and governance have become intertwined in insidious ways.

Social Science Tradition

While there was a lack of theoretical engagement with the idea of communication within media disciplines, it has, all this while, been taught and studied as a subfield in select social science departments in the country. There has been no creative engagement between the two, only suspicion and mistrust about the encroachment of boundaries. Notwithstanding the distance, social sciences have thus far nurtured the field theoretically and historically more than any other discipline. However, due to a lack of continuous engagement and research, the social science disciplines are not much informed about the intricacies in media, especially in a rapidly changing environment. Overall, media courses have been neglected in the repertoire of courses developed within mainstream social science departments, and most courses remain under-theorised. Needless to say, universities have contributed variously to the expansion and growth of the departments and schools of media studies. But most of these institutions have not sufficiently engaged with or contributed to the growth of the discipline and its disciplinarity, let alone engage with other disciplines. Thus, media courses in India have been insular, disconnected and, often, invisible. A typical example is its missing interface with policy studies.

The emerging media environment today is characterised by a move from scarcity to the abundance of media technologies and issues. It reveals ambiguities and uncertainties as well as promises and possibilities. It generates manifold issues of enquiry, all of which require multilayered thinking and approaches on the part of media scholars. The changing domain of media policy and governance forms an important object of concern. It is important to analyse and debate media policy to develop a broad consensus among stakeholders in order to sustain a vibrant democracy. These discussions will inform us how and where it is formulated and the actors and advocates actively involved in its framing. Any theoretical endeavour on media policy needs to proceed with an awareness of the different sites where policy is being made and the dynamics of power that exist between them. The conventional comfort of policymaking has been transformed during the last three decades due to policies (liberalisation, privatisation and globalisation) embraced by the government. It opens up a series of questions and issues related to the future of media education. Media policy is the backbone of any development related to the media sector in the country. It starts with the basic premise of conventional understanding that the media advances the public good. The shift from a welfare state to a neoliberal state offers manifold dimensions and issues to our ways of looking and thinking about the media.

How do we then visualise these developments in the media sector within the existing curricular framework? To what extent do our curriculum have to engage with the transformations within the media sector? What kind of pedagogy should we use to engage with media education in India? Since there is a disconnect between media research and media teaching, our priority and focus should be to engage with media education from an educational perspective. This perspective should focus not only on teaching and learning but also on knowledge in the field of media education. Much of the teaching in the field has been divided into theory and practice, with a hope to cater to the needs of the media industry and academia. This binary has been consciously propagated by a section of the industry that believes in the pedagogy of learning by doing. It does not realise that teaching media is beyond the needs of the industry. Besides, no practice can do without theoretical assumptions. Hence, theory should not be an alternative to practice; there is a need for both. Practice must not be done in isolation from society. Before we initiate practice, be it in print, television or new media, we must ask ourselves why are we doing it? Whom are we serving for? These questions will clarify the purpose and intent behind the production work and practice.

Media education does not belong to the media industry. Further, media education cannot be rendered unimportant because of the revolutionary transformation in media technologies and culture. These technologies might have resulted in increased uncertainty in the creation, circulation and acquisition of knowledge, but this differentiated media-induced knowledge requires urgent attention. The more the uncertainties the greater the need for media education.

Conclusion

This chapter sought to highlight that at a conceptual level the term *media education* is yet to cohere as a distinct field of enquiry. Although there are scholarly contributions across mediums and institutions, they do not provide sufficient insight into the development of the knowledge dimension of media education. Policy studies is a neglected field in media education. Even though early contributions were immense, the recent engagement in the field, especially when the field of media policy has emerged as a level playing field in India, is minimal,

The chapter showed how the educational potential of the media has been limited to training-oriented programmes, which undermined the importance of knowledge and soft skills related to the discipline. It also highlighted that the revolution in technology has led to academic institutions constantly focussing on updating and upkeeping themselves with these transformations and the grammar of new media technology. While other scientific disciplines have gone through periods of fruitful debate and discussion on the status and growth of the discipline, rarely have communication studies had the privilege of such inquiry. The past three decades have shown the pace of introduction of media courses and curricula to cater to the growing market and industrial media requirements. But rarely has the academic community spared time to reflect on and engage with factors that may shape certain areas for future investigation and identify grey areas that need to be explored further. Therefore, in the emerging media studies and media policy and governance disciplines, further articulation is needed in the new field, new curriculum, pedagogic engagements and policy analysis through hands-on projects. The next chapter engages with an analysis of pedagogy and teaching-learning strategies with a focus on PBL. PBL in media policy and governance projects has been exemplified in Chapters 4–7, followed by a discussion on the professional development of media and governance educators in PBL. The concluding chapter examines the future of media education at the intersection of pedagogy and technology.

References

Agarwal, B.C. 'Culture, Communication and Development: An Indian Perspective.' In *Third Survey of Research in Sociology and Social Anthropology*, edited by M.S. Gore, 296–325. New Delhi: Manak Publications, 2000.

Banerjee, Indrajit. 'Asian Media Studies: The Struggle for International Legitimacy.' In *Internationalizing Media Studies*, edited by Daya Kishan Thussu, 179–188. London: Routledge, 2009.

Belavadi, Vasuki. 'What Ails Media Education in India?: A Teacher's Perspective.' (2002). Posted July 2016. http://www.thehoot.org

Bhaskaran, Theodore S. *The Message Bearers: The Nationalistic Politics and the Entertainment Media in South India*. New Delhi: SAGE, 1981.

Brosius, Christiane and Melissa Butcher. *Image Journeys: Audio-Visual Media and Cultural Change in India*. New Delhi: SAGE, 1999.

Butcher, Melissa. *Transnational Television, Cultural Identity and Change: When STAR Came to India*. New Delhi: SAGE, 2003.

Chakravarty, Sumita. *National Identity in Indian Popular Cinema, 1947–87*. Austin: University of Texas Press, 1993.

Chatterji, P.C. *Broadcasting in India*. New Delhi: SAGE, 1987.

Das, Biswajit. 'Communication Research in India.' In *Identity, Culture and Communication*, edited by Yogendra Singh, 158–209. New Delhi: Oxford University Press, 2014.

———. 'Media Education as a Development Project: Connecting Emancipatory Interests and Governance in India.' *Revista Comunicar* 16, no. 32 (2009): 65–82.

———. 'Mediating Modernity: Colonial Discourse and Radio.' *Media and Mediation: Communication Processes* vol. 1, edited by Bernard Bel et al., 229–255. New Delhi: SAGE, 2005.

———. 'The Quest for Theory: Mapping Communication Studies in India.' In *Media and Mediation: Communication Processes* vol. 1, edited by Bernard Bel et al., 35–66. New Delhi: SAGE, 2005.

———. 'Strengthening Media and Communication in India.' A Pilot Project Report Submitted to UGC, CCMG, Jamia Millia Islamia, New Delhi, 2012.

Das, Biswajit and Vibodh Parthasarathi. 'Media Research and Public Policy: Tiding Over the Rupture.' In *The Handbook of Global Media and Communication Policy*, edited by Robin Marsell and Marc Raboy, 243–260. London: Wiley-Blackwell, 2011.

Das, Biswajit, Vibodh Parthasarathi, and Guy Poitevin. 'Investigating Communication: Remooring the Contours of Research.' In *Media and Mediation: Communication Processes* vol. 1, edited by Bernard Bel, Jan Brouwer, Biswajit Das, Vibodh Parthasarathi and Guy Poitevin, 66–93. New Delhi: SAGE, 2005.

Desai, Mira K. 'Journalism Education in India: Maze or Mosaic.' In *Global Journalism Education in the 21st Century: Challenges and Innovations*, edited by Robyn S. Goodman and Elanie Steyn, 113–136, Texas: Knight Centre for Journalism, 2017.

———. 'Reviewing Communication/Media Education in India: Many Players, Diverse Directions but Lost Focus…?!' *Journal of Global Communication* 1, no. 2 (2008): 118–131.

Eapen, K.E. 'Education for Communication: Indian Scenario.' *Media Asia* 9, no. 2 (1982): 99–104.

Farmer, V.L. 'Mass Media: Images, Mobilization and Communalism.' In *Making India Hindu: Religion, Community and the Politics of Democracy in India*, edited by David Ludden. Delhi: Oxford University Press, 1996.

———. 'Depicting the Nation: Media Politics in Independent India.' In *Transforming India: Social and Political Dynamics of Democracy*, edited by F.R. Frankel, Zoya Hasan, Rajeev Bhargava and Balveer Arora, 254–287. New Delhi: Oxford University Press, 2000.

Freire, Paulo. *The Politics of Education: Culture, Power and Liberation*. Connneticut: Bergin and Garvey, Westport, 1985.

Gupta, Nilanjana. *Switching Channels: Ideologies of Television in India*. New York: Oxford University Press, 1998.

Gupta, S.K. 'Sociology of Communication.' In *Survey of Research in Sociology and Social Anthropology* vol. 2, 151–167. New Delhi: ICSSR/Satvahana, 1985.

Hartmann, Paul, Bhivarao Rajdhar Patil, and Anita Dighe. *The Mass Media and Village Life: An Indian Study.* New Delhi: SAGE, 1989.

Hughes, Stephen P. 'The Music Boom: in Tamil South India: Gramophone, Radio and the Making of Mass Culture.' *Historical Journal of Film, Radio and Television* 22, no. 4 (2002): 445–473.

———. 'Music in the Age of Mechanical Reproduction: Drama, Gramophone, and the Beginnings of Tamil Cinema.' *The Journal of Asian Studies* 66, no. 1 (2007): 3–34.

Israel, Milton. *Communications and Power: Propaganda and the Press in the Indian National Struggle, 1920–1947* no. 56. Cambridge: Cambridge University Press, 1994.

Johnson, Kirk. *Television and Social Change in Rural India*. New Delhi: SAGE, 2000.

Joseph, Ammu and Kalpana Sharma, eds. *Whose News? The Media and Women's Issues*. New Delhi: SAGE, 1994.

Joshi, P.C. *Communication and National Development*. New Delhi: Anamika Publishers, 2002.

Krishnan, Prabha and Anita Dighe. *Affirmation and Denial: Construction of Femininity on Indian Television*. New Delhi: SAGE, 1990.

Kumar, K.J. 'The Changing Media Scenario in India: Implications for Media Education.' *Children and Media: Image, Education, Participation*. Goteborg, Sweden: UNESCO, 1999.

———. *Media Education, Communication, and Public Policy: An Indian Perspective*. New Delhi: Himalaya Publishing House, 1995.

Manuel, Peter. *Cassette Culture: Popular Music and Technology in North India*. Chicago: University of Chicago Press, 1993.

Mehta, Nalin, ed. *Television in India: Satellites, Politics and Cultural Change*. New Delhi: Routledge, 2008.

Mitra, Ananda. *Television and Popular Culture in India: A Study of the Mahabharat*. New Delhi: SAGE, 1993.

Nandy, Ashish, ed. *The Secret Politics of Our Desires: Innocence, Culpability and Indian Popular Cinema*. New Delhi: Oxford University Press, 1998.

Narayan, Sunetra Sen. *Globalization and Television: A Study of the Indian Experience, 1990–2010*. New Delhi: Oxford University Press, 2014.

Ninan, Sevanti. *Through the Magic Window: Television and Change in India*. New Delhi: Penguin Books, 1995.

Pandian, M.S.S. *The Image Trap: MG Ramachandran in Film and Politics*. New Delhi: SAGE, 1992.

Parthasarathi, Vibodh. 'Construing a "New Media" Market: Merchandising the Talking Machine, c.1900–1913.' In *Media and Mediation: Communication Processes* vol. 1, edited by Bernard Bel et al., 165–198. New Delhi: SAGE, 2005.

———. 'Interventionist Tendencies in Popular Culture.' *Communication, Culture and Confrontation: Communication Processes* vol. 3, edited by Bernard Bel et al., 47–69. New Delhi: SAGE, 2010a.

———. 'Articulating His Master's Voice: Reflection on the Ecology of Early Recorded Sound.' In *Social Sciences: Communication, Anthropology and Sociology*, edited by Yogendra Singh, 189–210. New Delhi: Pearson, 2010b.

Pinkerton, Alasdair. 'Radio and the Raj: Broadcasting in British India (1920–1940).' *Journal of the Royal Asiatic Society* Series 3, 18, no. 2 (2008): 167–191; 1–25.

Prasad, M. Madhava. *Ideology of the Hindi Film: A Historical Construction*. New Delhi: Oxford University Press, 1998.

Prasad, Nandini. *A Vision Unveiled: Women on Television*. Delhi: Har-Anand Publications, 1994.

Rajagopal, Arvind. 'The Rise of National Programming: The Case of Indian Television.' *Media, Culture & Society* 15, no. 1 (1993): 91–111.

———. *Politics After Television: Hindu Nationalism and the Reshaping of the Public in India*. Cambridge, UK: Cambridge University Press, 2001.

Rangnathan, M. 'A Statutory Body for Media Education.' *Vidura, Journal of the Press Institute of India* 43, no. 4 (2006): 31–32.

Rao, Shakuntala. 'Glocalization of Indian Journalism.' *Journalism Studies* 10, no. 4 (2009): 474–488.

Rao, Ursula. *News as Culture: Journalistic Practices and the Remaking of Indian Leadership Traditions* vol. 3. New York: Berghahn Books, 2010.

Rogers, E.M. *Diffusion of Innovations*. New York: The Free Press, 1995.

Saeed, Saima. *Screening the Public Sphere: Media and Democracy in India*. New Delhi: Routledge, 2013.

Sanjay, B.P. 'Communication Education and Media Needs in India.' A Study Conducted by Asian Media Information and Communication Centre of India. Chennai: AMIC-INDIA, 2002.

———. 'News Media Teaching in India.' In *Making News*, edited by U. Sahay, 28–37. New Delhi: Oxford University Press, 2006.

Shah, Amrita. *Hype, Hypocrisy, and Television in Urban India*. New Delhi: Vikas Publishing House, 1997.

Singh, Yogendra, ed. *Identity, Culture and Communication*. New Delhi: Oxford University Press, 2014

———. *Social Sciences: Communication, Anthropology, and Sociology*. New Delhi: Pearson, 2010.

Sinha, Dipankar. 'Communication: The Challenges of Globalization, Information Society, Identity and Development.' In *Social Sciences: Communication, Anthropology and Sociology*, edited by Yogendra Singh, 231–247. New Delhi: Pearson Longman/ Centre for Studies in Civilizations, 2010.

Ståhlberg, Per. 'Lucknow Daily: How a Hindi Newspaper Constructs Society.' PhD diss., Department of Social Anthropology, Stockholm University, 2002.

Tere, N.S. 'Commentary—Increasing Journalism Education in India: Concern for Quality.' *Asia Pacific Media Educator* 22, no. 1 (2012): 127–133.

Udupa, Sahana. *Making News in Global India: Media, Public, Politics*. Cambridge: Cambridge University Press, 2015.

UKIERI. 'Vision for Media and Communication Education in India'. New Delhi: CMS Academy, 2015.

Verghese, B.G. 'The Media in a Free Society: Proposals for Restructuring.' *Economic and Political Weekly* 12, no 18 (1977): 731–740.

Vilanilam, J.V. *Science and Communication*. New Delhi: SAGE, 1993.

Yadav, J.S. 'At the Cross Road'. *Vidura* 40, no. 4 (2003): 13–15.

Section 2

Pedagogic Practices: Project-Based Learning

4

Enumerating Media Diversity

Athikho Kaisii, Nabeela Inayati and Vibodh Parthasarathi

Introduction

The media plays a vital role in shaping public opinion and politics in society. Politics and the media have a symbiotic relationship, and this is more so in a democratic society where the media is considered as the oxygen of democracy. The media can shape political discourse and manipulate and influence the decision-making process. Free and independent media is vital for every democratic society. Democracy as a system of governance can exist and flourish with a vibrant, independent and free press, devoid of any external influence and intervention (Keane 1991). The condition of a democratic regime is reflected in its media. Hence, studying the intricacies of politics and the media is required as a precondition for understanding the health of democracy in a society.

Diversity is a prerequisite for democracy (Curran 2011; McCann 2013). The term *diversity* in the media refers to the plural character and diverse nature of representation, ownership, content and accessibility of the media (Kleiman 1991; Horwitz 2005; Hill 2006; Parthasarathi 2022); it is a precondition for any healthy engagement between media and democracy. For Napoli, media diversity can be broadly seen in the forms of source, content and exposure (with the possibility of multiply subcomponents) (Napoli 1999), and Valcke has categorised it into supplier/provider diversity, product diversity, and exposure/use diversity (Valcke 2011).

Course Description: Media and Politics

This is the first case study on projects in media policy for the master's programme in media governance. This master's programme engages with the media's representation of political processes and the salience of formal institutions in light of the challenges posed by the present media milieu.

Further, an attempt is made to map the trajectory of the ideological strands of communication and critical issues such as how communication reshapes the state and the political sphere. The chapter is divided into three modules and each module is further divided into four subunits.

Module 1: Media and Democracy

This module intends to provide a basic understanding of the theoretical strands, which will help in understanding the relationship between media and democracy, and moves on to interrogate the media and its representation.

Module 2: Ideology and Media

The media being a part of the democratic institution has transcended its visible boundaries in a democratic set-up. It has become a part of the structural categories and an instrument of structural modifications. Hence, the media plays an ideological role. As an ideological apparatus, the understanding of the media requires critical scrutiny today than ever before. In this module, an attempt is made to map the trajectory of the ideological part of the media and critical issues such as how it reshapes and redefines power and political spheres.

Module 3: Democracy in Transition

In this module, students are introduced to structural changes in the wake of the growth and expansion of media in the form of new media and mediated politics. This new module highlights the character of communication and the understanding of democracy, electoral processes, information, participation, liberalism and public opinion. It aims to highlight how legitimacy and trust have been affected by shifting the media from a catalyst to one of the actors in democracy.

The course concept map (Figure 4.1) is a depiction of the chapter's content (modules and sub-modules). This further highlights and describes the content of the course as well as the description of each module noted previously.

Figure 4.1: Concept Map of Course I: Media and Politics

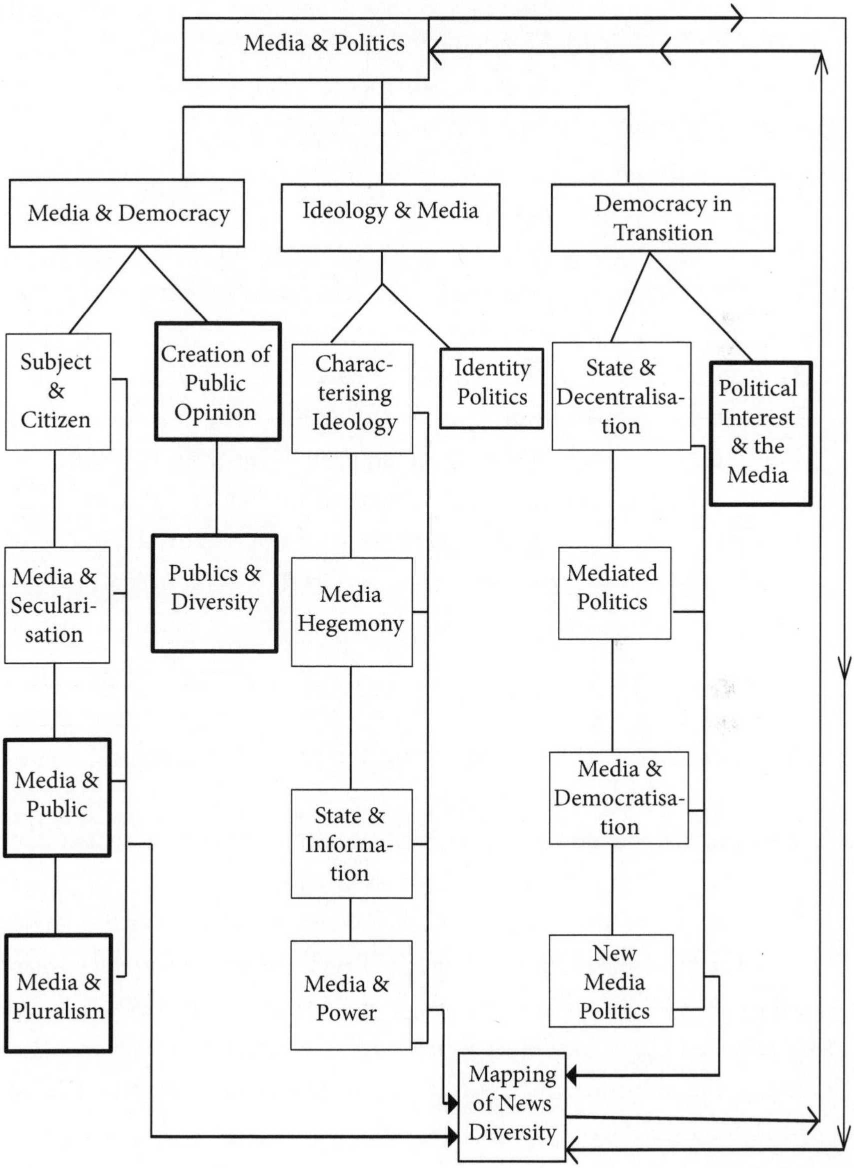

Source: Authors

Notes:

- The black boxes are the subunits of each module. The bold boxes constitute parts of the hands-on project.
- The subunit Media and Pluralism in the first module constitutes an important component of mapping news diversity.
- The course concept map indicates that the mapping of news diversity as a theme for the workshop is cutting across all the modules of the chapter.

Instructional Objectives

The course aims to impart a fundamental understanding of the nature of the interdependence of media and politics in a democratic regime. The following are the major instructional objectives of this chapter:

- To build up an understanding of how moving from the subject to citizen, which is both legal and right-based, is a key factor in the growth of a democratic nation state, freedom of expression and the right to information.
- To impart the need to interrogate the notion of public, secularism and pluralism from the perspective of the media.
- To develop an understanding of how the media shape and reshape the understanding of ideology, domination and hegemony, which also influence the power equation and its dynamic.
- To help in understanding the transitory stages of democracy, viz., along the line of the information revolution and its impact on decentralisation, electoral processes, participation and legitimacy.

Course Learning Outcomes

After going through this course, students are expected to be able to:

- underline that the media is the core element that defines and shapes issues that a citizen faces daily in a democratic country.
- describe how secular is information and entertainment, how public opinion is created and how the media represent the diverse nature of a particular society.
- analyse how information and news are not free from ideologies that perpetuate hegemonic domination and shape power equations.
- analyse the influence of the media on the growth of identity politics and the changing nature of participation in politics.
- substantiate the role and importance of new media in politics.

Keywords

The basic requirement of a citizen in a democratic setup is to be aware of their rights and entitlements as well as to participate in civic and public life in society. The kind of politics a state or nation follows affects the citizens and defines the media accordingly. The state through its policies propagates the dominant ideology reflected through the media since it is the instrument of the state. Media concentration may be studied accordingly. The recent liberalisation policies have affected the monopoly of the state with the privatisation of the media sector. This duopoly of the media industry has allowed access to a diversity of voices and sources. These voices have resulted in the assertion of a plurality of identities that adds to the ongoing debates on identity politics. Given these intricacies, concepts such as citizenship, diversity, ideology, identity politics, pluralism, media pluralism and secularism are clarified as follows.

Citizenship is a right and legal status of an individual belonging to a particular territory in a nation state. It is based on equality and participation in a democratic regime. Citizenship is a license for a person to enjoy the provisions enshrined in the statute of a country as well as an obligation to abide by it.

Diversity goes beyond plurality; it describes various components of a plurality that are internally different. Plurality merely suggests the presence of many; diversity points to many that are different. It means multiplicity that is not reducible to one whole. In other words, various cultural communities exist independently, so the issue of comparison does not arise. And their existence is not dependent on the survival of the other but in their parallel existence.

Ideology is a science of ideas. It means world views: a system of values and beliefs that an individual, group or society holds as true or important. It is a belief system of a particular class or group, not merely an individual attitude, and is, therefore, social. Ideology is identified as a controversial and debatable topic since it represents culture, tradition and a way of life.

Identity politics as a political process and movement is considered a corrective measure to counteract a dominant political structure that allegedly engenders injustice against certain groups and communities. It is more of an exclusionary politics based on the need to secure equality within its constituency. In practice, though, what is considered provisional often gets streamlined and attains permanency since identity is continuously produced and reproduced by political projects based on existing issues and with a vision to the future.

Pluralism is an ideology that recognises the coexistence of various cultural groups or communities in the same social space. It is an antithesis of monism (elitist and Marxist). It insists that an analysis of a social system or group be done on the basis of the nature of politics and power within. Pluralism stresses on tolerance and acceptance, not so much on the role and status of these variegated communities that operate in the public sphere.

Media pluralism as a concept embraces different aspects ranging from concentration, the pattern of ownership, representation, accessibility and competition to a diversity of information, thought and opinion. It means an opinion that is not unduly influenced by a dominant view or majority community. It also implies a plurality of content, access to diverse views and a wide range of choices.

Secularism is a concept that seeks the separation of state and religion and philosophy and theology. It is based on the principle that religion is a personal affair, and so equal treatment must be given to all religions. It means becoming rational and scientific, distancing oneself from parochial beliefs and avoiding religious symbolism or tokenism.

Introduction to the Hands-on Project

It may be underlined that each module has a variety of projects, and each project comprises a few workshops. The first module of the course introduces media and democracy and helps in understanding media diversity in India. It also helps in understanding the relationship between media and democracy. The mushrooming of media organisations all over the country has given birth to the idea of analysing media diversity in India. Thus, the workshop in this module has been designed to help in analysing broadcast television news as an approach to studying media diversity in India. This module also highlights the conceptual difference between pluralism and diversity. Plurality, according to this module, refers to the existence of many components, but it does not specify the nature of that many. Diversity, on the other hand, refers to the existence of many that are different. The workshop helps in understanding media diversity through news analysis in a classroom scenario.

The project focuses on different elements in a news story and how students can study those elements through quantitative and qualitative techniques to find out about media pluralism. This workshop attempts to give hands-on training to students and helps in understanding essential statistical tools, such as MS Excel. During the workshop, students are trained to analyse news broadcast on television. The workshop provides insights into how media organisations follow certain trends or break the rules to define their own style of news broadcasting to grab eyeballs. The idea of the workshop is to go beyond the theoretical teaching of plurality and equip students with the skill to understand the content being fed through media organisations. During this workshop, students are asked to analyse news based on news value and explore the tone and distinction within different news organisations to help them understand media and democracy in India.

To this end, the workshop gives hands-on training to analyse news. News mapping in India is a new concept that is still being explored, and it gives a sense of what news is all about. Students might not know the term *news value* or trends being followed in a newsroom and the treatments given to a news story; therefore, the project workshop familiarises them with the terms and the tools required to analyse news. The students are supposed to familiarise themselves with the following variables:

- Themes of news stories
- Geography of the news
- Voices of actors in news stories
- Demography of actors in news themes
- Treatment of news stories
- Sources of advertisements within news bulletins
- Types of advertisements within news bulletins

These variables will help students in measuring news stories and analysing various aspects of news bulletins. These are further discussed in detail in the following sections.

Project Concept Map

Let us look at the relationship between the variables and their subdivisions in the project module by depicting it with the help of a concept map (Figure 4.2). With the use of these variables, one can measure news stories. After going through the concept map, students can easily list the themes and sub-themes and understand their linkages.

Figure 4.2: Concept Map of the Workshop: Mapping News Diversity

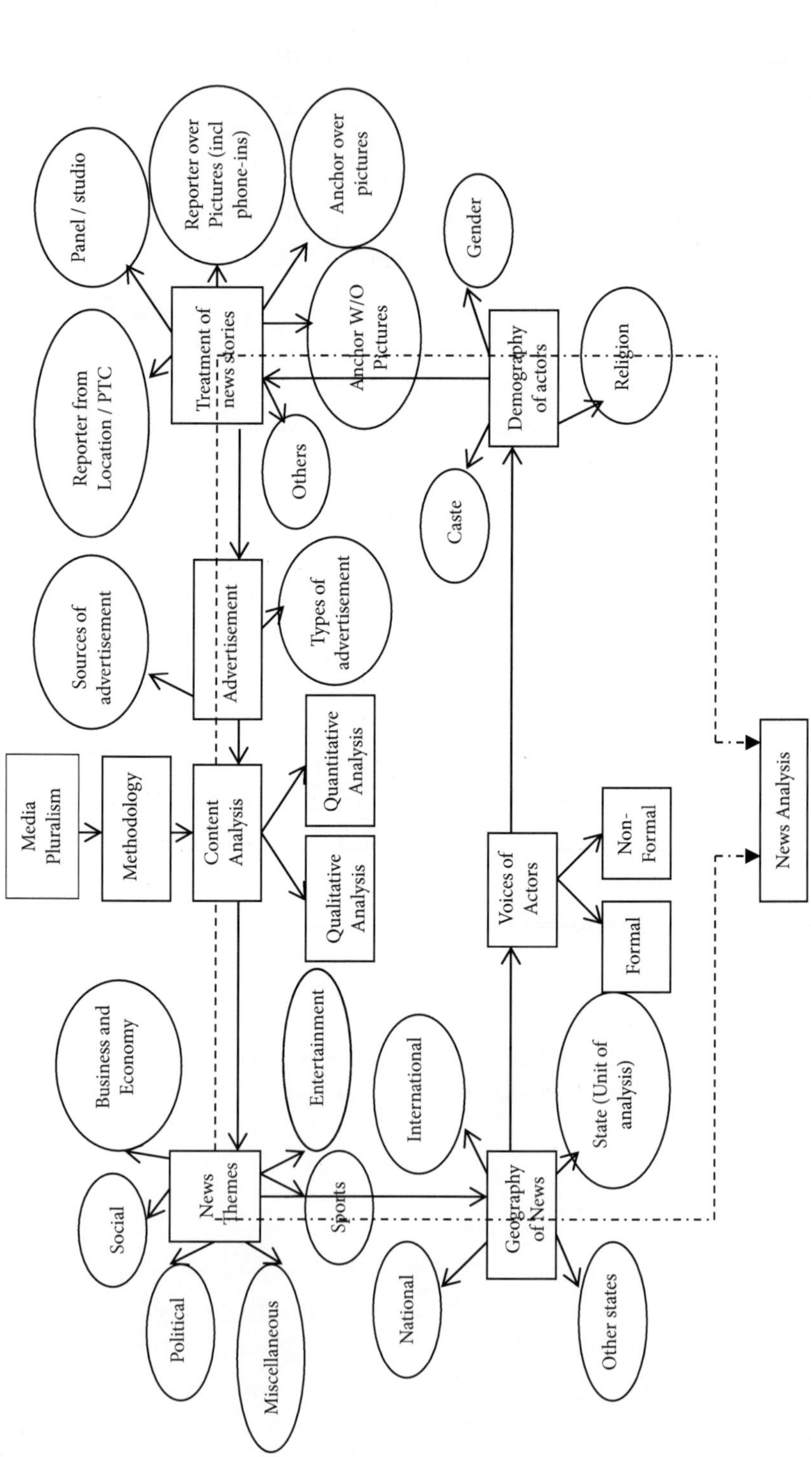

Source: Authors

Course Instructional Design

Through this hands-on project, teachers will help in analysing news while giving an understanding of news value. News analysis provides an insight into various aspects of news, such as how news is treated as a commodity and is designed for a stratum of the audience while giving a perspective on the diverse nature of news. The teachers shall ensure the following during the hands-on project:

- They must ensure that the variables used to analyse news, such as news themes and the geography of news, should be exhaustive and clearly explained to the students.
- They must demonstrate to the students that these variables have emerged from news stories and explain how to map these variables in the order of preference given to them.
- They should introduce to the students the idea of news value and give them a context and theoretical background.
- Readings on media pluralism should be given to the students while mapping news and asked to apply the theoretical knowledge that will help them find a nuanced meaning.
- They need to demonstrate to students how each variable depends on the other and that their comparison can give better results.
- Students should be asked to consume news regularly and analyse the trends followed by news channels.

Project Learning Outcomes

By the end of the workshop, the students should be well versed in news mapping and digging out details of the plural nature of news. In addition to this, they should be able to:

- describe the various methods applied in analysing news.
- analyse the trends followed by news channels, the treatments given to news stories, common themes around which news stories revolve and the pattern of reflection of the actors' voices.
- examine advertisement sources or their types and how they are affecting the media organisations.

- present and interpret news in the form of graphs and tables.
- interpret results and explain why and how a particular variable overpowers the other.
- develop the ability to correlate various variables, such as how the geography of an actor can affect the caste of the actor, et cetera.
- analyse the ownership pattern of any media organisation and how it affects their news stories.
- list the findings and details on a media organisation and start building a narrative based on such findings.

Key Concepts

We have listed four key concepts that will be helpful for students in understanding the terms used during the project. These concepts are often used during the project workshop.

News value

This is sometimes referred to as news criteria. It determines how significant a particular news story is and how much importance is being given to a news story by a media outlet. News value can vary according to the culture, time and space in which a news story exists.

Voices of actors

These are expressions and opinions from both formal and non-formal spheres of the society in a news story; they may represent anyone ranging from a religious/cultural group, a non-identity group or a civil society to a government body or a political party.

Formal and non-formal sphere

The formal sphere represents the voices of political leaders, experts and government bodies. In contrast, the non-formal sphere represents interest groups, identity groups and common people who form the nucleus of society.

Interest groups

These are those non-identity groups that are formed to fight for the common good of the society; they do not have any political, religious, caste or ethnic inclination to their formation. They are not intended to capture formal power or control government structures.

Setting Up the Hands-on Project

Students are introduced to the workshop after they have been familiarised with the course Media and Politics. It runs in sync with the first module on Media and Democracy. This module introduces media pluralism and media diversity, which is important to understand the theoretical background to map news diversity and practically approach the idea of diversity.

From the theoretical modules, one can relate to how media pluralism reflects society's identity, institutions and government bodies and how democratic the media organisations are. Further, one can explore media democracy and media hegemony through the other two modules and how all this is affecting the news industry.

This mapping exercise has been planned to help in understanding that pluralism does not explicitly deal with news stories. Nevertheless, it helps in understanding the larger context of media ideology, identity politics and the creation of public opinion.

Project Instructional Design

The hands-on project attempts to explore media diversity with the help of certain variables that have to be planned to be well executed. The instructor/teacher should be well-versed in the variables before reaching out to students. The instructor should know the importance of news value in a media organisation and should have an eye for news and be interested in watching and analysing news content.

During the first week of the project, students are introduced to the concept of time calculation (of the voices of the actors) and time slot; the theory classes of the course Media and Politics are also taught in the first week. During this time, they are also given training on how to use MS Excel. Later in the week, they are introduced to a template designed specifically for the workshop. They are informed about how to fill in the template and logically analyse news according to the template. They should be told that news must be mapped from left to right and top to bottom, which will help them map news according to the preference given to the variables. The teachers need to show the students a few clippings in the class and practically explain to them how to analyse news stories according to the given themes. Further, the class should be divided into groups of two, and each group should be assigned a news channel. It should be made clear that each group will enumerate a news channel for fifteen days.

In the second week, students start with the news-mapping process by filling in a given template. Teachers could ask students to discuss their problems in detail and mark them with red so that they could follow the news stories and give further insights. During the process, students are asked to come up with various issues such as the caste of the actors and their geographical locations because caste in India is subject to geographical boundaries. (A person with a particular surname may be a high caste if born in one part of the country but a lower caste in another.) By the end of the first week, students are asked to submit their mapping sheets for assessment so that they may be provided with more insights into how news ought to be analysed without ambiguity, which is a crucial step to knowing the level of their understanding to reduce further discrepancies in news analysis. After the first quality check and a detailed discussion on every mistake, students generally begin to understand the process better; therefore, it becomes easier for them to analyse the remaining few days.

Students will continue the analysis through the third week. By this time they will have become more comfortable and focused to complete the remaining exercise. As the sample of five days will be divided among two students, they should have ample time to clean the data during this week. Students will map the remaining five days during this time. By the end of the week, they will be given training on how to clean the data, make charts and graphs, and present the findings.

Further, during the fourth week, students must tabulate the findings in the form of graphs and pie charts. They will be asked to give the final presentation during this time and work on a narrative of their respective channels, which is required to be submitted for their term exam.

Planning the Project

The project has to be planned keeping in view various aspects of news analysis, such as the unit of analysis: whether it is the state or the nation. The media organisations to be analysed must be carefully selected. If the unit of analysis is a particular region or state, regional channels catering to that state should be selected; otherwise, national channels should be taken as a sample. After choosing a news slot, one has to then check its assortment of news stories. A template should be designed keeping in mind the types of news and their occurrence within that particular time slot. The template should map various news elements with clarity on each and every term being used; this should be the first and foremost objective. The template can have different criteria for mapping news, based on the selection of news channels. After the template has been finalised, the teacher should explain to students how to use MS Excel.

During the project workshop, seven regional news channels catering to the audience in Uttar Pradesh were mapped. Thus, the template that was designed for the project measured the themes of the news, the geography of the news, the voices of actors in news bulletins, the demography of actors in news bulletins, the treatment given to news stories, the sources of advertisement and the types of advertising. An exemplary template is shown in Figures 4.3 to 4.6 as a sample.

This section deals with the pre-planning that the instructor needs to do before conducting the hands-on project workshop. The template clearly defines the themes and sub-themes through which students can map news effectively. So, the teacher must collate all the information and make it available to the students whenever the need arises. The teacher should:

- collect the sample of the news slot from the local cable operator or the respective news channels.
- look at the footage carefully and chalk out a template design according to the news stories.
- list out a series of questions based on the template. If we look at the template sample (see Figure 4.3), we can list questions under the miscellaneous category.
- ensure that the alignment of the template's variables is in the order of preference given to the variables. The simplest example that can be given is that the sports category in the template (see Figure 4.3) has cricket and non-cricket sections. As cricket is a popular game in India and students will find more stories on cricket rather than any other sport, the teacher should place cricket before non-cricket and follow the same style in all the other variables as well.

Figure 4.3: Themes of News Stories and Geographical Origin of the News

Political (POL)					Social (SOC)				Business) (B & E)		Ent-mnt.		Sports (SPT)		Misc.		Geographical Origin of News					
Functioning of Political Parties	Functioning of Organs of the State	Protest and Demonstration	Conflict/Terror/War	Corruption/Scam	Cultural/Religious	Crime/Social Conflict	Welfare (Health and Education)	Environment/Natural Disaster	Functioning of Govt./Regulation/ Debates/ Discussion (Tools used)	Corporate & Markets	Hollywood	Non-Bollywood	Cricket	Non-Cricket	Misc.	Code	Central UP	East UP	West UP	Other State	National	International

Figure 4.4: Voices of the Actors from Formal and Non-Formal Sphere

Voices of the Actors from Non-Formal Spheres			Voices of Actors from Formal Spheres			
Non-Identity Activist Group (Interest Group)	Identity Group (Regional/ Religious/ Gender/ Ethnic/Caste)	Vox Populi	Ruling Party	Opposition(s)	Govt. Officials	Experts

Figure 4.5: Demography of the Voices of Actors and Treatment of News Stories

Caste									Religion		Gender		Ranked as a function of investment in stories					
Name	Brahmin	Kshatriya	Vaishya	Shia	Sunni	Other	OBC	SC/ST	Majority	Minority	Male	Female	Reporter from location (PTC)	Reporter over pics (incl Phone-in)	Panel Studio Interview	Anchor over pic's (incl Agency)	Anchor reads (without pics)	Other

Figure 4.6: Source of Advertisement and Product Category

Ad Source (who is advertising?)		Product Category (What is being advertised?)					
Govt/Public Sector Companies	Domestic/Foreign Pvt. Companies	BF	F&B (Edible)	CD	FMCG Non-Edible	Service Sectors (Non-Financial)	Others (Self-Promotion/ Other Channels Programme)

Once the template has been designed properly, the instructor can conduct the hands-on project workshop while taking care of some important steps discussed further.

Conducting the Project

This part of the hands-on project deals with how well the teacher can train students to interact in the classroom effectively. The following need due consideration.

- The teacher should divide the class into groups of two. Each group should be asked to map one news channel.
- Discussions in detail should be the priority of the teacher.
- Before asking students to start mapping news, the teacher should ask them to bring to the class some news stories based on the template.
- After a few classes on the template, the teacher should test whether students can easily handle MS Excel or not as students need to know how to prepare charts and graphs.
- The teacher should try to inculcate in students the ability to look at news from the perspective of analysing it without preconceived notions.
- The teacher must ask students to ensure that they clean up the data, mark their doubts and discuss it with their teacher.
- They must also ensure that students do not let their opinions colour the news analysis process.
- The teacher should explain at every step how each variable depends on the other.

Students should develop an understanding of these points and, at the end of the hands-on workshop, be able to evaluate them and read between the lines.

Pre-Project Workshop Exercises

Some pre-project workshop assignments can be helpful to students in understanding content analysis of news. They should be asked to open their emails and filter them according to people they are close to or most frequently receive emails from. After looking through the mails for five minutes, they should be asked to grab a pen and a paper and categorise them based on whether they depict anger, fear, hatred, love or friendship. After this exercise, they will have a fair idea of how a template is developed based on content and not on the instructor's opinion.

Further, after having introduced the template, they can be asked to bring news stories from their favourite news channels and categorise them under different themes. The students will be trained to prepare a codesheet to enlist the data under different heads for further enumeration and analysis.

Project Workshop Design

The primary objective of the hands-on project workshop is to analyse media pluralism and its representation in television news. The hands-on project is designed to ensure that all aspects of the news market are considered and news is analysed to highlight the strings attached to the broadcast industry. This is done by feeding data in the template and applying the codesheet used during the process. The template should be designed in a way that is exhaustive and clear. The teacher should explain the template's variables well in advance with proper examples so that any ambiguity can be avoided. The teacher should prepare a note on the variables and ask students to go through it in detail. Discussion on various elements of news before mapping begins can also prove beneficial.

The template used during the hands-on workshop was designed keeping in mind the nature of news. The following template explains each variable in detail and can be given to students, as this explains in detail all the variables used in analysing the news.

TEMPLATE

1. News Themes

1.1 Political (POL)

1.1.1 Functioning of Political Parties: This variable measures the conflicts or execution of work within a political party or between two parties.

1.1.2 Functioning of Organs of the State: It measures the conflicts, resolutions and orders at the Centre. Government orders and their execution will be measured under this category without taking into account political parties.

1.1.3 Protest and Demonstrations: This measures the outcome of resentment that may result in protests or demonstrations and has a political inclination or questions the functioning of the state.

1.1.4 Conflict/Terror/War: The spread of terror or a war-like situation will come under this theme. It also measures the conflict between a state and its people or between nations.

1.1.5 Corruption/Scam: This will measure all kinds of corruption and scam or unethical activities carried out within the national boundaries that affect the functioning of the state.

1.2 Social (SOC)

1.2.1 Cultural/Religious: This variable measures cultural and religious aspects of society. Religion and culture play important role in society and, thus, there is a need to measure them.

1.2.2 Crime/Social Conflict: Social crime can range from petty theft to robbery or murder. This variable measures social conflict, which can be defined as a quarrel between individuals or within an individual that might result in suicide.

1.2.3 Welfare/Health/Education/Sanitation: All news pertaining to development or news related to health, sanitation or education will be covered under this theme.

1.2.4 Environment/Natural Disaster: This measures the degradation or deployment of the environment or the sudden outcome of a natural disaster that affects society.

1.3 Business and Economy (B&E)

1.3.1 Functioning of Government/Regulation/Debates/Discussion (Tools Used): This variable measures regulations, laws and policies related to the economy (not polity) approved by government.

1.3.2 Corporate and Market: This measures the ups and downs in the market. The prices of various products and the share market comes under this variable and is measured in terms of economic benefits to the country.

1.4 Entertainment (ENT)

1.4.1 Bollywood: As the Indian entertainment industry is booming with pride, there is a need to measure news from the industry.

1.4.2 Non-Bollywood: This variable measures news from the entertainment industry except the Indian entertainment industry.

1.5 Sports (SPT)

1.5.1 Cricket: As cricket is India's most talked about and widely played sports, there is a need to consider news from the discipline.

1.5.2 Non-Cricket: Any news from any other sports except cricket comes under this category.

1.5.3 Misc. (MIS): This theme measures everything that does not fall under the above-stated themes, e.g., accident.

1.6 Geographical Origin of News

1.6.1 Place: A place that comes within Uttar Pradesh is to be accordingly named under this category.

1.6.2 Other State: A place within the national boundaries but outside Uttar Pradesh.

1.6.3 National: Any news that is of national importance and concerns the nation falls under this category.

1.6.4 International: News from outside India or that concerns India but originates from any other country comes under this category.

2. Voices of Actors

2.1 Voices of Actors from Formal Spheres

2.2.1 Ruling Party: Voices of people who speak on behalf of the party in power are measured under this category. Whether it is the ruling party in a particular state or at the Centre, the voices are explicitly measured based on the party in power.

2.2.2 Opposition(s): This measures voices of the actors from the opposition. It also considers the ruling party and decides the opposition party according to whether it is in the state or at the Centre.

2.2.3 Government Officials: These are voices from the government officials.

2.2.4 Experts: These are voices from different specialised fields or subjects.

2.2 Voices of Actors from Non-Formal Spheres

2.2.1 Non-Identity Activist Group (Interest Groups): These are not voices from actors who do not have any political inclination or represent society's factions.

2.2.2 Identity Group (Regional/Religious/Gender/Ethnic /Caste): These are voices from identity groups that represent different factions of society.

2.2.3 Vox Populi: This is the voice of the common man, who do not have any vested interest.

2.3 Demography

2.3.1 Caste: This is the variable to measure the caste of the speakers, which is measured in terms of upper caste, OBC and SC/ST. The upper caste is further divided into Brahmin, Kshatriya and Vaisya—Sunni and Shia in the case of Muslims.

2.3.2 Religion: This measures the religions of the speakers, which is binary in nature and measured in terms of minority and majority.

2.3.3 Gender: The genders of the speakers are also marked to segregate them into male and female.

2.4 Treatment of News Stories

2.4.1 Reporter from Location/(PTC): This was taken into account to measure the treatment of news stories in terms of investment. If an in-house reporter reports from the location, the news story will fall under this category.

2.4.2 Reporter over Pics (incl Phone-in): If the news comes from a reporter over images or narrates the story over the phone, it will come under this category.

2.4.3 Panel/Studio Interview: This will include panel discussions or interviews in the studio. This type of treatment is quite popular these days as it cuts the cost of sending a reporter out to cover stories. Channels will rather invite expert advice in the studio.

2.4.4 Anchor over Pics (incl Agency): This measures news stories where the anchor reads over images. This way of gathering news also helps in cutting cost.

2.4.5 Anchor Reads (without pics): This is the cheapest way of reaching out to the audience; thus, this measures only news that involves anchors from inside the studio.

2.4.6 Others: Another graphical representation of news is taken into account under this category.

2.5 Advertisements

2.5.1 Advertisement Sources.

2.5.1.1 Government/Public Sector Companies: This variable measures advertisements and represents the source of an advertisement. If the advertisement is from the government sector, it will fall under this category.

2.5.1.2 Domestic/Foreign Private Companies: Advertisements by the private sector or foreign private companies will come under this category.

2.5.2 Product Category.

2.5.2.1 Business and Finance (BF): Advertisements related to the economic sector, such as real estate or investments, come under this category.

2.5.2.2 Food and Beverages (F&B) Edible: All food and beverages come under this category. Tobacco has also been included here.
2.5.2.3 Consumer Durable (CD): Consumer durables, typically household appliances with long useful life, fall under this category.
2.5.2.4 Fast Moving Consumption Goods (FMCG) Non-Edible: All kinds of fast-moving goods that are not consumer durables come under this category.
2.5.2.5 Service Sectors (Non-Financial): All kinds of products and services that aim to benefit society as a whole come under this category.
2.5.2.6 Others (Self-Promotion/Other Channels Programme): All kinds of promotional advertisement by a news channel or any other channel fall under this category.

Analysing the Parameters of the Template

The project provides hands-on training in analysing the news. The template should be approached in a way that makes the variables more viable. The template tells you the order and preference of the variables and how the variables have been clustered together in terms of political news, social news, demography of actors, voices of the actors, et cetera. Examining the following steps will help in analysing the parameters of the template effectively.

- Follow the golden rule of news analyses by mapping news according to the order of appearance of variables in the template.
- Students should look at the template from left to right and top to bottom.
- Students should be instructed well in advance that their personal opinions cannot creep into their analyses. They should look at news from the broadcasters' perspective and what they want people to see.
- First, analyse the category or nature of news, whether it is political, social, sports or entertainment news. In the same way, after analysing the themes, students are supposed to analyse the sub-themes of a given news story.
- During this process, most of the students commit the mistake of analysing the sub-themes before the central themes.
- The story should be coded according to the codes given in the template.

- After coding stories, students should analyse the geography or origin of the news story.
- After this analysis, students should check whether or not the actors are speaking on behalf of society, government, a political party, et cetera. The voices of such actors should be calculated in terms of the time given to each and every voice and the demography of the actors.
- At the end of the news analysis, analyse the treatment given to news stories based on whether the news being broadcast comes from a reporter from the location, an anchor over pictures or an anchor reading without pictures, et cetera.
- Ask students to analyse the source of advertisements: whether an advertisement is from a public sector or a private sector and what kind of advertisement is it, according to the template?
- Finally, ask them to tabulate the data and construct a narrative based on their findings.

How to Do the Hands-on Project

This exercise will require understanding how news stories are based on news value. And through this exercise, one must look at news stories from the perspective of finding diversity within an organisation and across different organisations. Approaching the subject according to the following steps will help in reaching the required output.

- Use the pre-project workshop exercises to familiarise yourself with content analysis that is used to analyse news.
- Understand that news mapping is a process that requires news to be considered and analysed as a commodity.
- Familiarise yourself with the supplied reading material.
- The next step is to look at the news footage given to you and start with the process of mapping news.
- Carefully do basic research on the news channel you are mapping.
- Dig out details like ownership pattern, stakeholders and advertisers in the channel or the group. This will help in carefully mapping advertisements and finding the representation of voices of the actors.

- Identify and list the castes of the actors beforehand. One can file an RTI to obtain such information.
- The next step is to send the mapping sheets to the teacher for feedback. This is an important step to avoid further discrepancies.
- Finally, compile all the data after completing news analysis to make charts and graphs. (The number of charts and their details is further discussed below.) This will help in correlating the variables and looking at the results carefully.

The following charts are required to be made during the data tabulation process:

I News Themes

1. Proportion of News Themes in Headlines Only **(Pie Chart %)**
2. Proportion of News Sub-Themes in Headlines **(Pie Chart %)**
3. Proportion of News Stories Under Various News Themes **(Pie Chart %)**
4. Proportion of News Stories of Various Sub-themes in Entire Bulletin (**Pie Chart %)**

II Voices of Actors in News Stories

5. Profile of Time Given to Voices (both formal and informal) **(Column Chart)**
6. Proportion of Voices **(Column Chart %)**
7. Profile of Time Given to Sub-Themes of Voices **(Column Chart)**
8. Proportion of Time Given to Sub-Themes of Voices **(Column Chart)**

III Demography of Actors in News Stories

9. Proportion of Caste of Actors in News Stories **(Pie Chart %)**
10. Proportion of Class of Actors in News Stories **(Pie Chart %)**
11. Proportion of Gender of Actors in News Stories **(Pie Chart %)**

IV Origin of News or Geography of News

12. Proportion of Origin of News in News Stories **(Pie Chart %)**

V Treatment of News

13. Story Treatment **(Pie Chart %)**

VI Advertisements

14. Ad Source **(Pie Chart %)**
15. Product Category **(Pie Chart %)**
16. Combined Graph of All News Channels **(Column Chart)**

- There are in total sixteen graphs that need to be presented. Tabulate the data according to the given number of graphs that cover each variable and represent all the template sections.
- The next step is to look at the results reflected in the graphs and put together an argument around them. Highlight the main findings and mention in your report the reasons for the results.

How Will Students be Evaluated?

Student evaluation for the hands-on project workshop can be done based on three outputs:

- Class Response and Correct Understanding of News Analysis: This forms the first step to evaluate students, as news mapping is a process that can give erroneous results if the template is not well-understood. So the teacher should do a quality check after every five days of news mapping. Quality check is a process where the teacher looks at the footage and cross-checks it with the mapping sheet to see whether or not the news has been mapped properly.
- Final Presentation/Group Presentation: The number of graphs has been discussed hereinafter. Students need to follow the same style, and the teacher should make sure that they have worked around all sixteen graphs during the final presentation. Students are also expected to explain the graphs in detail.
- Narrative: This is the outcome of each student's work; it will reflect their understanding of the hands-on project and whether they could understand and analyse media pluralism.

They need to mention the findings they have derived from the news mapping exercise as well as the arguments that have been incorporated to support those findings.

Assessment of students carries 25 per cent weightage. Overall, students can be tested for their grasp of ideas and how effectively they deal with the subject. They may be assessed for their ability to:

- understand media pluralism.
- identify key components that exist in the media industry and accordingly develop a better understanding of news.
- derive results and correlate various news-story elements and see how the voices of the actors or treatment given to a story may or may not depend on the ownership pattern, et cetera.

Key Things to Focus

As students will be working on news analysis, they should develop the capacity to watch the news with patience and try to grab as much news as possible. They will also be working on the demography of the actors, so they require an understanding of the caste system in India; they should, therefore, follow a few web feeds in that regard, which will help them enhance the quality of their work. They need to follow proper instructions as follows.

Basic Requirements for the Hands-on Project Workshop

Students should prepare themselves for the hands-on project and try to understand the variables as much as they can. They can do so by taking care of the following:

- Students should make an effort to look at the template as many times as possible and clarify doubts before mapping news.
- As they are dealing with complicated subjects, news can be vague at times; they may come across some grey areas. Therefore, they should always ask the instructor before mapping such news stories.
- Students should follow the order of appearance of variables.
- They should also make themselves comfortable with MS Excel.
- Students should focus on assignments and take deadlines seriously; otherwise, the quality of the outcome could be hampered.
- They should develop an understanding of the workshop and how it can help in understanding theory in a better way.

Guidelines for Students

Students are expected to follow the following guidelines:

- Students should familiarise themselves with the variables, themes and sub-themes that form the nucleus of the workshop.
- If in doubt, they must clear it with the instructor.
- Once familiarisation is done, they should focus on news value and evaluate news according to the footage provided.
- Students should keep taking notes in class and while mapping news. They should put down on paper every piece of news that is vague or specific elements or news that are unclear, such as the geographical origin of news, et cetera.
- They should highlight all grey areas and clarify them with the instructor as much as possible.
- Discussion in the classroom about grey areas will prove beneficial to students, as it will give a platform to their classmates to share their opinions and discuss similar problems faced by them.
- Students should familiarise themselves with the basic concepts and keywords.
- They should do basic research on the caste of the actors and always map them when known.
- While researching the caste of the actors or ownership pattern of a news channel, students must ensure the participation of all the group members.
- They must look at news from the perspective of a viewer and not an analyst because looking at news from a viewer's perspective will let them map it without any biases.
- After mapping it, students should be able to correlate various variables.
- They should always focus on quality checks and ask the instructor for feedback from time to time, as a tiny mistake can result in data discrepancy.
- Students must follow their teacher's instructions in class and after quality checks because they may not revisit them.
- They should understand the structure of the hands-on project workshop and the idea behind it.

Self-Evaluation by Students

Before writing and submitting their work, students should try evaluating their work individually based on the following:

- Whether or not the format of the PowerPoint presentation is correct and visually sound.
- Introduction: Check whether the channel has been introduced and a brief about media pluralism and the study's objective are given.
- Slides: The slides should be handed over to every student to cross-check if the number of graphs are correct or not.
- Under what headings the article/PowerPoint presentation should be written.
- Make sure spellings are correct.
- What conclusion are you aiming for? Whether the presentation/narrative reflects the idea of media pluralism or, if not, are there some other interesting findings? It should be strictly based on findings backed by data.

Illustrative Case Study

Here is a description of the hands-on project on news analysis that will provide an overview of the hands-on workshop. This project is designed solely for mapping regional news channels. However, it can be used to map and assess both national and regional news channels. The idea of finding diversity in plurality among different channels is something to aspire. The template has been designed in a way that can be used to analyse both regional and national news channels.

With 36 sessions of 60 minutes each, the hands-on project workshop can be taken as an illustrative case for group exercise.

- A group of two students mapped each news channel.
- The template was introduced to them, and they were asked to discuss it in detail with the instructor.
- A basic framework was introduced to them, and they were supplied with proper instructions on how to work around the variables.

- Each student in the group was asked to do background research on the news channel that was given before getting into the process of news mapping.
- Every student was expected to familiarise themselves with the template structure, the terms used in the template and the objective of the analysis.
- Further, students were supplied with reading material on media pluralism and asked to review the same literature review. This was required to bridge the gap between theoretical knowledge and practical training.
- Discussion on news stories and their elements were always welcomed, which enhanced the quality of their work and provided the students with a perspective.
- The hands-on project dealt with regional news channels catering to the state of Uttar Pradesh. Uttar Pradesh was taken as a unit of analysis during this workshop. Five regional channels with significant presence in Uttar Pradesh were mapped.
- Each student gave a PowerPoint presentation, during which their major findings were discussed.
- The students were asked to work in groups, but each student was marked according to their presentation and narrative.
- The students submitted the narratives as well as PowerPoint presentations.
- The students worked in groups, as a team, and had fruitful discussions during the presentation and amongst themselves.

Questions on Presentation

Each student's final presentation is based on a long mapping process, which increases the chances of forging data in some cases. So, students should be frequently asked about the news stories, the news organisation, major sources of revenue, et cetera, through which to evaluate their understanding of news mapping. The following questions are important:

- How diverse is the news, or are they circulating the same news time and again?
- To what extent do 'regional channels' cater to the states?
- Whether channels catering to a particular region/state have represented diverse religious, cultural and regional communities of the state?
- Can you describe some news stories because a particular variable shows a sudden increase or decrease?
- What constitutes a particular segment of news?

- How is pluralism different from media pluralism?
- How and why is democracy essential for media pluralism?
- What are the most common trends followed by your channel?
- What is the difference between interest groups and identity groups?
- If a person is speaking on behalf of a religion or community, what are the parameters to evaluate the voice on and map it?

Evaluation and Assessment

Students can be evaluated based on the time they took to analyse news, their understanding of news analysis, the final presentation and their narrative on the process of news mapping. By the end of the hands-on project workshop, the students are expected to have gained the ability to:

- look at news from the perspective of analysing it.
- locate and put together an argument on media pluralism and how democratic the media is.
- synthesise data graphically and interpret it.
- develop an eye for news and interpret nuanced meanings in news.
- see a pattern in news followed by a news organisation and how that is affecting the news analysis process.

Assessment (components)

Students have to be evaluated throughout the hands-on workshop based on elements (i.e., components of the workshop) described as follows:

News Analysis and Class Response: Students should be evaluated based on their news analysis, understanding of the process of mapping news and understanding of mapping news according to news value.

Presentation: They should also be evaluated based on the final presentation and the ability to convey their understanding of news analysis.

Narrative: Another possible way to evaluate them is to ask them for a brief note on the news analysis of their respective channels. Some may not have the ability to communicate their understanding effectively but be able to put it in writing.

Assessment (content)

This evaluates students' understanding of the contents of the hands-on project workshop.

Concepts: As this is a practical exercise, students should be guided to be well-versed in key concepts. The conceptual knowledge of news value or pluralism or some common terms used during the workshop can sharpen their skills to analyse news. Readings on the subject will prove beneficial for a better understanding of the concepts.

Technicality: Students will also be required to analyse and derive quantitative results. The ability to demonstrate data in the form of charts, graphs and bar diagrams is essential to the hands-on project.

Narrative: Students should know that the final presentation is yet another step to achieve stability in their narrative form. They should spend sufficient time in background research of media organisations and try to incorporate relevant information about ownership patterns, et cetera, which will help them build a strong argument. The narrative form gives a platform for them to put together their findings and arguments through the correlation between different variables which can be divided into:

- whether or not a piece of background information has been provided.
- whether or not the basic argument and nature of pluralism of news channels have been advanced.
- whether or not the findings of the analyses vis-à-vis news stories and the plurality of media organisations have been discussed in detail.

Assessment (presentation)

The assessment of presentations made by students may be based on the following areas:

Content: Presentations made by students should not be text-heavy but should focus on whether the idea of news analysis and media pluralism have been communicated in the introduction and whether or not students have reviewed their findings and built an argument around them, making sure the presentations have a proper structure with correct grammar and spelling.

Argument: Students must acquire the ability to build an argument without any vague information with data derived from news mapping. The reasons and arguments should be backed by valid data derived from news analysis.

Coherence: They must ensure that the slides, graphs and charts in their presentations are intelligible, a link has been provided between slides and proper headings have been given to the slides. There must be clarity in the delivery (speech) of the presentation.

Creativity: The presentations should have linkages between various variables of the template and produce high-quality content that is visually approachable.

Organisation: The presentations should reflect students' ability to organise and present data derived from the variables at a given time and flip through different slides without creating chaos.

Criteria for Grading

The following template, which is used to record the level/standard of work to be done by students, should be helpful for both students (for organising their hands-on project presentations) and teachers (to be able to evaluate and grade the presentations objectively).

Grade Criteria	A (Excellent)	B (Good)	C (Average)	D (Poor)
News Analysis	For mapping news with sound knowledge of the geographical boundaries of the state and without any bias; proper research-based marking of caste and religion during news mapping; mapping news based on the preference given to the variables.	For appropriate mapping based on the preference given to the variables but confusions over the caste of the actors and geography of the news.	For mapping some parts of the news based on the preference given to the variables but partially going against it because of confusion over caste, geography, etc.	Mapping news against preference given to the variables and no sound knowledge of the geography of the state and caste of the actors.

Grade Criteria	A (Excellent)	B (Good)	C (Average)	D (Poor)
Narrative	For clearly and coherently prepared reports with proper introduction and sound arguments knitted together into the findings. Proper research and understanding of the readings provided. Correct spelling, grammar and punctuation.	For clear reports backed by coherent findings and arguments but the findings and arguments have not been weaved together sufficiently. Proper research and understanding of the readings provided, with correct grammar, spelling and punctuation.	For clear reports but fewer findings. Arguments not strongly presented; an average understanding of the readings. Language and grammar average.	For confused reports, without a focus on the findings; loosely written and lack understanding.
Presentation	For clarity in speech and presentation, the linkage between various slides with proper headings. Well-organised display of the findings. Good explanations of the variables and concepts used.	For clarity in speech and presentation, with appropriate connections between slides but an average display of findings.	For clarity in speech but failure to establish links between slides. Presenters not being able to put their findings.	For missing to connect the slides. Failure to explain the slides and being less organised.

References

Curran, James. *Media and Democracy*. London: Routledge, 2011.

Hill, Brian. 'Measuring Media Market Diversity: Concentration, Importance, and Pluralism.' *Federal Communications Law Journal* 58, no. 1 (2006): 169–194.

Horwitz, R.B. 'On Media Concentration and the Diversity Question.' *The Information Society* 21, no. 3 (2005): 181–204.

Karppinen, Kari. *Rethinking Media Pluralism*. New York: Fordham University Press, 2013.

———. 'Making a Difference to Media Pluralism: A Critique of the Pluralistic Consensus in European Media Policy.' In *Reclaiming the Media: Communication Rights and Democratic Media Roles*, edited by Bart Cammaerts and Nico Carpentier, 9–30. Bristol, UK: Intellect, 2007.

———. 'Media Diversity and the Politics of Criteria: Diversity Assessment and Technocratisation of European Media Policy.' *Nordicom Review* 27, no. 2 (2006): 53–68.

Keane, John. *The Media and Democracy*. Cambridge, UK: Polity Press, 1991.

Kleiman, Howard. 'Content Diversity and the FCC's Minority and Gender Licensing Policies.' *Journal of Broadcasting & Electronic Media* 35, no. 4 (1991): 411–429.

McCann, Kim P. 'The Diversity Policy Model and Assessment of the Policy: Debates and Challenges of (Media) Diversity,' *Sage Open* April–June (2013): 1–12.

Napoli, Philip M. 'Deconstructing the Diversity Principle.' *Journal of Communication* 49, no. 4 (1999): 7–34.

Parthasarathi, V. 'Institutional Constraints and Accordant Interests: The Speckled Life of an "Ownership Bill" in India.' *Journal of Digital Media and Policy* 13, no. 1 (2022): 75–89.

Valcke, Peggy. 'Looking For the User in Media Pluralism Regulation: Unravelling the Traditional Diversity Chain and Recent Trends of User Empowerment in European Media Regulation.' *Journal of Information Policy* 1 (2011): 287–320.

5

Market Structure, Ownership and Industry

Pradosh Nath, Prashant Kumar and Vibodh Parthasarathi

Introduction

One of the most important aspects of contemporary societies is the intense commercialisation of the media. Much of the cultural contentions associated with the media can be traced to specific economic attributes of the industry. Understanding the market and firms and their structure is necessary for the larger curricular goal to train students in media, research and policy analysis. The course Introduction to Media Economics, which is part of the first semester in MA in Media Governance, seeks to explore the working and organisation of media markets. It examines technological trends shaping market structures, terms of competition across sectors and the dynamics of conglomeration and co-evolution over the last twenty years in India. The course aims to disseminate knowledge about various underlying issues relating to media ownership such as revenue, control and cross-media ownership across different media industry segments—print, television, radio or telecom. Comprehending the links between economic parameters such as profit, revenue and sales will sharpen students' ability to discern shifts in horizontal and vertical integrations within a company, across holdings, competition and market share. The immediate ability to conceive, comprehend and operationalise broader institutional trends will help students undertake a more extensive policy analysis exercise in the latter part of their coursework. Construing the market structures in this manner will provide a base to account for other mediating institutions, such as public, democracy, state and civil society, in policy analysis. We believe that this broader insight into media economics or parameters of media ownership will help the graduates in consultation papers, recommendations issued by regulatory authorities, performance parameters and understanding licensing issues when they enter the world of work in the field of media policy and media governance.

Course Description

This course is designed to provide training on the techniques of discerning basic economic parameters of the media market and understanding of business history with particular reference to the media. The course aims to acquaint students with the facets of media firms to understand the media market and ownership. The practical learning of developing and using quantitative data and learning to collect, identify, collate and analyse economic data in relation to ownership parameters or business models will enable a comprehensive understanding of media economics. It will help in identifying various economic variables to explore the commercial nature, expansion and diversification of media business.

With this broader goal, the hands-on project provides practical training in identifying a company, data in annual reports, IPOs and business history and using information available publicly on company websites to explain fluctuations in the market or company and the reasons for it.

The course is divided into three modules. The first two modules are conceptual ones that provide theory and concepts while the third module is framed as a hands-on project. The depth of engagement with different variables identified in this course provides basic but rigorous training, which will prove useful in further policy analysis while also preparing the students professionally.

Module 1: Enterprise and Industry in Media

The module proposes to give a comprehensive perspective of the media industry as a commercial entity. It begins with fundamental questions in economics and gradually unfolds the typical commercial characteristics of the media industry. It intends to familiarise students with basic economic issues, economics actors and concepts to identify economic variables and their measurements. In the process, the module also brings in distinctions that the media industry stands for vis-à-vis other industries. In doing so, it addresses the history of media firms, ownership pattern of the firms, identification of stakeholders and the nature of expansion and diversification of the firms' business.

Module 2: Dynamics of the Media Market

The question 'how does the media industry function?' is answered by developing an understanding of the media market dynamics. This module is premised on making familiar with the constituents of supply and demand of the media product to understand the supply chain from production to the market. The carrier of the supply chain is linked to revenue generation and pricing strategies, the distinctive characteristics of which are discussed in this module. Also discussed is the role of advertisement that is central to shaping the dynamics of the industry.

Module 3: Market Structure and Industry

This module is introduced as a hands-on project primarily based on the use of analytical tools and techniques for a learned and critical understanding of the actual facets of media ownership and market. The project takes up studies on various media companies, some media segments and various project parameters. It locates the structure and implications of the media industry, product (contents), revenues and identifies power related to different ownership and concentration patterns and other imperatives in cultural production.

Course Concept Map

See Figure 5.1 for the different concepts associated and linked with the course Introduction to Media Economics.

Figure 5.1: Concept Map of Course II: Media Economics

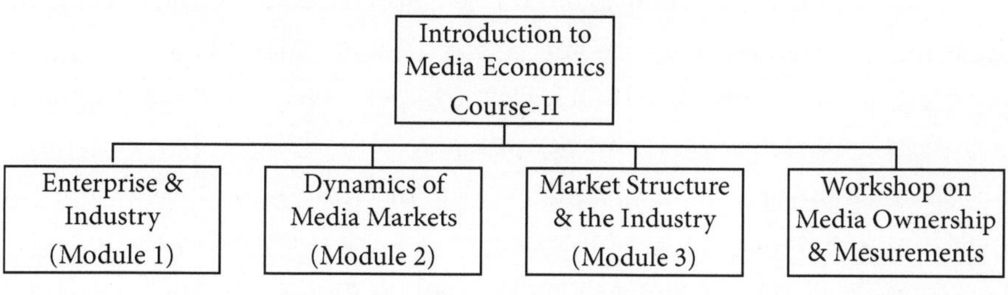

Instructional Objectives

In this course, teachers will assist students in acquiring a foundational understanding of ownership and the media market. The following are the broader instructional goals of the course:

- Develop an understanding of the economics of media industries by analysing interrelated facets of media firms, ownership, media market and its supply and demand.
- Promote an understanding of the history of (media) firms, ownership pattern of the firms and nature of expansion and diversification of business as part of understanding the market.
- Develop practical skills to analyse media economics and understand its relevance to subsequent analysis of policy, government data and reports.
- Explain and illustrate different concepts such as ownership, market, media and business to understand media ownership.
- Identify economic variables, economic actors, stakeholders, economic concepts and measurements of media to critique the economics of media industries.

Learning Outcomes

After going through the first two modules of this course, students will be able to:

- describe the parameters of ownership, market, media revenue, profits, market, goods, supply, demand and their interrelationships to evaluate the economics of media industries.
- define, compute and demonstrate knowledge of economic variables, economic actors, stakeholders and economic concepts and measurements.
- evaluate profit after tax (PAT), earnings per share (EPS), initial public offer (IPO) and employee stock ownership plan (ESOP).
- describe and determine subsidiary companies, mergers and acquisitions, promoter(s) and non-promoter(s) groups of a company in the market.
- demonstrate the theoretical application of the concepts of economic parameters of media ownership in practical explanations.

- differentiate between media firms, media markets and media environment and discern their relevance in policy analysis exercises.

Introduction to the Hands-on Project

The first two modules introduce concepts from enterprise and industry aspects in media ownership and media market dynamics. The third module is designed to help students understand the contexts of media ownership to discern an overall understanding of media economics as taught in theory classes. The final module is taught in a hands-on project workshop format. The workshop aims to make students competent in using qualitative and quantitative methodological tools to identify and critically analyse various aspects of media economics as discussed in the classroom. The immediate aim is to train students to practically locate multiple media companies that make up the media market, analyse elements of media ownership measurement and look into its various parameters. The central focus is to equip students with analytical tools like MS Excel and basic economic formulas for a critical understanding of ownership and market. Hence the workshop takes up studies on various media companies and segments and looks into multiple ownership parameters. At the end of the workshop, students will have gained a practical, hands-on approach to locating key content parameters, revenue, profits, different types of ownership, business expansion and the market.

This hands-on project is designed to give students practical training in data analysis, an understanding of media ownership and the ability to present various aspects of economic data and collate it in a way that will feed into the broader goal of policy analysis. Some students may be familiar with MS Excel while others not so. The project is also designed to train students who do not have formal MS Excel or mathematics training. Students are expected to generate primary data relating to the media firm and media market based on secondary data sources and MS Excel. They must also be aware that some of the results should be expressed as numbers, tabular forms or graphical presentations. The aim of collating such results is to help them to illustrate elements of media ownership.

The hands-on project is structured to deal with the following aspects:

History of the firm
Students will learn to identify a media firm from a select list of channels and services. An exercise to explore the history of the firm, identify ownership and track its evolution to its present stage will be undertaken. It will cover questions such as how it began? Is it an initiative from an established business house or a new entrepreneur? Are they from a media background?

Ownership pattern of the firm
This aspect deals with questions such as: Who owns the company? Is it a professionally managed company? Is it a listed company? What is the type and nature of international linkages in terms of ownership?

Nature of expansion and diversification of business of the firm
Students develop an account of the firm's expansion, if any, from the beginning, and its diversification from the media business.

Major revenue sources of the firm
Students learn to survey the accounts of the firm and its various revenue sources, grading them in order of their importance, from the most to the least in terms of a share of the revenue.

Observation
Students use theoretical knowledge and analytical tools to understand the industry, firms and the market.

Presentation
Students demonstrate all the aspects previously mentioned, collate economic data and analysis in the form of key findings, and present them in class.

The project concept map (Figure 5.2) illustrates elements of media ownership and the sections that illustrate its links with the market. Some of these concepts will be dealt with in class, and the rest as part of the hands-on project workshop. Both teachers and students will need to carefully observe and understand the logical linkages between the concepts and the project requirements to deepen their understanding of media ownership and market concept.

Figure 5.2: Concept Map: Media Structure and Industry

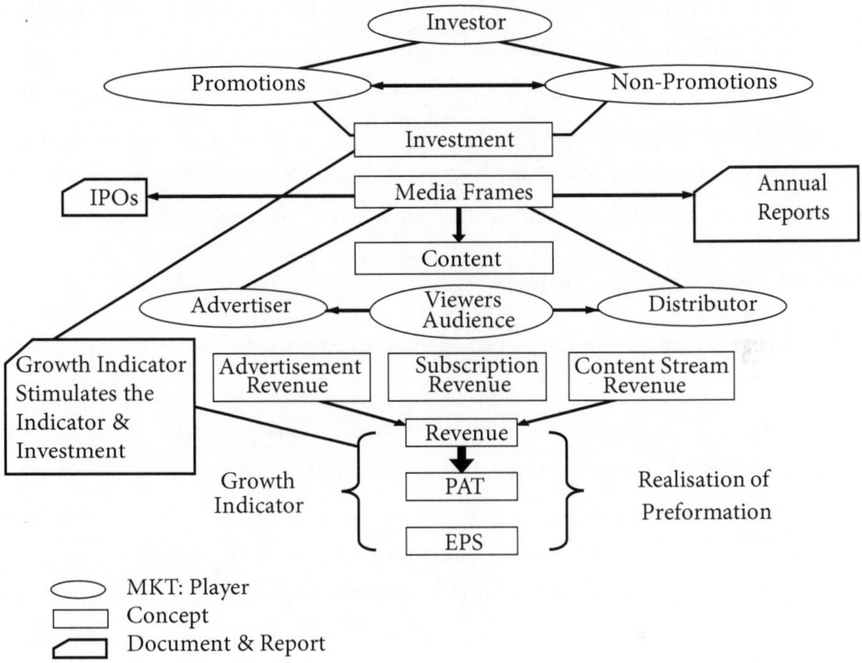

Source: Authors

Course Instructional Design

The project aims to give students a practical and in-depth understanding of media economics, ownership and market. Teachers organise teaching-learning timetables to facilitate students in the following manner:

- Help students identify and illustrate characteristics of primary and secondary data related to media economics.
- Impart knowledge in the theory and methods of analysis of media ownership and measurement, which will also assist in subsequent policy analysis.
- Impart practical skills in applying basic research tools and techniques of economic analysis of primary and secondary material.
- Enable students to use research tools and techniques such as technical analysis, which looks at the shareholding patterns and calculates EPS, PAT, et cetera, and graphical analysis of information gathered from annual reports, IPOs, et cetera.

- Expose students to media ownership, firm and market behaviour through analysis of public data such as market shares, firm websites, annual reports and IPO of various media firms.
- Develop the ability to compute relevant parameters of media ownership, revenue, profit and the market.
- Impart the knowledge to synthesise different forms of economic data to argue or compare different economic facets of ownership and market.

Project Learning Outcomes

At the end of the hands-on project workshop, students should be able to:

- distinguish and collate different dimensions/parameters of media ownership and media market for a coherent understanding of firms or market behaviour.
- identify and illustrate behavioural parameters, shifts and dimensions of media ownership to explain business histories, models and commercial imperatives.
- identify and make use of primary and secondary material, such as annual reports, firm websites and IPOs of media firms, for qualitative analysis.
- apply key economic concepts technically in quantitative and qualitative analysis and illustrate revenue, EPS and PAT as parameters of media ownership.
- present and interpret graphical or tabular data after analysing financial information gathered from annual reports, IPOs, et cetera.
- derive analysis of market data, government data and reports for broader policy-analysis exercises in the long run, et cetera.
- practically/technically identify, derive, compare and demonstrate the theoretical application of concepts of media economics.
- interpret graphical and economic data to explain movements and shifts in the firms' or market behaviour.
- analyse theory and methods of analysis of media ownership and measurements.
- organise economic data in the form of reports to substantiate or argue out different issues of understanding policy and the role of stakeholders.

Key Concepts

Students will need to understand the following key concepts that are central to understanding media economics. They need to understand them individually before exploring their interlinkages. They are also expected to practically illustrate them in the hands-on project to understand the factors influencing media ownership and media business.

Media market

This is a designated market area and could refer to a space of singular or multiple media such as the broadcast market, et cetera. Simply speaking, it is a market, a region, where people can offer and receive media offerings such as television, radio, internet, newspapers, et cetera.

Integration

Integration is a type of strategy or management employed by media firms/companies to create a competitive advantage in the marketplace. There are two types of integration:

- Vertical integration: Vertical integration describes a style of management control that brings large portions of the supply chain, that is, creation, production, distribution and exhibition, under common ownership and one corporation. Such integration increases a company's power in the marketplace and also helps a firm reduce costs and improve efficiency by decreasing transportation expenses and reducing turnaround time, among other advantages, for example, a newspaper company that owns a newspaper printing plant, a paper (raw paper) company, ink company, distribution and transportation company.
- Horizontal integration: Horizontal integration describes a type of ownership and control strategy of a firm to increase market share by taking over, merging with or buying out another firm that is in the same industry and in the same stage of production to increase its reach. For example, within a conglomerate, the content used in broadcasting television will be used in broadcasting radio and the content used in the hard copy of its newspaper will also be used in its online version.

Diversification

Diversification means risk management. There are various types of diversification like:

- Concentric diversification: In concentric diversification, a company or a firm acquires or develops new products or services or enters a new market. The addition of tomato ketchup and sauce to an existing processed item such as Maggi, a brand from Food Specialties Limited, is an example of technology-related concentric diversification.
- Horizontal diversification: Under horizontal diversification, a company or a firm acquires new products that are different from its core business but may appeal to its current business, for example, a notebook-making company entering the pen market with its new product.
- Conglomerates diversification: Under conglomerates diversification, a firm or a company markets new products or services that have no technological or commercial synergies with current products but may appeal to new customers. The conglomerate diversification has a minimal relationship with the firm's current business. Therefore, the main reasons for adopting such a strategy are, first, to improve the profitability and flexibility of the company and, second, to get a better reception in capital markets as the company gets bigger. Even if this strategy is risky, it can also, if successful, provide increased growth and profitability.
- Diversification (finance): It's a strategy of reducing risk by investing money in various assets.
- Diversification (marketing strategy): Corporate marketing strategy seeks to increase profitability by capturing a larger market share by selling a greater volume of new products in the new market.

Merger and acquisition

- Merger: Merger is a process whereby two or more companies come together to expand their business. This decision is usually mutual between or among the companies involved; it is done to acquire equal profit in the newly created entity. In a merger, both companies can retain their respective names or pick either of the two by mutual consent. An example of this is Sony Ericsson, where both the companies (Sony and Ericsson) retained their names following the merger.

- Acquisition: An acquisition is a purchase/takeover of one business or company by another company or business entity. Consolidation occurs when two companies combine to form a new enterprise and neither of them survives independently.

Competition

Competition is defined as the degree to which competitors compete for the same resources. In media economics, audience and advertisers are resources for which companies or firms compete, as they are required for business growth and survival.

Intellectual property

Intellectual property is the 'creation of the mind, inventions, literary and artistic works, and symbols, name, image, and designs used in commerce' (World Intellectual Property Organization, 2009). Intellectual property includes literary and artistic works, broadcast and other performances, patents and copyright.

Investment

The term 'investment' means putting money into any work or in a business to see the original investment appreciate over a period of time. Numerous investment decisions are made for growth, such as purchasing stock, bonds or mutual funds, et cetera.

Stock and stock market

Stock (also known as capital stock) is the founders' original capital invested in a business. Broadly, there are two types of stock:

- Common stock: Common stock (also known as corporate stock) is a stock purchased online or through a broker. It carries voting rights that can be exercised during corporate decision-making and is offered in different types of classes. For example, Viacom offered class 'B' shares of common stock to individual investors in New York Stock Exchange (NYSE).
- Preferred stock: Preferred stock is a higher class of stock that is restricted to designated buyers of the shares. They do not carry any voting right but legally receive a certain level of dividend payments before other shareholders.

- Stock repurchases: Stock repurchasing (or buy back) is a process by which a company acquires its stock or shares from the market to increase the market value of the stock or shares. The market value of a company's shares is directly dependent on the earnings over the shares or earnings per share. By repurchasing their own shares, companies reduce the number of shares held by the public and increase the earning per share if the profit remains the same as before the repurchase of stock. Thus, the higher the earning per share, the higher the market value of the shares, and vice versa.

Revenue

It is the total income raised by a firm or company during a financial year by selling certain products and services. In the context of media ownership, these products and services could be media contents in any form, that is, news or entertainment such as movies, serial, et cetera. Revenue streams indicate broad divisions of revenue into categories or streams such as:

- Revenue from advertisement: Advertisement revenue is the amount received by a media firm for telecasting and promoting a certain brand or product of a company for a fixed duration, for example, a Lux soap ad. on a particular TV or radio channel. Advertisements account for the maximum share of the total revenues.
- Revenue from subscription: Subscription revenue is the amount received by a distributor directly from subscribers for subscribing to a particular media. The contribution of this medium towards the total revenues is not very large but still is a reasonable part of the total revenues.
- Pay-per-item: Pay-per-item is a revenue model for media types packaged in individual offers and is often sustained through sales. An example of this is pay-per-view channels, movies, cable, movie tickets at the local theatre, CD or DVD.
- Merchandising: Merchandising offers a secondary or ancillary income to media companies. Media franchises with a larger fan base typically offer related media items for purchase. An example is Disney, which produces and sells merchandise for all of its big-budget movies and TV shows. Merchandising efforts can generate more income than a company's primary media product. For example, the original Star Wars movies earned more income through merchandising than through ticket sales.

- Revenue from other sources: Other sources of revenue include shared service and sales of television software. The contribution of this medium to the total revenue is significantly small.

Subsidiary companies

A subsidiary company is a branch or a part of the higher entity or company. This higher entity or company is usually known as the parent company. The parent company can have absolute or partial control over the subsidiary company. For example, NDTV Imagine is a subsidiary of NDTV Ltd.

Dual product market

A dual market is a market where one company is involved in two economic activities, that is, selling two different products in the same market.

Picard (1989) explains that the media industries are unique in that they function as a dual product market, that is, while they produce one product, they participate in two separate goods and services in the market. In the market, media industries also sell their content. For example, all news channels, such as NDTV, Aaj Tak, et cetera, reach their audience with news as content while also being involved in advertisements. Figure 5.3 demonstrates this link:

Figure 5.3: Media Goods and Services

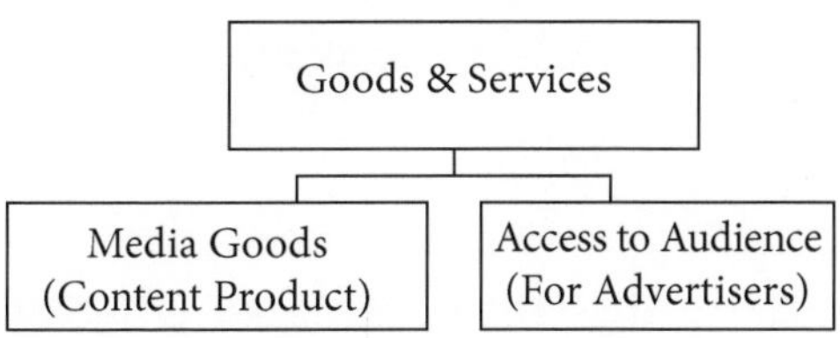

Types of goods

Goods are also called products. The following are different types of goods:

- Tangible and non-tangible goods
    - Tangible goods: Tangible goods are those that can be touchable or are in solid form.
    - Non-tangible goods: Non-tangible goods are those that are not in solid form and cannot be felt or touched.

- Public and private goods
    - Public goods: Public goods are those goods that are non-rival and non-excludable in nature. Every individual can enjoy its benefits and consume as much as they want without excluding others or themselves. Thus, public goods are non-rivalrous and non-excludable in nature.
    - Private goods: Unlike public goods, private goods are rivalrous and excludable. Its owner can exercise the private property right and can prevent others to consume it. Examples: Movie ticket, private house, rented room, et cetera.

To understand the concept of public and private goods more clearly, clarification has been provided in Table 5.1.

Table 5.1: Public and Private Goods

	Excludable	**Non-excludable**
Rivalrous	**Private goods** food, clothing, cars, personal electronics	**Common goods (Common-pool resources)** fish stocks, timber, coal
Non-rivalrous	**Club goods** cinemas, private parks, satellite television	**Public goods** free-to-air television, air, national defence

Source: Ostrom Elinor. *Understanding Institutional Diversity. Princeton*. NJ: Princeton University Press, 2005.

Setting up the Hands-on Project

After the initial theoretical and conceptual orientation in media economics in the class, this hands-on project workshop is introduced by the teacher. Students are expected to be familiar with the aforementioned concepts and the learning objectives of both the course and the project, that is, to understand various economic factors influencing the media and its market. The key concepts are covered in the first three classroom sessions before the hands-on workshop. Ideally, the module begins by mapping the context of media ownership and locating various components, such as type of ownership, promoters, non-promoters, revenue, profit, et cetera, of media firms theoretically so that students can gain a sufficient theoretical understanding of the dynamics of the industry before applying analytical tools. The concepts of media economics and its methodological application are introduced as a pedagogic technique through a simultaneous theory-and-application format during the hands-on workshop itself. This exercise is designed to train students to locate background features of the economics of ownership and grasp their influence in the larger policy context. The hands-on workshop will train students to describe the linkages between the concepts and sub-concepts, plot them technically and interpret graphs and tables to explain ownership and market parameters. This also involves data sorting, presentation in graphical tables, assignments on business histories and a final presentation, after which students are expected to submit the write-up.

The hands-on project is covered in sixteen classes of ninety minutes each. As a pre-workshop exercise, teachers assign to students the task of learning how to use MS Excel and identify sources of economic data such as media websites, annual reports or IPOs and how to read/identify relevant data sources. This exercise also familiarises students with the rich repertoire of movements and shifts in the market. Also, selected readings in media economics are assigned to students to help them understand media economics.

Teachers prepare short instruction sheets that are handed over to students before the process begins. This instruction sheet covers the timetable, key concepts, basic instructions on using MS Excel, the nature of assignments expected from students and a timeline that indicates what and when the portions will be covered. The training on data sorting is expected to take a month and includes short exercises. Some portions such as one on MS Excel will require teachers and students to do intense work. Graphical data presentations are to be made at the end of the month. Assignments on business history are to be submitted at the end of the second month of the project workshop while the final presentation and submission of the write-up are expected to be submitted at the end of the third month.

Project Instructional Design

The sessions in this course are divided into modules that cover the course materials and the hands-on workshop; this requires teachers to be familiar with theories, approaches and methods in media economics in general. Teachers are also expected to be familiar with the basics of mathematical calculations, economic formulas, computers, et cetera, and to be able to read and present financial data and have a fair understanding of media segments, media sectors, movements in media markets and the nature of the stock market.

Students are taught how to use MS Excel for basic quantitative analysis in media economics. Some of the students might be familiar with MS Excel; nevertheless, this project workshop will begin with the basics of the spreadsheet programme. The teacher must be capable of training students to generate primary data using secondary data available publicly and by using tools such as MS Excel. For this purpose, teachers are expected to have had exposure to economic data available online, such as annual reports and IPOs of firms, BSE, NSE, SEBI and the websites of the companies. They must already have known how to identify shareholding patterns, profits, revenue, et cetera. This section details the guidelines on what teachers need to do to plan and execute the hands-on project workshop.

Planning the Hands-on Project

The teacher should plot the project-workshop work before the workshop begins. This project workshop could include preparing detailed instructional sheets, notes, exercises and hands-on exercises, which need not be given to students. The following is a list of guidelines that the teacher needs to follow before beginning the process:

- Make a list of possible companies (Aaj Tak, NDTV, etc.) or media segments (TV news, FM radio, etc.) that you may want students to analyse.
- Arrange a computer and projector so that students can be comfortably instructed during the hands-on project work.
- Have a working knowledge of and familiarity with the websites of Bombay Stock Exchange (BSE), National Stock Exchange (NSE) and Security Exchange Board of India (SEBI) and a basic understanding of security and the stock market.
- Aggregate and understand the economic aspects of each segment or media company; identify IPOs and their details.

- Identify the economic elements around which the hands-on project work could be designed and prepare a short exercise for students.
- Familiarise yourself with the economic groundings of media and technology, and the vocabularies and consequences of different actors, such as the state, media, citizens, consumers, civil society, global institutions, networks and policies.
- List a series of selected readings so that students can deepen their understanding of ownership and market and their interrelationships with policy.
- Map a series of pre-project workshop exercises for students.
- Draw up questions and tasks within each segment to help students better understand the company, segment and media market.
- Divide students into individuals and groups for segment-wise analysis depending on their familiarity with MS Excel or background in economics.
- Develop pre-hands-on exercises and see that students are familiar with the keywords or concepts of media economics.

Conducting the Hands-on Project

The hands-on project workshop maps out the contents drawn out in the next few pages. Before this, teachers should lucidly explain to students the goals of this exercise and ensure that students attend classes and do the activities outlined for this exercise. The instructors should provide students with notes on key concepts; they are also expected to illustrate key parameters of MS Excel, data sorting, reading and presenting the data in tables and graphs and how each of these parameters will be evaluated. Students will also be informed that they are expected to interact with the instructors at each stage, especially during MS Excel exercises.

- The first three classes are devoted to introducing the aims of the hands-on project, its relevance, theories and instructions on identifying firm sites, stock market sites, collecting annual reports and IPOs and identifying the firm or market segment of the assignments.
- Students should be instructed to present economic data related to media firms and markets in graphs or charts.
- They should be instructed that the graphs to be prepared include:

(i) total number of shares
(ii) shareholdings by promoters and non-promoters
(iii) subcategories of institutions
(iv) subcategories of non-institutions

- Teachers should provide illustrative examples of practical training on MS Excel and of analysing economic data collected through quantitative and qualitative methods.
- Students should be divided into groups, media segments or firms finalised for analysis and clearly instructed on the homework and classroom assignments.
- They should be made aware that data can be mined from secondary sources; they should be told how to formulate primary data to answer a particular economic query.
- Teachers must inform students to analyse the units within each financial year and specify the units in their graphical or tabular presentation.
- When discussing each parameter, teachers need to draw linkages with broader revenue issues, the market and ownership, even referring to the readings on economics assigned to students.
- Students need to be instructed to critically read financial information in annual reports and IPOs and identify its various components to understand market shifts.
- Review all the exercises and data presented by students to see if the numbers are entered and plotted correctly.
- Students should be instructed to divide their work into three stages in the following order:

(i) Tabular presentation,
(ii) Graphical presentation and
(iii) A mix of both, along with a detailed illustration of economic parameters.

- Instruct students to collate economic data for a broader narrative to illustrate the parameters of ownership and the market.
- Three more classes should be assigned to students, over and above the scheduled sixteen classes for the workshop: two for students' interim presentations and narratives and one for the final presentations.

Pre-Hands-on Project Exercises

The pre-project workshop exercises could be included in the first three to four sessions of classroom instructions, which could include the following:

- Exercises to test students' familiarity with microeconomics concepts.
- Short exercises to explain the concept of market and provide an overview of media ownership.
- Basic instructions on and exercises in MS Excel.
- Short commentaries on select readings provided to students.

Box 5.1 presents a brief example of a pre-project workshop exercise.

Box 5.1: Example of a Pre-Project Workshop Exercise

Example of a Pre-Project Workshop Exercise

- Do a review of two articles on media ownership.
- Analyse non-financial pages of the last three annual reports along with the IPO document of a particular company.

Aim: To familiarise the students with elements and concepts of ownership (for article) and economic data available in larger reports like annual reports and IPOs of firms.

Key: Students should take note for the following:

- In the case of an article review, they need to pay attention to ownership and its parameters.
- In the case of an AR and IPO review, they need to look at the company's business history, its present scenario and the changes that have taken place in the last three years.

Exercise: Students will need to write an analysis report of 1,200–1,500 words.

Hands-on Project Design

The Template

This exercise intends to train students to analyse, interpret and present economic data about ownership and the market. The teachers have to link key concepts and theoretical elements discussed in the classroom, along with quantitative illustration and presentation. Therefore, it is recommended that teachers follow the order elaborated in Box 5.2, or a similar order to indicate elements of ownership, and explain to students how to apply the methodological tools. This will help in identifying a segment, a firm within a segment, its various components and a broader location within the media market, and also in analysing and presenting shares and profits, mergers and acquisitions, et cetera. In the process, the following components (Box 5.2) will be dealt with both in the class and as practical exercises, which will help students understand evolution, ownership, components, firm behaviour, economic parameters of the firms and media markets. Further elements to be mapped could be added, at which point the complexity of the calculations will increase, or the elements could be combined based on what is being studied, student capacities or contents of the course. This hands-on exercise will be useful to map the concepts related to revenue vis-à-vis investors, PAT and EPS, and tools to plot the relationships, as also evaluate its economics.

Box 5.2: Elements of Ownership

Contents

1. Company Introduction
2. Business History of the Company
3. Ownership
4. Parameters
   (i) Shareholdings by Type of Investors
      (a) Total number of shares
      (b) Holdings by promoters and non-promoters
      (c) Holdings by institutions and non-institutions
      (d) Holdings under the subcategory of institutions
      (e) Holdings under the subcategory of non-institutions
   (ii) Subsidiary Companies
   (iii) Merger and Acquisitions
   (iv) Revenue
   (v) PAT
   (vi) EPS
5. Conclusion

All the aspects identified in Box 5.2 are to be illustrated theoretically and practically during the hands-on exercise. The aim of planning the contents in this order is to illustrate the elements of media ownership and also the nature and extent of interlinkages among the elements. The fourth point in the above exercise is to clarify the connections between investments. The revenue of a (media) company impacts its EPS (earnings per share) and profit; for example, a higher revenue will lead to higher EPS and profit, which will attract more investors and, hence, more profit, leading to a cycle of growth. And, more investment requires a greater number of equity shares to be issued so that the total equity could rise. If a merger or an acquisition occurs, the company's profit will increase or decrease depending on the financial status of the company being acquired.

Teachers should ask students to do short exercises before they go on to do longer ones. At each stage, students are expected to collate data for their final presentations. The instructor must pose questions related to the companies. Accordingly, students will then identify and fill in the details as part of their initial attempts to chart a business model or business history map. (For example, see Box 5.3.)

Box 5.3: Project Workshop Exercises

Project Workshop Exercises: Identifying the Firm

1. The first economic element should begin with an introduction to the company and its business journey; the list should look like this:
   (i) Introduction to the company.
   (ii) When was the company incorporated?
   (ii) Other products and diversifications in the company's portfolio.
2. The second element should plot the business history of the company in chronological order:
   (ii) What changes happened in what year?
   (ii) What were the turning points in the company's history?
   (ii) A list of achievements of the company.
3. The third element should be to identify some parameters of ownership:
   (ii) Name of the owner(s).
   (ii) What was the type of ownership (public or private)?

Time: 1 week

After having identified a firm, the teacher must guide students to begin analysing its different parameters. These parameters are intended to illustrate the firm's holdings, its link to revenue models, its holdings and how it would influence costs. The things that the teacher must note before beginning to analyse the parameters are:

- The company's inception and listing dates have to be mentioned. Reasonable year-wise economic information has to be collected to further investigate an identified economic issue.
- The timeframe for each unit has to be limited to a particular financial year.
- The instructor has to instruct students to specify the unit of shareholdings (in millions).

Box 5.4: Mid-Project Workshop Exercise

Mid-Project Workshop Exercise: Determining Economic out of Relevant Secondary Documents

This is a longer exercise that will look into the parameters of ownership in detail. The parameters that need to be chalked out are as follow:

1. Parameters:
   (i) Shareholdings by Type of Investors:
      (a) Total no. of shares
      (b) Holdings by promoters and non-promoters
      (c) Holdings by institutions and non-institutions
      (d) Holdings under the subcategory of institutions
      (e) Holdings under the subcategory of non-institutions
   (ii) Subsidiary Companies
   (iii Merger and Acquisitions
   (iv) Revenue
   (v) PAT
   (vi) EPS
2. Conclusion
3. Bibliography

Time: 2 weeks

The following slides are a sample of the PowerPoint to be included in assignments to help students understand one of the parameters. Students need to identify elements of shareholdings, plot them in MS Excel and create a table or graphs based on the date. For example, the following illustrations show the parameters of shareholdings: Slide 1: a tabular format of different investors; Slide 2: a company's shares; Slide 3 promoters and non-promoters; Slide 4: a graph of institutions and non-institutions.

I. Shareholdings by the type of investors

Equity holding by the type of investors						
XYZ Ltd						
(No. of shares)						
	Mar-05	Mar-06	Mar-07	Mar-08	Mar-09	Mar-10
Total Shares	0	0	0	0	0	0
Promoters						
Indian						
Individuals & HUF						
Central & State Govt.						
Corporate Bodies						
FIs & Banks						
Others						
Foreign						
Individuals (NRIs)						
Corporate Bodies						
Institutions						
Others						
Persons acting in concert						
Non-Promoters						
Institutions						
Mutual Funds (UTI)						
Banks, FIs, Insurance Companies						
Insurance Companies						
Financial Institutions & Banks						
Central & State Govt.						
FII's						
Venture Capital Funds						
Foreign Venture Capital						
Others						
Non-Institutions						
Corporate Bodies						
Individuals						
Nominal Invest Upto Rs 1 Lakh						
Nominal Invest Over Rs 1 Lakh						
Others						

Slide 5.1

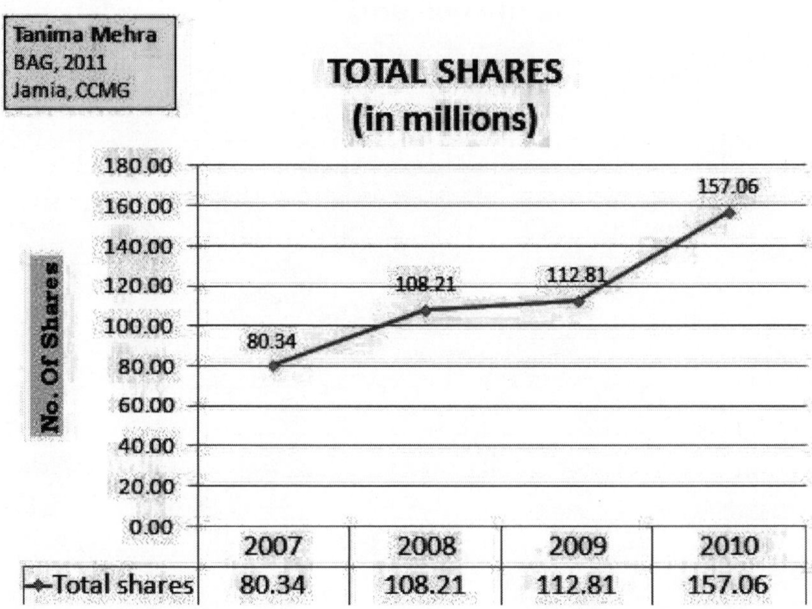

Slide 5.2

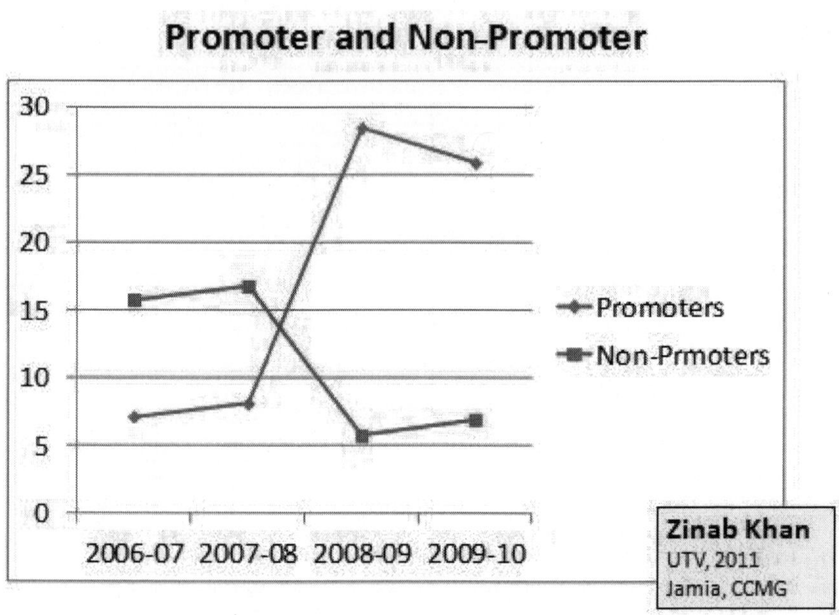

Slide 5.3

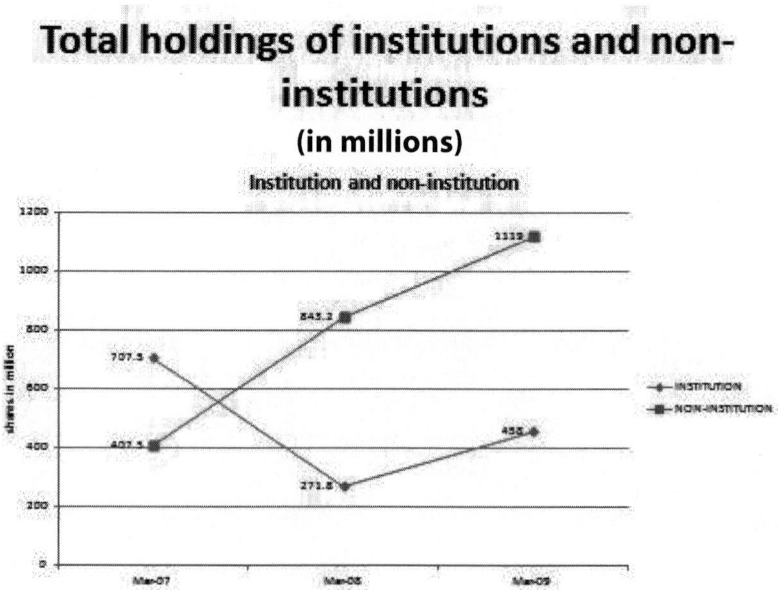

Slide 5.4

Similar exercises are required for other points, such as promoters and non-promoter et cetera, so that the workshop covers the entire variables given under the 'parameters' section. The idea is to get students to address each element through practical tasks so that they can make their final presentations, learn about media ownership and demonstrate their understanding of it.

How to Analyse the Parameters in the Template

The hands-on project workshop aims to link the conceptual part of learning (mentioned previously) with the technical part. The key questions and order of unravelling economic elements are mapped as links to be built into the broader aim of understanding media and its market. Students will need to relate market behaviours, revenue models and other elements to identify key elements of media economics. The conceptual elements are the clues that need to be further explained as quantitative data is analysed and collated into explanatory frameworks. At each stage of plotting the exercises, the concepts will be referred to in the classroom and the links drawn. The conceptual, thus, is a guide to the technical part detailed hereinafter. The graphs and tables are used to display trends. Students are expected to interpret the trends, the percentage of cases below or above a standard and the relationships between the variables.

How to Do a Hands-on Project

The instructional design is intended to help students link the theoretical concepts of media ownership with the practical and gain competency in basic quantitative techniques. The project workshop provides intense hands-on training in quantitative and qualitative tools. This exercise begins with the basics so that students who have not had formal training in economics can also learn and apply quantitative methods. It also trains students to collate and present economic data so that they can form a broader understanding of the dynamics of media markets. Teachers can design the project workshop in any other manner, provided that there are logical connections between the economic parameters.

Students must be prepared to work hard as this is an intense, time-bound exercise that requires them to write term papers, do homework and give PowerPoint presentations. The project requires students to pick a media firm as a case study and analyse its behaviour using qualitative and quantitative analytical tools of media economics and policy measurement. Ideally, students with and without MS Excel knowledge are grouped together.

Knowledge of the spreadsheet programme is crucial to the project, as mapping analyses done on MS Excel go on to shape the final presentation. At each stage, students must consult their instructor, who will check the calculations and tables and give feedback.

Students must strictly follow the structure mentioned below. This is primarily a group exercise. Students are divided into groups of four or five, corresponding to their tutorial groups, with each given one company to analyse. It is recommended that the groups are kept small in size so that students can undertake statistical analysis. Students are assigned four media segments to study: TV news, TV entertainment, mobile telephony and FM radio. More media segments can be added to this, depending on the accessibility and expanding market base of other media.

Each group is assigned one industry segment, and each student is asked to select and analyse one company or service provider within each segment. The instructor can change the segments depending on the interest, course orientations, class size and prior training or abilities of students. The exercise has two components: data presentation and assignment submission. Students should be told to divide their work as follows:

- In the first stage, students are taught tabulation. They are required to make tabular presentations of all the parameters in the contents mentioned previously.
- In the second stage, they are required to make graphical presentations.
- In the third and final presentations, they could mix both or make a presentation that illustrates media ownership.

During the eight-week hands-on exercise, the following timeline is important (Figure 5.4):

- The first interim presentation on data sorting is expected in the first week of the workshop.
- The second interim presentation on the graphical representation of data is expected at the end of the first month.
- A three-page write-up on the business history of a company must be submitted by the fifth week.
- The final presentation and submission of the write-up are due in the last week of the exercise.

Figure 5.4: Timeline Tree Diagram

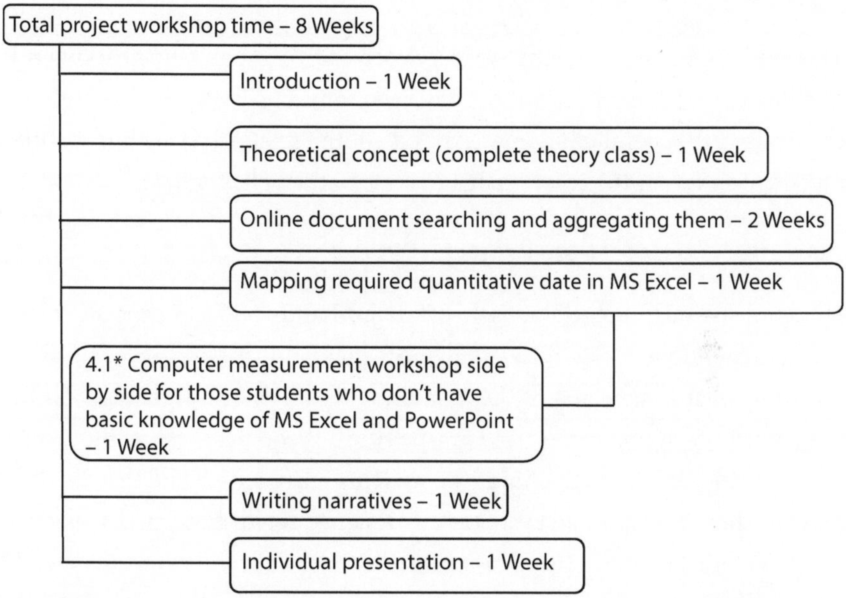

* This can be skipped if students already have MS Excel and PowerPoint knowledge.

Source: Authors

Evaluation of Students

Students are evaluated based on the following outputs:

- How correctly a company and its data (for a financial year) have been identified.
- Individual interim presentation of graphs and tables with relevant interpretations.
- Narratives within the presentation.
- Final presentation to illustrate the economics of ownership or a firm.
- How deeply the presentations have incorporated reviews of IPOs and annual reports.

Assessment carries 25 per cent weightage.

Overall, students are tested for their ability to grasp ownership measurement analysis and repeat this exercise for various media firms and other companies. They are also assessed for their ability to identify secondary data from websites and reports, sift through primary economic data and grasp theories, concepts and methodologies of media economics.

Key Things for Students to Focus On

This exercise requires students to work closely with computers and use classroom learning to understand methods of basic economic analysis. It will help students understand that conflicting interests and commercial drives within the media market are a few of the contexts that operate in the policy sphere.

Planning the Hands-on-Project

Students should prepare themselves for the hands-on workshop by keeping the aforementioned lessons in mind and being familiar with the concept map, knowing what is expected of them and how to do their assignments on time. They must try to understand and grasp critical theoretical and methodological issues during classroom teaching. The students must understand that the hands-on workshop concepts and exercises are designed to illustrate media ownership and the market context. They are expected to follow the following guidelines:

- They should go back and look at the concept map and envision and map out what they are expected to learn and how.
- They must be familiar with the concepts of media ownership and market so that they can work towards identifying their various elements conceptually and technically.
- They should have also gained basic knowledge of what quantitative and qualitative data are.
- They should identify a media company and segment after consulting their instructor.
- They should also source and examine IPOs and annual reports available online.
- Students should be familiar with the websites of Bombay Stock Exchange (BSE), National Stock Exchange (NSE) and Security Exchange Board of India (SEBI) so that they know how to identify economic materials available online and use them as financial data for analysis.
  The links to the websites are:
  BSE India website: http://www.bseindia.com
  NSE India website: http://www.nseindia.com/
  SEBI website: http://www.sebi.gov.in/sebiweb/

- They should bookmark the websites of the companies they are working on.
- They should have a basic idea of MS Excel and MS PowerPoint.
- They are expected to sort and clean the quantitative data before presenting it.
- At each point, they are expected to consult their teacher.

Guidelines for Students in the Classroom

Each student is expected to participate in class and do the following:

- Search and identify IPOs, promoters and non-promoters and other details.
- Identify the various elements of media ownership and the market and link their primary data for analysis and to explain theoretical concepts.
- Identify media websites and company information.
- Use MS Excel to create tables and graphs on key economic parameters.
- Create PowerPoint slides from the MS Excel data.
- See that the data they use or generate are of a single financial year.
- Make proper entries so that the correct data is generated.
- Time the presentation to cover all aspects.
- Have a fair idea of the number of slides to include (consult the instructor for the number of slides (maximum or minimum), if any.
- Present data in a coherent manner as part of interim presentations and stick to the deadlines set by the teacher.
- Demonstrate how media economic is relevant in understanding the context of policies.

Students' Self-Evaluation

The hands-on project exercise requires close consultation with the instructor, as it involves real analysis of media segments, firms, et cetera. However, students can personally evaluate their PPT slides for presentations on certain basic parameters, including the following:

- that a proper format introduces the company, its history, ownership.
- that slides of tables and graphs illustrate various economic parameters.
- that quantitative data has been presented correctly.

- that tables are inserted in the correct order.
- that graphs are plotted correctly.
- that headings are appropriately placed.
- that their slides cover the parameters to capture the concept of media ownership and demonstrate an ability to collate and interpret primary and secondary data.
- that appropriate conclusions are given, followed by proper references, including those of websites.

Illustrative Case Study

This section details what possible cases could be developed and the rationale behind each of them.

Universe of cases

The exercise could pick one industry segment or channel from the clusters given in the following box.

1. Business
2. Hindi
3. English
4. Regional–South
5. Regional–West/East

Teachers, however, should ensure that they are familiar with the cluster or industry and the media firms within them. Within each such segment or cluster is a list of companies and service providers, and a student needs to select one company or service provider from the given list.

Illustrative case

The following design could be used, and the segments chosen for analysis are given in the following box.

1. TV–News
2. TV–Entertainment
3. Mobile telecom
4. FM radio

But the segments could also include other sectors such as the newspaper. The segments may be altered by teachers depending on their interest, course orientations, class size and prior training or current abilities of the students. Students may be divided into four to five groups corresponding to their interactive counselling (IC)/tutorial groups. This is a group as well as an individual exercise. Each student is given one company to analyse, present its data and write an assignment for submission. It is recommended that the groups are kept small for ease of mathematical analysis. The groups may be expanded or reduced based on the combination of data to be explored.

Past work

The sample (see Figures 5.5 to 5.7) illustrates some parts of an assignment of work done by a student with the help of teachers who have authored various chapters in this book. It demonstrates the work of a student, and how she identified a company from the allocated media segments, in this case, the TV–entertainment sector, and explained media firm or market behaviour by connecting different elements of economic variables. Students need to follow a similar pattern of understanding ownership or a firm or market behaviour, regardless of the segment or channel clusters that they take up for the study. The following example is just a sample and not a full illustration of all the slides that explain ownership. A PowerPoint format is used to prepare slides for the presentation. Also, the final write-up incorporates some of the slides, explains the growth and evolution of a firm and its revenue, and includes growth strategies, among others, to illustrate theoretical concepts and link them to the data.

This model example illustrates parts of both the PowerPoint presentation and term paper that Tanimaa Mehra developed to study B.A.G. Films & Media Ltd. to illustrate ownership and other parameters. The data is from a single financial year of the firm. Also, the data has been plotted correctly and the units specified clearly. The student has effectively illustrated the expansions and diversifications of the company as well as its mergers and acquisitions. The student writes:

> B.A.G. Films & Media Ltd. was incorporated as B.A.G. Films Private Ltd. on January 22, 1993, at New Delhi, was converted into a public limited company vide Special Resolution passed on 03.03.2001 and renamed as B.A.G. Films Limited on March 29, 2001 .... B.A.G. Films started in 1993 with a talk show

on Doordarshan called Aaj Ki Baat ... looking at the ownership pattern of the company we find that the company is promoted by a team of core media professionals, having more than 15 years of experience in the Indian Media industry. The initial promoters of the company were Ms. Anurradha Prasad and Mr. Rajiv Shukla. Ref. Student, 2010

Figure 5.5: Total Number of Shares

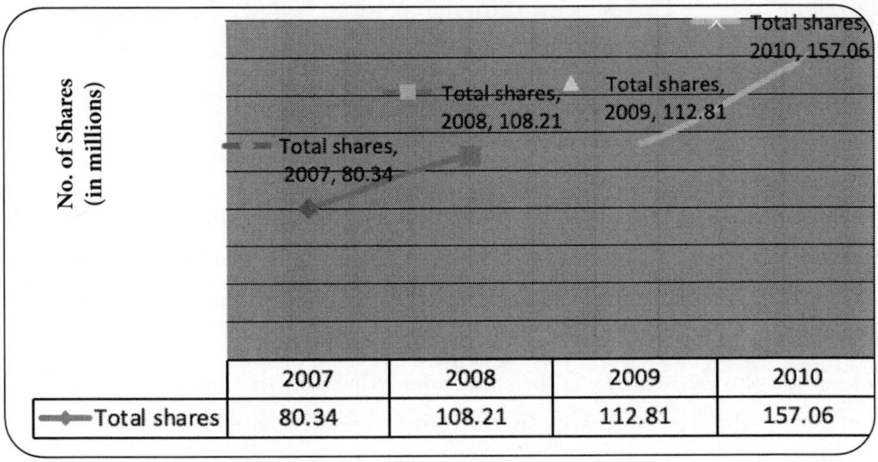

Source: Tanima Mehra (Student), 2010

Figure 5.6: Shares of Investors

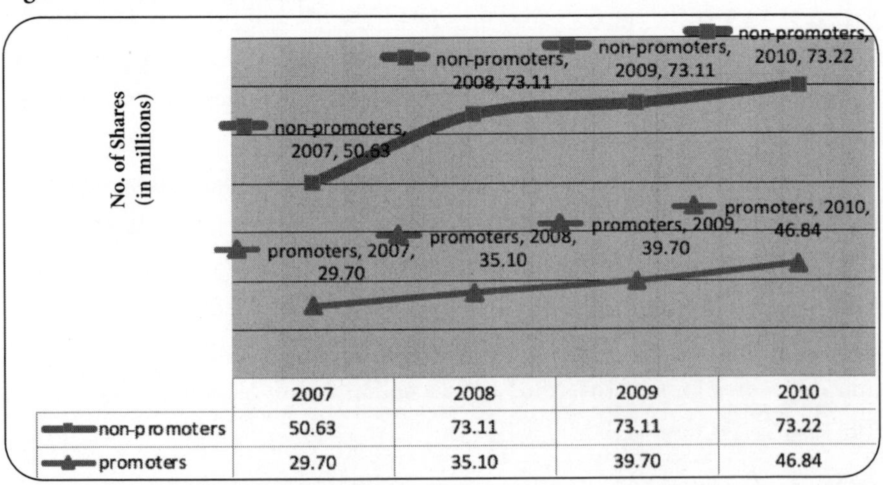

Source: Tanima Mehra (Student), 2010

She concludes:

> Looking at the broad categories of investors, we find an increasing trend in both types. Promoters are steadily increasing due to the steady rise in ARVR Communications Pvt Ltd. (which was initially known as Anu Films Communications Pvt Ltd). As for the Non-Promoters, we can further divide this type into Institutional and Non-Institutional. In these two subcategories, we find a positive trend in the non-institutional category but a downward trend in the institutional category. (Student, 2010)

The student plotted the total number of shares (Figure 5.5), shares of investors (Figure 5.6) and subsequently explained the financial performance of B.A.G by examining the trends of the total revenue, profit after tax and earnings per share, even ascertaining the interlinkages between financial accounting, especially between PAT and EPS (Figure 5.7). For example, she plotted sales and revenue graphically and linked it to the performance of the company's projects and identified its transition:

Figure 5.7: Total Revenue and Its Components

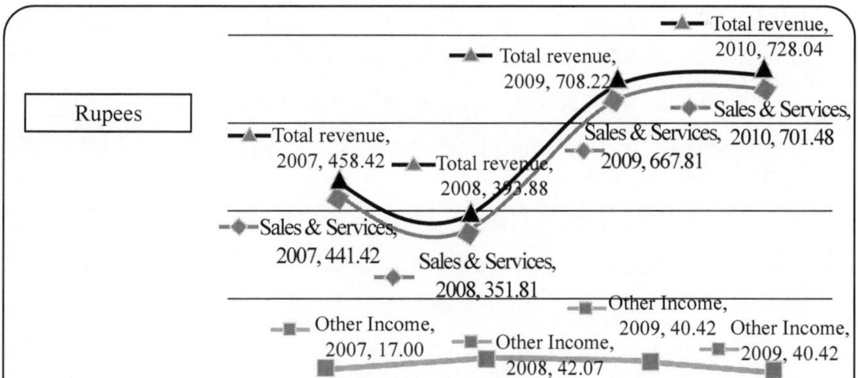

	2007	2008	2009	2010
SALES & SERVICES	441.42	351.81	667.81	701.48
OTHER INCOME	17.00	42.07	40.42	26.57
TOTAL INCOME	458.42	393.88	708.22	728.04

Source: Tanima Mehra (Student), 2010

Finally, as part of the conclusion, the overall performance of the company in the given time frame was assessed and its future performance indicated.

Questions on Presentation

This subsection details the cues with which to gauge students' understanding of the elements of media economics taught in the class. The following are some of the cue questions and common mistakes of students. The questions are also indicative of possible further exercises that the instructor may plan in future.

Questions

- What is the aim of the exercise and what companies, websites and reports have been identified?
- What is the difference between qualitative and quantitative data?
- What is the ownership pattern of the company/firm given to the student (public, public limited, private, private limited)?
- Name the main promoter(s) of the company/firm.
- Trace the business journey of the firm.
- Questions regarding subsidiary company, if any: How many subsidiary companies does the company own and in which areas do they operate, et cetera?
- Did merger and acquisition take place in the company? If yes, what are the consequences or impacts of the merger and acquisition (for instance, did it lead to an increase or decrease in the company's performance, etc.)?
- How many market shares have been captured by the company in its area of operation?
- How do you establish a link between EPS and PAT?
- What are the reasons for the change (increase or decrease) in the share of the promoter(s) and non-promoter(s) over a period of time? If stagnant, why?
- What are the reasons for the change (increase or decrease) in institutional and non-institutional investors and their subcategories over a period of time? If unchanged, why?
- Can you explain media ownership and the commercial dynamics of the media market?

Most common mistakes or ineptitudes of students or their ineptitudes

- Confusion over types of ownership.
- Incorrect graphs because of insufficient knowledge of conceptual and technical techniques.
- Unable to link slides and draw connections between economic variables.
- Confusion about the relationship between EPS and PAT.
- Inability to explain the slope of a graph that depicts, for instance, merger and acquisition, financial crises, et cetera.

Evaluation and Assessment

Each student is evaluated based on the quality and volume of material collected, appropriate use of the material and depth of analysis using the material, as also the application of theoretical understanding of media economics and its presentation through coherent illustration.

By the end of the hands-on project workshop, students will have gained the following skills:

- The ability to determine relevant documents or data from various online sources (online search of IPOs and AR documents).
- The ability to demonstrate conceptual knowledge of ownership and market as a whole.
- The ability for theoretical, conceptual and technical illustrations and to critically evaluate various parameters of ownership.
- The ability to review the relevance of economic data in collected documents.
- The capability to map, in the form of a write-up, related quantitative data from the collected documents.
- The ability to synthesise and organise data graphically in support of their arguments.

Assessment (components)

Student assessment is a continuous procedure throughout the hands-on project workshop exercise.

Document review (IPOs and annual reports)
IPOs and annual reports are the main and important documents that need to be reviewed first. Students need to identify and extract related qualitative and quantitative information from these documents. Quantitative information (data) needs to be mapped in an Excel sheet for further use after sorting and tabulating it in a meaningful manner.

Individual narratives
Students need to individually produce a write-up of about 1500 words, including graphs.

Final individual presentation
Each and every student will have to make a PowerPoint presentation, which should include logically sorted data and details of the company's history and growth represented coherently in graphs.

Assessment (content)

The following are the evaluation criteria used to evaluate students' work based on the contents of their assignments.

IPO and annual reports review
Students need to collect financial information such as control, ownership, forms of integration, shareholding and other details from these secondary documents and organise them to explain or argue the economic aspects of media markets. They will also need to differentiate and derive data related to different media segments, cross-media ownership, business concentration et cetera, which inform the economic structure of a media firm and its industry. For assessment, these will have to be reliably placed to illustrate, argue or establish the relationship between different economic components.

Various concepts
While the hands-on workshop is focused on imparting practical skills in basic quantitative techniques, students should remember that they will

also be assessed for theoretical comprehension of key concepts of media economics. They will need to refer to selected readings provided to them and illustrate in their presentation of economic data knowledge of the concepts.

Technicality

Students will need to demonstrate their ability to extract quantitative data and use it in their assignments. They will have to demonstrate their ability to apply tables, formulas and graphs to indicate institutional economic parameters and their implications in explaining media firm or market behaviour and illustrate holdings, shares, mergers and revenue, among others.

Narrative

Students should remember that the final presentation is a narrative that illustrates media ownership and market. They will need to provide evidence through a coherent narrative that links business history and ownership (culled from companies' websites), locates the shifts of media segments and weaves in economic data. Students will be assessed based on how well they present the data, its correctness and how well it illustrates their assignment objectives.

Assessment (presentation)

Student presentations will be assessed based on the following:

Content

Questions raised should be addressed precisely and coherently in the final presentation. The presentation should be related to the matter. The written assignment should have a clear introduction, the main body should logically map the parameters of media ownership and it must present a compelling conclusion. Students will need to present economic data in a manner that explains media ownership, history, expansion, graphs of shares, ESOPs, types of holdings, PAT and EPS. The facts of the research and reading should be valid. Sources used for research have to be appropriate and up to the mark. The text should be checked for spelling and grammar.

Coherence

The PPT presentation should demonstrate a clear connection between the economic variables. Students must be able to deliver a presentation that explains ownership patterns and provides an overview of the economic drives that shape media markets. There must be clarity in the presentation and suitable references to the concepts taught in class must be provided. They must have fulfilled all assignment requirements by the end of the workshop.

Argument

The argument presented must reflect the ability of the student to explain related graphs and economic variables; it must also present a logical interpretation of graphically plotted data, such as in explaining the slope of a graph (if there is any increase or decrease and stagnation or oscillation—why?). It should be based on factual data collated during the workshop exercises. No imaginary or hypothetical generalisation and conclusion should be made.

Creativity

Students need to be creative. The interconnection between the presentation and the slides has to be inventive, resourceful and ingenious.

Organisation

The presentation must display the student's ability to organise literature, conceptual indicators and primary and secondary economic data. The organisation of these items must establish the links between the introduction, intermittent arguments and conclusion.

Criteria for Grading

Table 5.2 is the assessment grid with criteria to meet for respective grades.

Table 5.2: Assessment Rubric

Grade criteria exercises	**A-Grade (Excellent)**	**B-Grade (Good)**	**C-Grade (Average)**	**D-Grade (Poor)**
Use of secondary sources of economic data	Excellent conceptual knowledge of ownership gained from various document reviews (i.e., ARs, IPOs and TRAI reports, etc.); excellent grasp of key concepts of ownership parameters.	Good knowledge of key concepts; uses a singular source to illustrate the presentation or arguments.	Average use of concepts and reports; has not been demonstrated clearly in the presentation.	Has used few or none of these.
Technical	Sound knowledge of MS Excel and MS PowerPoint. Knows how to plot graphs, has correctly plotted the units, knows the exact reasons behind the shapes of the graphs and links it to media revenue, costs, investments etc. Demonstrates the relevance of explanations of the parameters	Has fair idea how to plot graphs; knows the reasons behind their shapes. Draws good explanatory links to the parameters to understand market or ownership.	Very little knowledge of graphs and the reasons behind their shapes. Errors in plotting or interpretations; has not identified larger links or trends.	Confusing report; most of the graphs are missing; no Idea about graphs made and no clue about their shapes. No connection to the parameters
Presentation	Clarity in connections between PPT slides and graphs/tables. Clarity in connections between different data; clarity in establishing interrelationship between market or firm's economic variables. Clear illustration of the commercial/ economic nature of ownership and market. Organised presentation.	Clarity in explaining connections between PPT slides; clarity in explaining links between parameters. Good organisation and display of material. Minor mistakes in reading economic movements.	Clarity in speech. Some missing connections between slides; presenter unable to fully explain the gaps. Incorrectly plotted graphs. Display and organisation of material average.	Connections between slides weak; presenter unable to explain links and gaps. Display and organisation of economic data weak.

Grade criteria exercises	A-Grade (Excellent)	B-Grade (Good)	C-Grade (Average)	D-Grade (Poor)
Narratives	Clearly and coherently presented report. Media websites accessed and materials used. Clear introduction of company business history/journey. Properly plotted graphs; clearly explained the shapes of the graphs (increasing, decreasing or oscillating etc.) to indicate trends; a clear conclusion. Appropriately used sources. Correct grammar, punctuation and spelling.	Clear report with appropriate evidence, but format not tightly knit. Evidence and research good; trends partially interpreted but could be more expansive. Appropriate use of resources. Correct grammar, punctuation and spelling.	Graphs plotted correctly or incorrectly; poor content or linkages between slides; poor explanation of trends; lacks conceptual clarity. Format not tightly bound. Language and grammar average.	Confusing report; unsound content explanation and conclusion. Inadequate research. Poor language.

Additional Readings

Alexander, Alison, et al., eds. *Media Economics: Theory and Practice*. London: Lawrence Erlbaum, 2004.

Caves, R. *Creative Industries.* Cambridge, MA: Harvard University Press, 2000.

Cowens, T. *In Praise of Commercial Culture*, Introduction, 1. London: Harvard University Press, 1998.

Doyle, Gillian. *Media Ownership: The Economics and Politics of Convergence and Concentration in the UK and European Media*. London: SAGE, 2002.

———. *Understanding Media Economics*, Chapters 1, 2, 3, 8 and 9. London: SAGE, 2002.

Harold L.V. *Entertainment Industry Economics: A Guide for Financial Analysis*, Chapters 1 and 2. Cambridge: Cambridge University Press, 2007.

Hesmondhalgh, David. *The Cultural Industries*. Los Angeles: SAGE, 2007.

Hoskins, Colin, Stuart McFadyen, and Adam Finn. *Media Economics: Applying Economics to New and Traditional Media*, Chapters 1–13. London: SAGE, 2004.

Picard, Robert G. *Media Economics: Concepts and Issues.* Newbury Park, California: SAGE, 1989.

Throsby, David. *Economics and Culture*, Chapter 6. Cambridge: Cambridge University Press, 2001.

6

Document Analysis for Media Policy Research

Vibodh Parthasarathi and Ritu Sinha

Introduction

Unprecedented changes in the economy and polity of India in the last two decades have made us witness massive shifts, in scale and forms, of Indian media in recent times. The complex terrain of the international and national policy arena in a globalised world has altered the relationships between social institutions and diverse sectors of society to bring about a remarkable change in media and other disciplines such as polity and economy. It has posed new challenges to scholars and the pedagogy in the field of media and communication studies. Therefore, the shifting media policy environment and the technological expansion are decisive factors in defining the contours of the multifaceted, rapidly growing Indian media.

Therefore, it is imperative to acquire knowledge of the tools and techniques to comprehend the existing set of policies guiding the broader landscape of Indian media today. At the same time, it becomes crucial to understand the process of policy formulation and get acquainted with the relevant debates and areas of concern. It must be said that the domain of public policy and the associated field of policy research aid us in unravelling the intricate topography of media in the contemporary period. Exposure to the realm of policy studies in India is similarly vital to throw light on India's entire policy scene and the concern of media policy globally. The course/paper Policy Research and Evaluation focuses on these concerns and issues.

Course Description: Policy Research and Evaluation

The mushrooming media sector in India and other developing countries and its growing complexities have opened up new leaves in media and communication studies. Policy research has offered new methods and techniques to comprehend the world of media by focusing on media-related and other relevant policies.

The course Policy Research and Evaluation is designed along similar lines. The course aims to familiarise students with substantive issues, approaches and theoretical perspectives in policy research by opening the window to policy studies. After having done so, it equips the learners with the skills to understand policy processes and policy analyses. The course, therefore, is designed to impart skills to develop a critical understanding of the process of policy formulation and analyses. It provides knowledge of policy processes and approaches to policymaking institutions, instruments and actors. The course shall facilitate learning by imparting knowledge of the tools and techniques involved in the process of policymaking.

Learners are, therefore, introduced to the basic technique of policy formulation. The last segment of the course is in the form of a workshop where they are exposed to certain tools and techniques to initiate the policy analysis process.

Module 1: Approaches to Policy Studies

All the students are introduced to the development, initiation and implementation of public policy—in this case, in India. Providing the rationale behind how different approaches to policy analysis tend to view and prioritise institutions, instruments and actors, it familiarises students with the past and current approaches to policy studies in the field of communication. In doing so, it addresses issues concerning the identification of stakeholders and vested interests in the policymaking process; it debates on public interest from the vantage point of commerce and the property of jurisdictional quandaries and complexities of national law and governance within a global media system.

Module 2: Contexts of Public Policy in India

While everyone agrees on the importance of media in public life, what does such an agreement lead to and how is it instrumentalised? With an increasing number of stakeholders and the widening deployment of media technologies, policy formulation and planning activities are no longer the sole domain of the state. It is evident that public policy in the media is no longer formulated at any one central site; instead, it involves intense negotiation between competing actors operating at various levels of jurisdiction. This module focuses on the concerns and methods that drive present initiatives, especially among non-state players and in broader media and communication planning debates. The module also highlights the complexities of the field by throwing light on a large number of indistinct policy arenas that overlap with the media policy field.

Module 3: Tools and Techniques of Policy Analysis

This last module of the course is designed in a workshop mode. It focuses on the primary stage of learning to analyse processes of policy formulation. It introduces a structured way to decipher government documents, including inquiry commissions and reports of various committees on various aspects of the media before the 1990s. One learns to identify key actors in the concerned media sector, reflect critically on quantitative and qualitative evidence provided and unravel arguments on policy options. Structured in a hands-on workshop mode, it provides a thorough grounding in a select set of techniques that are commonly used in understanding the process of policy formulation. The workshop identifies document analysis as one such technique; therefore, it is designed to equip the learners with skills for document analysis.

Course Concept Map

As shown in Figure 6.1, the course concept map is designed as an illustrative description of the course Policy Research and Evaluation. It describes the different components of each module and explains its linkages with the workshop exercise. Overall it throws light on different aspects of policy research and evaluation. The map elucidates that there are three modules in the course, and each of them has defined subsections. Each of these modules feeds into each other and is incomplete without learning about the others. It illustrates that a hands-on project is an indispensable part of the course but is strongly linked to the contents of the other two modules.

Figure 6.1: Course Concept Map

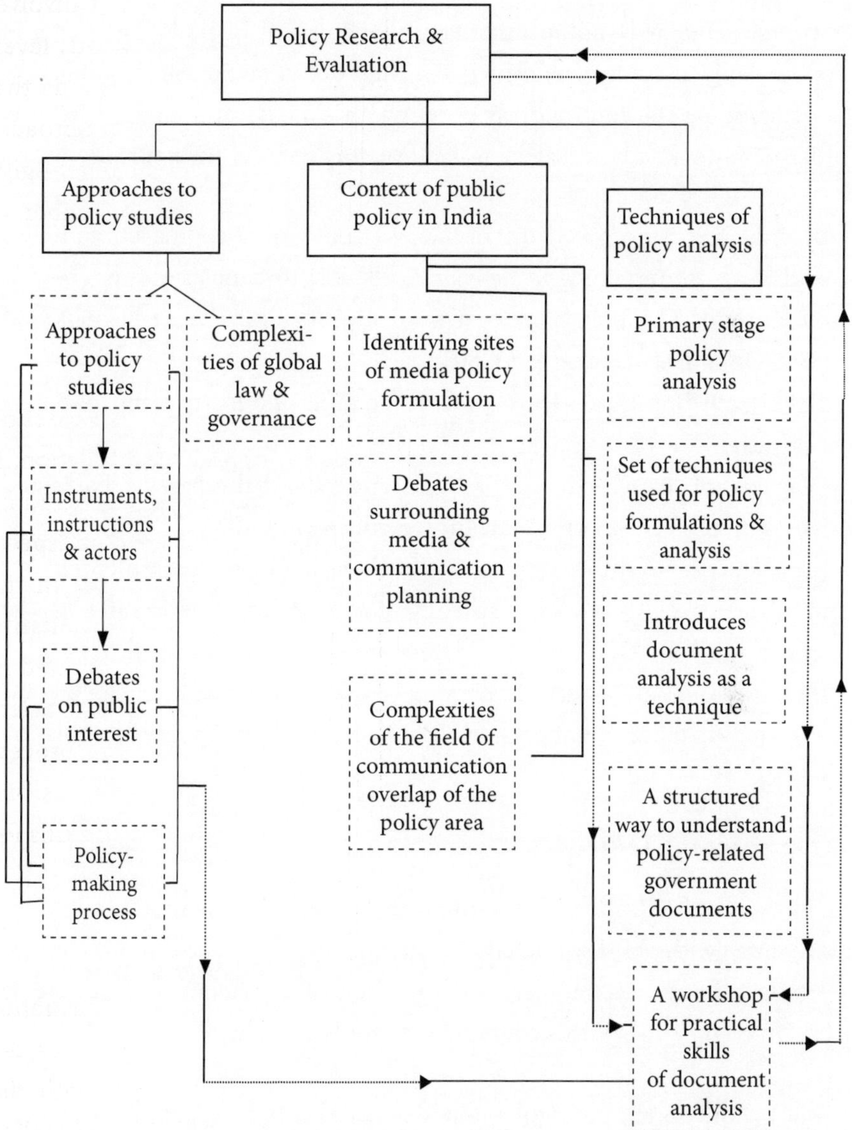

Plain lines show the components of the course.

Dotted lines show the linkage between the workshop exercise and other components of the syllabus.

Source: Authors

Course Instructional Objectives

This course aims at building a larger understanding of policy studies and policy research to comprehend media-related policies and their significance in understanding the continuously evolving media environment, in this case, in India. Enumerated here are the broad learning goals of the course.

- By providing basic knowledge of the past and current approaches to policy studies in communication, the course attempts to familiarise learners with the larger world of policymaking in the field of media in the pre-liberalisation period in India (i.e., up to the 1980s).
- The course familiarises learners with the tools and instruments of policy analysis.
- Learners are equipped with skills to understand the basic debates and issues in media and communication planning in India.
- Learners can examine documents such as reports, recommendations, inquiries, et cetera, as a basic instrument of policy analysis and an essential step in the policy formulation process.
- It focuses on making learners acquire an ability to assess these documents and analyse them to understand their relevance in the policy formulation process.

Course Learning Outcomes

Once the teacher fulfils the instructional objectives, learners should be able to acquire much wider media-related information and knowledge and get skilled in certain tools and techniques to comprehend the dynamics of the media world. On completion of this course, they should be able to:

- analyse the domain of public policy in India and decipher the process of policy formulations and policy analysis.
- examine and paraphrase the broader debates and subsequent issues surrounding the field of media and communications planning in India before liberalisation.
- analyse the characteristics and appropriateness of a select set of tools and techniques used in the process of policy formulation and policy analysis.

- describe and compare relevant theories, various approaches and methods used in policy analysis.
- demonstrate the ability to identify institutions, instruments and actors involved in the policymaking process.
- underline the importance of policy research in the policymaking environment in India.
- take stock of public policy and the policymaking environment in India before liberalisation.
- locate and describe the field of media and communications policy in the larger policy environment in India.
- relate and identify various steps involved in the policymaking process.
- demonstrate the capabilities and skills required for project planning and evaluation, which have become central to independent initiatives seeking to redesign the workings of media in India.

As shall be evident in the subsequent discussion and application of these learning objectives, most of the aforementioned objectives are achieved through the hands-on project on document analysis organised in practical workshop settings.

Introduction to the Hands-on Project

The first two modules of the course—Approaches to Policy Studies and Contexts of Policy Studies in India—aim to inform learners about theoretical approaches in policy studies, the state of policy studies in India and developing knowledge of media and communication planning in India since Independence. These modules reflect on the policy formulation process and aspects of policy analysis by highlighting the instruments, institutions and actors involved in policymaking. They highlight important debates on public interest and vested interest in the policymaking process that shaped the media environment in India before liberalisation. Overall, it contextualises media policy in India's larger domain of policymaking by looking into the arena of public policy and policy research.

Once the approaches, the policy formulation process and the general scene of media and communication planning during the pre-liberalisation period are made clear and comprehended well, the third module introduces the techniques and instruments of policy analysis. This module is designed in a workshop format to practically learn document analysis. Learners are exposed to various media-related government documents, such as reports, recommendations, et cetera, based on which media policy is formulated. These documents initiate the policymaking process; hence, it is essential to understand and evaluate them to reflect India's media policy scene. Evaluating these documents forms the primary stage of learning to analyse the policy or the policy formulation process.

Document analysis is the basic technique out of several methods and tools of policy analysis. It is the basic pre-step to understanding a policy and will indeed enrich the process of comprehending and locating a particular policy in the larger policy arena.

The hands-on project workshop allows students to learn the basic techniques of policy analysis and go beyond the theoretical understanding provided in the first two modules. Learners can practically apply the theoretical understanding by learning about policymaking and policy analysis techniques. By enquiring into pre-policy processes, they can enter the realm of policy research, and by handling government documents, they can experience policy analysis first-hand.

Project Concept Map

As shown in Figure 6.2, the concept map of the hands-on project on document analysis enables us to understand the function and importance of the government's policy-related documents. The diagram highlights these documents as both a tool for government and as a basic technique of policy analysis, aiding policy research and evaluation. The concept map elucidates the linkages between document analysis and the larger policy environment and policy research and evaluation. It also highlights the methods/parameters used for analysing the documents and the utility of analysing such documents. It draws attention to its relevance in the entire process of policy formulation and analysis. The process begins by explaining various components of policy research and evaluation, followed by marking document analysis as one of the techniques of analysing policies and policy processes. Policy evaluation and analysis are part of the policy process and are important for policy research

Figure 6.2: Concept Map for a Project on Document Analysis

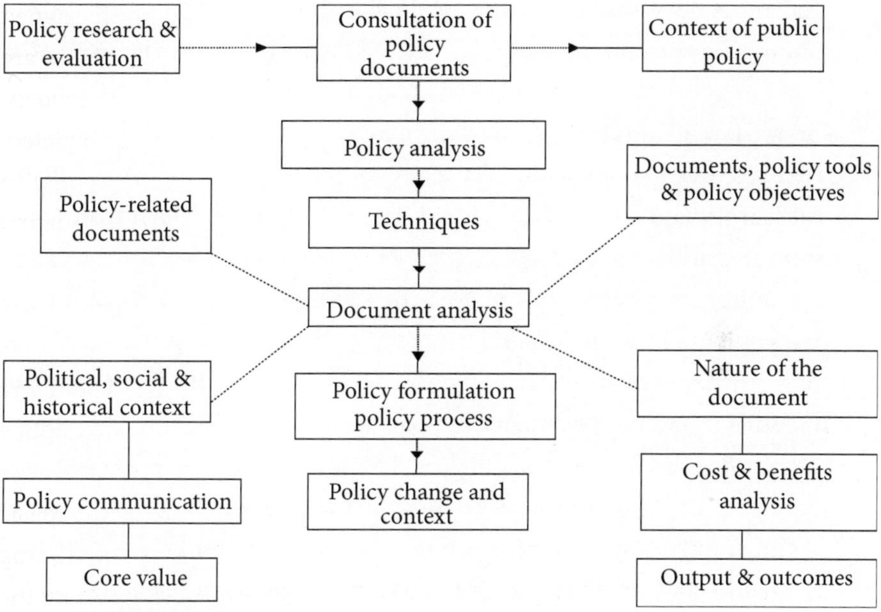

——— Plain lines with arrows show the location of 'Document Analysis' and its relevance in Policy Research and Policy Studies.

······ Dotted lines explain what documents use and the methods through which they can be analysed.

Source: Authors

and policy studies. The linkages are clearly shown on the map and explained with suitable dotted lines and arrows.

Project Instructional Objectives

The hands-on project workshop aims to give the learners a practical and in-depth experience of document analysis, which is one of the basic policy analysis techniques. This will be the entry point into the domain of policy research and evaluation. The goals of the workshop include the following:

- The exercise enables the learners to acquire skills to analyse documents that are crucial to the policymaking process and to develop abilities to understand the policy environment in general and equip them with techniques of policy analysis.

- As an important step in policy analysis, learners are introduced to the analysis of government documents, including reports of committees and inquiry commissions on various aspects of the media before the 1990s. The documents concerned are linked to media and communication planning in India. Through this exercise, they learn to realise that these documents play a decisive role in shaping the media environment in India before the 1990s.
- The learners are trained to develop skills to identify these documents, read them and understand a relevant policy through them. They learn to apply theoretical approaches and methods for identifying actors and institutions in a structured way and to understand the policymaking process.
- They are exposed to the making and formulation of these government documents and their relevance in policy research.
- By reading and analysing these documents, they are exposed to understanding the context of policy studies and the importance of commissions and inquiries in public policy formulation.
- The hands-on workshop also provides the skills to learn to analyse policy and policy processes and handle independent evaluation projects.

Project Learning Outcomes

The project workshop brings out certain abilities and skills to help evolve an understanding of policy research in India and its significance in understanding the media environment in general. On completion of the workshop, learners should be able to achieve the following, which the teacher needs to ensure, as also consider for student assessment. Learners should be able to:

- critically analyse the process of document formulation and evaluation.
- read, identify and analyse different components of policy-related documents and establish a relationship between them.
- deduce facts, collect evidence, organise them and collate the issues into comprehensive arguments.
- define interest groups/stakeholders/institutions by reading the documents, and differentiate them.
- interpret the documents critically in a larger policy arena, as also their relevance in the policy analysis process, by highlighting the objectives and interests of the documents.

- identify the author and target audience and locate them in terms of the industry regulations.
- examine institutional values, interests and the overall structure so as to define the nature of the policy-related documents analytically.
- apply various theoretical approaches and methods of documents analysis.
- recommend alternative suggestions while reviewing the documents.
- analyse pre-liberalisation policy documents, such as press commission reports, reports of inquiries on small newspapers, reports on newspaper economics, et cetera, and examine India's larger media policy scene and the state of Indian media.

Key Concepts

The project workshop involves certain concepts that are crucial for the entire document-analysis exercise. These are basic concepts that assist in outlining the field of policy research and analysis. These concepts throw light on the methods used in the process of document analysis. These are called key concepts because they facilitate learning the main components of policy studies. These are specific concepts that set up the document-analysis process and are the central concepts of policy analysis. The key terms enumerated here will be a useful reference to developing clarity of concept.

Policy process

In simple terms, a policy process involves debates or negotiations among a variety of actors, on a particular theme or problem of media and communication policy or any other field, and leading to either binding or non-binding rules in the form of laws, conventions, declarations, standards or norms. It is a very complex process involving various steps (see Figure 6.3). A policy process is limited in time and space. It typically provides a reference point for various actors from the state, market and society to articulate their interest and promote policy goals, principles and norms, and frame policy-relevant issues, thereby informing and influencing policymaking. Policy analysis and evaluation form one significant part of the entire process.

Figure 6.3: Policy Cycle

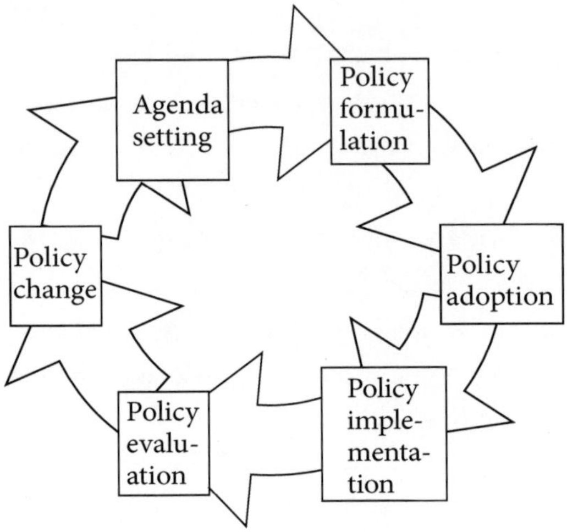

Source: Authors

Policy-related documents

These are inputs or outcomes of formal institutional processes at different levels (national, regional, international, etc.). These documents can be elaborated by individuals or organisational actors and include briefs, inquiry reports, other reports, policy statements, legislative and regulatory texts, conventions, et cetera. Such documents can be binding and non-binding.

Organisational actors/stakeholders

These entities (institutions, associations, corporations, networks, etc.) have stakes in the issues and participate in national and global media policymaking and governance processes. Actors can be governmental or multistakeholders; they can represent different interests (public or private) and operate at different levels (national, regional, international, etc.). They are entities such as individuals, groups and governments who consider information and make decisions.

Policy area

It is defined as a particular sector for which a set of policies are designed. There are numerous policy areas within the sphere of governance. Policy area is the substantive domain of policy, such as the environmental policy area or health policy area, over which participants in policymaking compete and compromises. Some of these policy areas are so vast that they contain other areas too.

The activities that take place within these policy areas often spill over from one area to other. A policy area is influenced by how people conceive the nature of a problem, what is causing the problem and the range of potential solutions.

Public interest/public good

The concept of 'public interest' has a long and contentious history in media policymaking. It serves as a benchmark against which all media policies are assessed. The concept represents perhaps the most direct mechanism via which policymakers, critics and researchers assess the past judgment of an individual media market and market system upon which advocacy of change is premised. It simply implies that policy outcomes should not cater to the interest of an individual interest group but rather serve the populace as a whole.

'Public good' can also be understood on similar lines, where the interest of the populace is the main objective. A policy is a public good if it is demanding collective action and regulation and, at the same time, is committed to the well-being of the public.

Cost and benefit

The concept of 'cost and benefit analysis' here is loosely based on the fundamental principle of weighing the goals and other alternatives within a policy, as well as the policy itself, in terms of benefits and costs. For any decision, we consciously or unconsciously evaluate its potential benefits and costs. We try to evaluate if its benefits are greater than its costs. The idea is also to find out which policy or objective of a policy gives the highest benefit against the costs incurred rather than against other components. The cost and benefit visualised here are in social terms, that is, pertaining to the populace. A list of all benefits and expenses, present and future, provides a clear understanding of the utility of any document or policy. Benefits and costs are also understood in monetary terms. Benefits and expenses, whether financial or social, are also seen in terms of future benefits and expenses and, hence, aid the analysis process.

For policy researchers, politicians and policymakers, the cost and benefit analysis is crucial since it is a form of evaluation and research that examine the continuance or discontinuance of a programme, the strategy of a programme and a technique of improvement or allocating of resources among competing programmes. For policy analysts, it is an important tool for evaluating and reviewing any policy.

Core value

It refers to institutional values and structures. The core value of an institution or a policy community is its larger aims and objectives, which initiate the policymaking process in its respective policy area. A policy is a window on the broader questions of power, priorities and possibilities in society. These define the core value of the documents so produced.

Policy community

The term 'policy community' is an important tool in the hands of policy researchers to understand or describe the policymaking process in industrialised societies. It is a grouping of interrelated policy actors pursuing the matter of public policy. It indicates the policy process in which organised interests and governmental actors shape the direction and outcomes of public policies. Thus, it broadly refers to a disaggregated system involving actors or potential actors who share an interest in a particular industry and interact with one another for mutual benefit.

Policy environment

A policy environment constitutes the structural, social, political and economic systems in which public policymaking occurs. Within this general notion of the policy environment, we can identify four major environments that influence policymaking: the structural environment, the social environment, the economic environment and the political environment.

Outputs and outcomes

Laws, regulations, rules and other such things produced by a policy process can be called 'outputs'. On the other hand, 'outcomes' are the results of any policy implementation. Outcomes can be intended or unintended and positive or negative. For example, the mid-day meal scheme introduced in government schools in India significantly reduced dropouts and increased literacy among the most deprived section of society. In this case, the predilection for education and the concomitant rise in retention numbers are the outcomes.

Setting Up the Hands-on Project

Learners are introduced to this workshop once they have been acquainted with the Policy Research and Evaluation course in the classroom. The workshop runs concurrently with two theoretical modules: Approaches to Policy Studies and Context of Public Policy in India. The two modules furnish the learners with a thorough introduction to policy studies in general and the relevance of policy research in the policymaking process in particular. At the same time, these modules also inform learners about the state of policy studies and media policy in India. The third module has been created as a document-analysis workshop; it focuses on the techniques of policy analysis where students will be given an opportunity to practically experience the basic techniques.

The project workshop involves learning in class and applying the techniques hands-on. The course focuses on the preliminary stage of analysis, which is a pre-assessment stage, or a stage for collecting evidence so as to be able to anticipate or predict the consequences of a policy on the environment. It is also a stage that helps in developing the knowledge and experience of the policy process in their respective policy areas. This exercise develops the fundamental skills required for the project workshop on mapping media policy shifts, which is part of the course Regulation and Theory in Practice.

Learners are introduced to the document-analysis exercise where they are exposed to a set of documents that had been instrumental in the policy process. These documents are crucial and must be studied by the learners since they serve as important tools for the central debates on policy and planning; they also help in the understanding of the concerns and issues that circulate in the government and private sectors and shape media policy and practices. These debates and issues are indicative of the core values and objectives of media policy in India.

During the hands-on project, learners are taught the methods of document analysis. Government reports and other important documents are circulated among learners to help them get involved and experience the exercise hands-on. These documents are the government's policy papers of the pre-liberalised era, that is, documents that have appeared until the 1980s.

A critical assessment of these documents helps learners develop an understanding of the relevance of media in the process of planning and development that defined media policy in pre-liberalised underdeveloped India. At the same time, it also unravels the process through which policy studies started taking roots in India and the growing relevance of policy research in governance and different disciplines.

The workshop will broadly be divided into sixteen classes of ninety minutes each. Class assessment, presentation and introduction will all be a part of these sixteen classes.

Project Instructional Design

Document analysis (what is to be done?)
After being introduced to the context of the hands-on workshop, students will be instructed on what exactly has to be done in this document analysis exercise. The exercise is composed of broadly two main aspects:

1. *Identifying the documents*
   The students first learn to identify the documents to be analysed. These are government documents in the form of recommendations, commission reports, inquiry reports on various aspects of media, which shaped the media environment in the pre-liberalisation period. Backgrounds of these documents will be provided to set up the contexts of the study and to familiarise the students with the environment in which these documents were produced. These will not be policy documents but policy-related government documents.
2. *Analysis of the documents*
   The core of the hands-on workshop is to analyse these documents. The students will read the documents and develop an understanding of the components of the documents. They will be provided with suitable concepts and a structured framework for the exercise. The analysis of the documents will involve a thorough understanding of the factors responsible for the origins of the documents and the environments in which they were formulated; and actors, instruments and institutions that influenced media and communication planning. The exercise will

also highlight the shortcomings of the documents while discussing their relevance within the larger media policy environment.

The analysis will be based on theories, approaches and qualitative methods that are used in contemporary policy research, which students will learn in the workshop and theoretical modules.

Features Open to Study

The exercise requires providing an appropriate context and background, linking it with the other two modules since it intends to impart preliminary techniques to interpret the larger policy environment. The introduction to the exercise creates knowledge among the students about its relevance and usage. It is followed by an exercise on the approaches and methods in policy studies. The exercise includes pre-workshop activities, too, which involves a general reading on the space, time and environment in which these documents are located and a general understanding of specific policy areas in which these documents are located (in this case, media policy). There can be another exercise dealing with the documents themselves in the middle of the hands-on workshop, and some more for students' self-assessment.

Planning the Hands-on Project Workshop

This covers the work to be done by the instructor before initiating the hands-on workshop for students. Students should also take note of these so that they can work closely with their teacher. The instructor should:

- make a list of possible policy-related government documents to be analysed by students.
- gather a preliminary summary of these documents by listing important areas/sections covered in the documents.
- highlight the main issues that reflect the need of the documents.
- identify, with the information on the documents, different areas to be probed, which can be useful in analysing the documents and then in the larger process of policy analysis.

- highlight each probe area that involves different issues of document analysis and can evolve as parameters for analysis.
- raise relevant questions within these parameters to make them as intense as possible and to cover all aspects of each probe area.
- select secondary readings for workshops related to a particular policy area and identify specific ones, if possible.
- divide the students into groups (a judicious mix of fast and slow learners for each sector).
- help students identify all kinds of literature related to the documents by introducing them to possible sources.
- help them prepare a list of four to five experts, participants and reviewers of the documents being examined by the students to set them up for interviews.
- invite experts, whose policy areas are located in the specific time and space in which the documents can be located, to discuss domain knowledge—those who can talk about the relevance of these documents in shaping the policy environment of the media industry.
- think up a pre-project workshop exercise that will help students in approaching the hands-on workshop.
- come up with and use step-wise (incremental) exercises in the workshop to help students systematically do their work.
- equip themselves with all the relevant debates within the area, time and space in which they are located.

Conducting the Hands-on Project Workshop

This deals with the planning of classroom instructions by teachers and their interactions with students.

- Devote the first few classes in setting up the aims of the workshop: Why should a hands-on workshop of this nature be undertaken? How is it designed and why is it designed in a particular way? And most importantly, how will the hands-on workshop be conducted (group/individual exercise in/outside the classroom)?.
- Also, be transparent about the evaluation criteria and explain them clearly in the first few classes.

- Devote maximum classes for a detailed explanation of substantive parts of the workshop (i.e., the parameters of analysis).
- To instruct students how to approach the exercise, utilise each session for a particular analysis parameter. So, if there are twelve parameters, each should be discussed separately in different sessions with suitable examples from different documents.
- Along with each parameter, discuss suitable concepts, key terms, relevant theories and models (if required) and secondary and primary sources of data. Also, identify how these can be obtained.
- Try and cover all the documents circulated to the students within each parameter through an interactive mode.
- Before each session, give students small exercises on different parameters: ask them to identify data from their respective documents that fall under the parameter and analyse two to three relevant secondary literature that can be utilised in discussing each parameter. The instruction should be given in a session prior to the session in which the exercise is to be done. This will drive students to study the documents on their own and then discuss them with you in the following sessions.
- Devote the last two to three classes for an overall analysis process, which involves mapping all the parameters.
- Devote enough time in resolving the queries and problems of the students.
- Review students' performances, in workshop exercises and interim presentations, throughout the workshop since the exercises require students to participate in every step. At the beginning of the workshop, introduce the students to the methodology of student participation, which will follow in future sessions.

Pre-Project Workshop Exercises

The instructor needs to begin with a pre-workshop exercise along with a general introductory lecture to set the background for the hands-on workshop and to build a context through general information on a policy area (as mentioned in the 'Features Open to Study' section). As discussed further, these are the areas around which the introductory lectures and pre-project workshop exercises should be designed so that students could begin with a brief overview of the state of media policy in India in a given period and are able to locate policy-related documents within a policy arena. The areas include the following:

- Basic theoretical understanding of what constitutes the field of media policy (i.e., theoretical requirements of policy areas).
- An overview of the genesis of media policy in India since the mid-nineteenth century, the main issues and the debates therein.
- An overview of the political economy of pre-liberalised India (i.e., general information about the time and space in which these documents are located).
- A brief overview of the state of media and communication planning in this period (i.e., general information about policy areas in their specific time and space).

The exercise can be of the following type (see Box 6. 1):

Box 6.1: Information on Policy Area

Basic Information of the Policy Area

Submit a 500-word write-up for each of the areas mentioned below, and state two suitable readings for each topic (either from the reading list or from previous semesters' courses). The suggested readings should directly throw light on the areas being studied.

- Media policy
- the genesis of media policy in India
- The state of media and communication planning in pre-liberalised India

Assessment Criteria

The write-up should not exceed the word limit and highlight all important arguments in the given area. The readings should be mentioned with complete references.

The assessment standards are mentioned in a section below.

Students are required to submit these write-ups within ten days. Each write-up should be submitted separately in hard copy, along with the soft copy.

The exercise format can vary and can depend on the teacher's choice, but the broad areas mentioned are mandatory to follow since they set up the contexts of the hands-on workshop.

Project Workshop Design

What follows is an elaboration of the ways to conduct the project workshop. The list of documents needs to be identified to begin the exercise. In this case, they are mostly government documents such as commission reports, recommendations and inquiry reports (as mentioned earlier). Students will be given the choice to choose a document, or it will be assigned to them by the teacher.

Template/s

Once the key policy-related documents (i.e., principal documents) have been identified and distributed, the larger exercise of reading and analysing the documents becomes important. The exercise is divided into smaller parts or parameters for acquiring systematic and complete knowledge of the text (i.e., the documents). All the students in a group study these parameters of analysis. The group distributes an equal number of parameters to each group member or is distributed by the instructor. If the text is handled by the students individually, each student contributes to the exercise individually. The resulting work must be brought together at the end of the exercise to form a larger narrative and a presentation on each of the specific documents. Each of these parameters carries a different set of issues and related analytical questions, which must be probed by using data from the primary (principal document) and secondary sources. These parameters, which are also methods of analysis, are created by the instructor with the help of suitable literature and are provided to students in a structured way for in-depth analysis of the documents. The parameters of the analysis are:

1. Context of the document:
   (i) Political, economic, social and historical background
   (ii) The environment in which it is formulated

2. Identifying the nature of the document:
   (i) What kind: distributive, redistributive or regulatory?

(ii) Is it regional, national or global?
(iii) The interconnections between levels, if any

Policy communities:
(i) Identify actors and interest groups
(ii) Identify targeted beneficiaries
(iii) Is there a beneficiary interest group?
(iv) Background of members

3. Core value:
(i) of the organisation or the players involved
(ii) of the document itself

4. Identifying the problem:
(i) What is the problem?
(ii) Is there a need-gap?
(iii) For whom and which section of the population: a group, a community, an organisation or a nation as a whole?

5. Envisioned targets and outcomes:
(i) Purpose and interest
(ii) Aims and objectives
(iii) Desired outcomes

6. Sources:
(i) Data used for identifying problems
(ii) Data used for planning and formulation
(iii) Data used for conclusion and implementation
(iv) What are the sources of data: research organisation, policy, document or any other?

7. Costs and benefits:
(i) What are the social costs: changes and effects?
(ii) Monetary costs if indicated: in formulation or implementation
(iii) What are the social benefits: changes and effects?
(iv) Monetary benefits and gains, if any

8. Recommendations:
   (i) What are the recommendations?
   (ii) Are there any indications of political and social acceptability of the recommendations?
   (iii) Future recommendations, if any

9. Implementation and results:
   (i) Possibilities of gains and benefits
   (ii) Any indication of social welfare or collective growth?
   (iii) Environmental changes
   (iv) Political gains

10. Shortcomings:
    (i) What are the gaps and failures?
    (ii) Inadequacies, if any, at the level of identification of problems, formulation and implementation
    (iii) Are objectives meeting the purpose?
    (iv) Who are the beneficiaries?
    (v) Is public interest the target or are other political and economic interests dominating?

11. Final outcomes and suggestions:
    (i) Evidence indicating policy area
    (ii) Evidence of policy process
    (iii) Alternative suggestions
    (iv) Concluding remarks.

How to Analyse the Parameters of the Template

Once each of these templates is understood by students, the exercise becomes analytical. The parameters in each of the templates need a critical investigation since these are also methods of analysis. The resources and methodology used for analysing these parameters and the documents as a whole will involve a few necessary steps:

Step 1: Gather knowledge about the time and space in which a document is located and the context of a particular policy area of the document.

Identify the role and significance of this kind of document in that particular time and space.

Step 2: Review existing theories, approaches and models present in the field of policy research.

Step 3: Collect primary and secondary sources to be used in the analysis.

Step 4: Read the primary source (the document) adequately.

Step 5: The primary source being utilised includes data collected by reading the principal document and conducting interviews with experts, members, reviewers, et cetera.

Step 6: Interviews should be collected to fill missing gaps, but only after reading the document.

Step 7: Secondary sources include newspaper articles, academic articles and literature available on government sites, national and international websites, other reports produced by civil society groups and other volumes of the same document (if any), et cetera.

Step 8: Primary and secondary data should be used throughout the analysis.

How to Do the Project Workshop

The exercise relies mainly on primary data collection, which involves reading the documents to be analysed. The documents have to be located in the historical development of the policy arena. The pre-workshop readings should be carefully done. Interviews with relevant people can be another form of primary source, apart from the documents. This workshop provides the scope for conducting interviews with members of the groups, institutions and government officials involved in the process of formulation of these documents, or with experts, such as the chairperson of the Press Trust of India, who can be interviewed for the relevance of press commission reports.

Along with primary information, the exercise will be comprehensive only when secondary sources of information are also utilised. The sources can be secondary literature, literature available on government websites, national and international websites or any kind of report or other volumes of specific documents, newspaper reports, project reports, et cetera. For students, an important step in the exercise will also be to familiarise themselves with and collect available information about these documents from different sources. It is important to note that students' familiarity with the theories, models and approaches, along with conceptual terms in the field of policy analysis, forms the foundation of the hands-on workshop. (These are also previously mentioned as necessary steps for analysing the parameters of each template.)

The procedure to do the hands-on project workshop is enumerated here in a few steps and with suitable exercises:

Step 1: Go through pre-project workshop readings to familiarise yourself with the larger environment of a policy area. Then get involved in the following exercise:

Revising the Approaches

Prepare a table to compare different approaches to policy studies. Point out the institutions, actors and interests expressed in each approach. Utilise the readings mentioned below.

1. Raboy, Mark (2006). 'Making Media: Creating the Conditions for Communications in the Public Good.' *Canadian Journal of Communication*, 31, 289–306.
2. Harvey, David (2005). *A Brief History of Neoliberalism*. London: Oxford University Press.
3. Geilhufe, L. Nancy (1979). 'Anthropology and Policy Analysis'. *Current Anthropology*, 20 (3).

Key: List the important differences, definitions and consequences of each approach in a table form.

Assessment criteria: All suitable readings should be referred to bring out the comparison, which should be finished within a week. Important concepts within each should be explained separately. For a detailed assessment, see a section on assessment below.

Step 2: Select appropriate documents for the project and read completely, highlighting small details in each section/chapter. Once this is done, an important exercise is required to bridge the missing ends of this step. The next exercise, as part of this step, is for students to assess their understanding of the documents and bring out the components for which specific data for the parameters mentioned in different templates need to be collected. The summary of the document will make the process of creating references to the document much easier and handier. The exercise is as follows:

Learning to Summarise the Document

Prepare a list of different chapters/modules mentioned in your document and list important points under each chapter/module briefly. Point out the keywords and phrases from different sections.

Key: A summary of the document with the main sections of the document, including introduction and conclusion/recommendations, the main highlights of each section, relevant data reflecting the policy area as well as data pointing the uses of the document.

Assessment: The ability to identify important points under each component of the document. The exercise should not exceed more than five pages (A4 size). It should provide a clear understanding and can be used as a brief introduction to the document. A description of all the components is required. For detailed assessment criteria, see the section on assessment below.

Step 3: Take suitable secondary readings on the document. The parameters within each template should be utilised for analysis, and appropriate primary and secondary readings should be taken.

This next step is to identify primary data from the document and collect secondary data to analyse the parameters. This is the initial step in the organisation of data. An exercise of this sort (shown in the following boxes) will help in this endeavour. This exercise needs to be executed after the list of parameters is provided and briefly introduced by the instructor. Two parts of this exercise must be done concurrently so as to be able to finish the exercise within two to three weeks.

Part I: Learning to Organise Sources

Bring out a list of ten suitable secondary readings that focuses on the document. Cull important points from each article.

Key: newspaper articles, articles from Economic and Political Weekly and other media-related journals, books, websites, government reports, et cetera.

Search articles by keeping in mind the time or period in which the document was prepared.

Assessment: The ability to create a pool of articles from varied sources (see Key in this box). Devote a paragraph each to enumerate the main points of an article. For detailed assessment criteria, see the section on assessmet below.

Part II: Exposure to Interview Method
Prepare a list of five experts who can provide useful information on the document. Also, prepare an interview schedule with a minimum of five questions.

Key: Authorities/personalities/people and heads of institutions involved in the formulation of the document (see the introduction to the document).

Also, identify some of the leading personalities of the policy area or those directly related to the policy area, such as media analysts, journalists, owners, media scholars and others, or people who can provide information on the document. Chalk out a specific timeline to meet and interview them.

Assessment: The ability to identify all five relevant people, with brief backgrounds and their importance. How will their inputs be useful? The ability to chalk out a timeline for the interviews and to select questions. For detailed assessment criteria, see the section on assessment below.

Step 4: Each group member should sort out data for each template according to questions appearing within each parameter. Make sure that the questions in each parameter are answered. Each parameter should be analysed by utilising both secondary and primary readings. Try and conduct interviews and collect information on possible sources, alongside the sessions on parameters.

Collect all relevant data, even from sources not cited in the aforementioned sections. While organising data around the parameters, learning the concepts and methods of analysing the document is also crucial to assess your progress. Hence, a mid-term assessment exercise is required. This should be done while learning the parameters. This is a self-assessment exercise to understand the utility of the reading material collected and other efforts taken for a comprehensive analysis of the document.

Self-Assessment Exercise
After reading the documents in detail and taking the aforementioned exercises, students are expected to review the material collected and assess if it is relevant and adequate for undertaking the analysis. Answering the following questions will help in this exercise:

1. Is the document clear to you?
2. Are there any gaps in understanding the documents? If yes, then identify them.

3. What and where are the information gaps?
4. Why are they there? Is it the lack of material referred to or has the material not been used effectively? Do you need some more material?
5. Have you been able to answer all the questions under each template?
6. What has not been done? What will you do to accomplish it? How will you address it?
7. Do you need to focus on some areas/segments more? What are those areas?
8. Are you able to identify a grey area? How do you plan to improve upon it?
9. Are you able to make sense of the material collected? What is it indicating? Is it leading towards a proper argument?
10. Have you been able to collect all your primary and secondary material? If not, then why? How and when will you be organising them?
11. Is your document providing you with a larger scenario of the selected policy area?

Note: If you answer these questions and do the needful, you are undertaking the exercise with the desired methodology.

Step 5: The self-assessment exercise will lead to an informed research-based articulation of arguments and a sound analysis of the document. It will fill in all the gaps, provide knowledge about zones that needs more information and help you tap new or existing sources for information. It will help in getting a good grip on the document. With this, you can proceed further with the analytical description of each parameter and narrative. Always remember to get involved in group discussions to share and learn information on different documents at different time intervals. The last part is meant to ensure that you have not missed out anything throughout the hands-on workshop. The following exercise will help you in revising for the final work.

Final Organisation

Make a checklist of the work done during the hands-on workshop. See if your list matches with the list mentioned below:

- Readings provided by the instructor while introducing the workshop
- Readings for the pre-workshop exercise
- Readings on approaches and methods
- Studied the document and listed its components

- Prepared a summary of the document
- Listed keywords and terms that appeared in the document
- Listed secondary readings and their brief descriptions
- Conducted interviews with experts
- Understood the parameters
- Understood the terms and concepts that appeared in each parameter
- Readings were given by the instructor, if any, on each parameter
- Organised data and issues to answer every question within each parameter
- Drawn linkages between parameters to develop a detailed analysis
- Discussed with other members and groups
- Exchanged information on different documents

Note: If your list matches the aforementioned list, move on to the next step of finalising each template and preparing narratives. If not, then try to accomplish the remaining task before moving on to the final step.

Step 6: Towards the end of the hands-on workshop, piece together all your arguments to explain the parameters, and bring out a complete description of the templates for the PowerPoint presentation. Although each parameter is handled by different group members individually, all of them should be put together for the final PowerPoint presentation. Exchange your work with others, and go through works done by other members. Carefully sort out all technical errors before the PowerPoint presentation.

Step 7: Put all the details together in a narrative form—give it an introduction and a conclusion. The introduction and conclusion should focus on the document and, at the same time, locate the document in the larger policy area and policy analysis process. The narratives should be developed by utilising both primary and secondary data of all kinds.

Step 8: Work towards a group narrative based on each parameter. Participate in group discussions to exchange information with other members of the group. Discuss your document with other groups and cultivate knowledge of other documents. Locate your document in relation to other documents and bring out an overview of the entire policy scene with all the documents circulated in the class.

The hands-on workshop exercise has to match the time period of the workshop; therefore, a systematic timeline must be followed. The following is a model of the timeline:

Timeline

Total time: 16 weeks

First week: for getting introduced to the hands-on workshop.

Two weeks: for identifying and reading the documents. The pre-project workshop exercises and other required readings (to understand the context of the documents) should be done by the end of these two weeks.

The documents should be read between these classes and all confusions must be cleared by the end of these two weeks.

One week: for collecting and identifying secondary sources and all possible materials needed for the analysis of the document.

Prepare a list of people who can throw light on the document or be useful for its analysis; also prepare a suitable schedule—within this week. The schedule for interviews should span the next four to five weeks.

For ten weeks: focus on one or two parameters each week.

Devote each week to understand a parameter(s) and to answer the questions within them. Learn suitable readings and related concepts for each parameter every week. Prepare slides for the parameters every week and conduct interviews according to the schedule.

One week: for writing the narrative.

Both individual and group narratives should be prepared by collating all material and slides from each parameter.

Last week: final PowerPoint presentations and group narratives.

Final touches are given by bringing together all the slides and group narrative to be produced in the final PowerPoint presentation.

How Will Students Be Evaluated

Student evaluation for the hands-on workshop can be done based on the following two output types:

- *Interim presentation*: Individual understanding of the document wherein a student is expected to make an individual presentation on the allocated document. They are required to explain the different components and broad areas covered in the templates.
- *Final outcome*: This will have three components:
  - *Individual narrative:* This will be an individual outcome of the document and will involve an individual's creative write-up.

- *Group narrative:* This is based on initiatives taken by a group. Each member will chip in data to produce a joint narrative on the document, utilising parameters from different templates.
- *Group PowerPoint presentation*: Each member of the group will do the presentation. The slides will be divided, prepared and presented by each member of the group. Healthy coordination is needed and linkages between the slides should be well chalked out. The group PowerPoint presentation also requires a brief introduction of the document by one member and a conclusion by another.

Assessment: 25 per cent weightage
At the overall level, students will be tested for their ability to grasp the idea of document analysis and to be able to locate the document in its different policy areas. Specifically, they will be assessed for their ability to:

- identify and read a government document (reports, inquiry reports, recommendations) that feed into policy.
- identify key/relevant issues from within the documents and map them chronologically to create a critical understanding of the document.
- understand the place of document analysis in the policy formulation and policy analysis process.
- utilise both primary and secondary data for qualitative analysis of the document.

The hands-on project workshop needs to be planned and organised—both at the level of the instructor where the workshop is designed and at the level of students when they undertake an extensive and detailed exercise like this—before being executed. The assessment weightage may vary but one-fourth of the total score/weightage may be preferable.

Key Things to Focus On

The students are expected to fulfil certain requirements before taking up the hands-on workshop exercise. They need to connect other modules of the paper with the third module, which is designed as a workshop. For this, they need to follow certain instructions from the beginning of this exercise. The instructions are as follows.

Basic Requirements for the Hands-on Workshop

- The students need to equip themselves with all the details of the workshop provided by the instructor in the class.
- They need to understand the purpose of the hands-on workshop and its relevance in the larger course structure of a particular paper (in this case, Policy Research and Evaluation).
- They also need to understand the basic requirements of an individual (such as clarity about collective exercise, no personal hostility between members, basic responsibility towards each member of a group and adjustment with group partners for an amicable work atmosphere) in the hands-on workshop since it is a group exercise.
- They need to have a clear understanding of the evaluation criteria of the hands-on workshop by looking through the finer details of different evaluation steps.
- Also, the students need to develop a clear understanding of the structure of the hands-on workshop.

Students' Role in the Classroom during the Hands-on Workshop

- Raise questions if there is difficulty in comprehending the instruction.
- Keep noting down important parts of the instruction (concepts, key terms, suitable examples cited, references of different readings, etc.).
- Try noting down carefully the explanatory parts of the instruction, and link it with the broader framework.
- Try and clear doubts by interacting with the instructor; give suggestions, and if they are incorporated, note them down. Suggestions are dependent on the amount of homework done before each class.
- Keeping in mind this basic pattern of classroom participation, look into the concept of document analysis and its various components.
- While identifying documents for a group, ensure the participation of all members of the group.
- Note down all the details of all the documents (yours in particular and other documents in general) provided by the instructor in the class.

- Try to understand the context of your document (vis-à-vis the larger policy arena) during the instruction itself, since that cannot be found just by reading the document.
- Also, note down the details of other documents for referencing, if needed, in your analysis. This will help you develop a comparative perspective (since all these documents are of a particular policy area) and make your analysis rich.
- Pay attention to each parameter and note down details and examples provided by the instructor.
- Note down the sources of your document (identified for each parameter) and others. This will ensure that you understand the exercise.
- Provide suggestions not just for your document; participate in discussions on other documents and give suggestions there too.
- Use a separate sheet of your notebook for each parameter.
- Come prepared with exercises given by the instructor so that classroom instructions are more participative, interactive and easier to fill gaps and understand.
- Remember to sort out all aspects of a parameter in the class devoted to its discussion. The time limitation of the workshop will not permit the instructor to revisit each parameter twice.
- Try and understand keywords and concepts and see how they are operationalised during the workshop/practical policymaking process.

Students' Self-Evaluation

Before writing out and submitting your final work, you should try to assess your work. The following are some cues to facilitate you to do so:

- Is the narrative/PPT format correct?
- Introduction: What should come here? Some reflections on the technique of document analysis and its uses in policy analysis. The introduction should have information on the policy area as well as the relevance of the document in understanding the policy.
- Under what headings/sections the article/narrative/PPT should be written? (Put down pointers on what you will write under each section and what material will be used for this, etc.).

- Conclusion: The conclusion is completely based on your analysis, and it should strictly be based on the evidence found and mapped by you during this exercise. At the same time, this should include the consequences of the inferences drawn on the policy arena and how document analysis becomes a crucial technique in policy research.
- References and bibliography: Ensure that all substantive information/data used in the output has been referenced. At the end of the narrative, have a bibliography recording all primary documents, secondary documents and interviews from where the information has been used.

Illustrative Case Study

Below is the description of a hands-on project workshop on document analysis conducted in the past with the students. The way it was shown can serve as an illustrative case for future policy project workshops.

The hands-on workshop covered over 16 sessions of 90 minutes each. The workshop was primarily seen as a group exercise.

- Each document was handled by a group of two to three students.
- The list of documents was provided to the students from where each group chose was given one document for the project.
- A framework of analysis was provided to read the document, identify various components and analyse it. The broad parameters were defined around which documents were screened.
- Every student was expected to familiarise themselves thoroughly with the text of the document, conduct background research and synthesize the information so obtained to present it finally in two forms: a presentation and a term paper/report at the end of the semester.
- The parameters were divided among the members and each member worked on a separate set of parameters provided for analysis.
- Each student was expected to make an individual presentation of the understanding of the document as a part of the interim presentation almost towards the end of the workshop.
- Suitable academic readings were also provided to bridge the gap between theoretical and practical, bring out the meaning and purpose of the exercise, and get informed about the environment in which the document has to be located.
- Further references of any kind were welcomed if needed by the students for the exercise. Such references were purely on students' initiative and so

were arranged by them. These were newspaper articles, journal articles and online information.

- The workshop dealt with the documents that appeared in pre-liberalised India, after Independence until the 1980s. These documents are important source material to understand the media policy scene in India, like Press Commission Reports, Inquiry Report on small newspapers, Indian Television Personality act, et cetera.
- The students submitted individual narratives as well as PowerPoint presentations. They also made Interim presentations individually.
- The students were expected to have group discussions and exchange information for a thorough analysis and locate their document in relation to other documents. For individual narratives, students were allowed to develop their bibliographies apart from the readings provided during the workshop. The structure of the narrative was similar to the structure of the term papers. The PowerPoint presentation was expected to be made by every member of a group dividing the parameters of the presentation.

It is important to note that this is just one sample of the output provided by the students. The variations will be welcomed. Though it is imperative to follow the parameters and answer all the questions within each of them, a number of innovative ways can be used to make the presentation lively and informative. The presentation totally depends on the creative ability of the students and also their technical skills. The input can be explained with the help of tables, pie charts, examples from other documents, colour variations, highlighted excerpts from the document to reflect on the parameters and many such innovative tools to make the presentation as communicative as possible. The linkages between different information in the document should be comprehensibly elucidated. It should reach out to the audience and bring out all the details lucidly.

Questions on Presentation

The students can be asked various questions based on the work submitted by them. Questions can be asked directly on the document, the methods used for the hands-on workshop and the targeted outcomes expected from an exercise of this nature. The following are some of the sample questions:

Questions in general

- What is your document focusing on?
- Why was this kind of document needed in that period?
- Were there any other documents that appeared earlier than this with a similar focus?
- How does your document initiate the policy process in the respective policy area?
- What is the main purpose of document analysis? Is it useful in understanding the policy area in which it is located? In what ways?
- Would you like to make any amendments to the process of analysis as a whole? If yes, then explain why?
- What are the new areas you would like to introduce for document analysis?
- Would you like to involve any other method of data collection, apart from those used in this exercise?
- How does document analysis facilitate policy research?
- Can you point out indistinct overlapping policy arenas after locating the document in its respective policy arena?

Questions on the templates

- Why are historical and political contexts required to understand a document?
- Why is it important to identify actors/stakeholders? What does it indicate?
- Why do you need to understand the nature of the document?
- Why do we need to understand the background of a policy community? Is it indicative of the changing policy environment?
- Why do we need to assess social benefits and costs?
- Is it necessary to know the core value of the document? Explain why?
- Why are the recommendations important?
- Is there any parameter that talks about the public interest? Does your document fulfil this yardstick?

Further Exercise

The project workshop provides an outline for analysing any kind of document located in any other policy area. A similar exercise can be done with any other policy-related document. The students can draw upon the parameters and methods suggested in the aforementioned section to make a concrete analysis and explain its relevance.

> **Exercise**
>
> Take the Report on the Indian Cinematograph Committee, 1928
>
> or
>
> Asok K. Chanda Committee Report on Broadcasting and Information Media, 1966
>
> As a primary document, analyse it to explain its relevance in the policy process and describe the media environment in the pre-liberalisation period.
>
> **Key**: Identify secondary readings and sources for collection of data on the document. Then map and analyse them, utilising steps mentioned in the workbook.
>
> **Alternate exercise**: A similar exercise can be done to understand documents in post-liberalisation era and of different nature.
>
> **Note**: These documents will be available with the instructor, and if not, then the information about their availability will be provided by them.

Evaluation and Assessment

As in any academic exercise, the evaluation and assessment criteria in this workshop should be both explicit and transparent. Evaluation is done based on a set of skills the teacher set out for students to learn during this workshop. The skills include the following:

- To be able to identify government documents that feed into policy processes.
- The ability to identify key actors, institutions and instruments involved in the document formulation process and how they play a crucial role in the larger policy formulation process.
- The ability to identify key issues within each document, highlighting the document formulation process and its significance in policy areas.
- To be able to identify and use relevant quantitative and qualitative data from the document.
- To understand the sources of data in the document as well as for the formation of the document.

- The ability to utilise both primary and secondary sources for the analysis of the document.
- To be able to absorb academic and other kinds of literature available on specific documents and in their respective policy areas.
- The ability to involve research techniques such as interview schedule and quantitative data analysis.
- The ability to utilise relevant theories, approaches and models in policy research.
- To be able to understand the larger policy analysis process and the relevance of document analysis in the whole process.
- To be able to build individual narratives on a particular document.

Evaluation (pattern)

Student evaluation will be an ongoing exercise throughout the project workshop. It may have three components:

1. Interim presentation by each student according to their individual understanding of the document.
2. Individual and group narratives (write-ups):

   (i) Individual write-up (2,000 words): This will be on specific documents covered by a student.
   (ii) Group write-up (5,000 words): Individual components will be grouped as one group report on one specific sector. This will also include an introduction, conclusion and references for a larger mapping exercise of each sector.

3. Group PowerPoint presentation: Here, each group will present a mapping exercise for their sector using PowerPoint slides. The slides will be divided among each member in equal numbers. The result of the final group PowerPoint presentation is dependent on equal participation and synchronised output.

Evaluation (content)

There following are an elaboration on why certain evaluation criteria have been used and the basis of the students' content.

Narrative: Students have to always keep in mind that the study of these documents is an analytical exercise. So, they have to invest a substantial amount of time and energy in reading primary documents, seeking information in secondary documents and scouring theories, approaches and models existing in policy studies. Assessment will be based on qualitative analysis of documents and extraction and correct use of relevant information. At the same time, students will be assessed based on the kind of resources used in their narratives: What secondary and primary sources have they used, besides those provided by the instructor? Last but most importantly, whether the students have effectively answered all the questions posed within each parameter.

Group narrative: Under this exercise, students must compile works done individually under different parameters and develop them into one comprehensive report. This will entail putting together all the verticals together and assessing them to come up with a common introduction and conclusion while analysing a given document. Assessment will be based on how well the parameters have been represented and integrated into the final exercise.

Evaluation (presentation)

The content aspect of the PowerPoint presentation will be based on group narratives. Here the presentations and the students will be evaluated based on the following skills:

Content: It is imperative to have a comprehensive, detailed analysis with all the parameters mapped and questions answered. The need is to elaborate on every issue with a clear introduction, main body and a conclusion. The presentation should ideally be free of punctuation and spelling mistakes, grammatical errors and enough evidence to support the use of primary and secondary research material and availability of data.

Coherence: There should be coherence in the presentation overall with connections between PowerPoint slides. The language used should be clear enough to bring out and draw connections between the PPT slides. Most importantly, if there are two presenters there should be no variations or gaps between the formats of the two presentations. During the presentation, there should be clear links between the introduction, main argument and conclusion.

Argument: Arguments should be clearly laid out and supported by evidence drawn from primary or secondary data. The arguments should be focussed on the topics concerned and not be a general account of things. There cannot be generalisations without any evidence. There should be clear connections between the arguments so that the entire presentation is coherent.

Creativity: This deals with the entire process, right from the beginning and reflected in the final presentation. The ability to build theoretical and other sources for a sound and comprehensive argument and to be able to use newer readings, evidence, methods of collecting evidence and a presentable language are all parts of the creative process. All this is used to established clear linkages between the parameters and the broad arguments.

Organisation: This is about how the presentation is organised: the time frame, length of arguments, designing of PPT slides, connectivity, language, usage of secondary and primary sources, sound technical output and connections between slides shown and presented along with clear diction.

Criteria for Grading

The criteria for assessment are based on a grading system from A to D grades based on specific parameters. These are shown in the following table:

Grades criteria Exercises	**A (Excellent)**	**B (Good)**	**C (Average)**	**D (Poor)**
Basic information of the policy area	Not simply a summary of the article but a critical evaluation and complete information of the respective areas. Both the references required in each area.	A summary and an evaluation were provided, but some of the points are missing. Incomplete information and references.	Merely a summary of the article, with insufficient information and just one or two references.	Incorrect or incoherent summary. No information. No references.

Grades criteria Exercises	**A (Excellent)**	**B (Good)**	**C (Average)**	**D (Poor)**
Revising the approaches	A complete analytical comparison between the approaches in a tabular form. Important institutions, actors and interests highlighted. Important concepts discussed.	Complete comparison but not analytical. Important institutions, actors and interests highlighted, and important concepts discussed.	Incomplete comparison. Wrong listing of institutions, actors and interests. Incorrect description of the concepts.	Wrong comparisons made. No mention of institutions or interests. No concepts discussed.
Summary of the document	A complete listing of different chapters/ sections of the document. All important information in each section. Key terms and concepts in each section.	A complete listing of different chapters/ sections. Incomplete information about different sections. Key terms and concepts mentioned.	An incomplete listing of different chapters/ sections. Incomplete description of information from each section. Key terms not mentioned.	A wrong and incomplete listing of different section/ chapters. No important information from the sections. No key terms mentioned.
Exposure to interview method	At least three interviews done with relevant people to fill information gaps in the mapping exercise with correct inputs. Relevant and detailed information about all the interviewees.	Just two interviews but still led to a reduction in information gaps. Incomplete information about the interviewees.	Interview(s) done but with wrong people or with relevant people but not posing relevant questions and hence no relevant answers obtained. No details provided about the interviewees.	No Interviews done.

Grades criteria Exercises	**A (Excellent)**	**B (Good)**	**C (Average)**	**D (Poor)**
Narrative	Clearly and coherently presented report, employing appropriate evidence. A clear introduction, the main body mapped policy shifts over the years, and a clear conclusion. Evidence of research and reading; appropriate sources used. Correct grammar, punctuation and spelling.	Clear report with appropriate use of evidence, but format not very tightly knit. Evidence and research good but could be more expansive. Appropriate use of resources. Correct grammar, punctuation and spelling.	Clear report but fewer resources used and not evidenced clearly, thus mapping exercise not robust and rich. Format not tightly bound. Language and grammar average.	Confused report without proper mapping of policy shifts, and thus unsound conclusion. Inadequate research and reading. Poor language.
Presentation	Clarity in speech; good connection between PPT slides and what is being said by the presenter; connection with previous and next slides; linkages between different parts of the presentation; succinct and appealing organisation and display of material.	Clarity in speech; fair connections between PPT slides and the presenter's ideas; links between slides, organisation and display of material average.	Clarity in speech; connections between slides missing at some junctures; presenter unable to fully explain gaps; display and organisation of material average.	Connections between slides weak; presenter unable to explain links and gaps; display and organisation of material poor.

Additional Readings

Brass, Paul R. *The Politics of India Since Independence*, vol. 1. New Delhi: Cambridge University Press, 1994.

Chandra, Bipan. 'The Fight to Secure Press Freedom.' In *India's Struggle For Freedom*, edited by B. Chandra et al., 102–113. New Delhi: Penguin Books, 1989.

Freedman, Des. 'Media Policy Silences: The Hidden Face of Communications Decision Making.' *The International Journal of Press/Politics* 15, no. 3 (2010): 344–361.

Moser, S.C. and G. Kalton. *Questionnaires in Social Research Methods*, 73–88. New York: Routledge, 2008.

Sidney, Mara S. 'Policy Formulation: Design and Tools.' In *Handbook of Public Policy Analysis*, edited by Frank Fischer, Jerald J. Miller and Mara S. Sidney, 79–88. New York: Routledge, 2007.

Wollmann, Hellmut. 'Policy Evaluation and Evaluation Research.' In *Handbook of Public Policy Analysis*, edited by Frank Fischer, Jerald J. Miller and Mara S. Sidney, 393–402. New York: Routledge, 2007.

7

Mapping Shifts in Media Regulation

Vibodh Parthasarathi and Aradhana Sharma

Introduction

There has been a radical and intense transformation in the dynamics of information and media over the last two decades. These transformations continue to imprint various facets of contemporary society. Multiple stakeholders are raising concerns in civil society regarding the legal and juridical implications and the nature of the policy implicated. This transformation has thrown up new challenges and insights to the existing set-up of the communication discipline. To address these challenges, a mapping of institutions, instruments and actors in the sphere of media policy can be the first step in identifying these changes. Mapping the sphere would involve identifying key juro-administrative mechanisms, stakeholder groups and civil society initiatives that have come to shape the framing and functioning of public policy.

In this chapter, both students and teachers can learn more about designing and presenting hands-on project workshops in this area of media policy. In the process, students will be able to present this workshop and develop a further understanding of mapping changes in media policy.

Description of the Course

This course, Regulation in Theory and Practice, grapples with the practical implications of regulation and theory in media industries. Over the past two decades, a set of renewed modes of thinking about and perceiving communication have appeared. These reflect the merging of existing social processes and intellectual conceptions with the beginnings of fresh ones.

The development of a policy-oriented model requires a firmer conceptual definition of media industries, taking into account significant changes in the role of cultural products in the economy and society. As noted previously, the course Regulation in Theory and Practice, taught in Semester 4 of the two-year MA in Media Governance, identifies and analyses the attempts to build instruments of media policy in India over the last twenty years. It further maps the response to the changing demands of openness and closure, access and ownership and convergence and diversity in this dynamic sector.

More directly, this course grapples with the evolving set of commercial, technological and institutional frameworks that have reshaped our thinking about media industries. It examines policy arrangements in different sectors of the media industry in India since the reforms process was set into motion in 1991 and the critical challenges to notions of regulation spawned by it. It emphasises equal engagements with primary and secondary writings generated from the government, industry and academic quarters in the still undefined field of media policy.

The first two modules of this course—Direction of Policy Thrusts and Engaging with Interests Groups—are taught theoretically and the third module on policy analysis is taught in a hands-on project workshop format to provide the students both a theoretical and a practical understanding of instruments of media policy. The hands-on workshop related to the theoretically taught modules does not follow but runs concurrently.

Module 1: Direction of Policy Thrusts

In this module, the students are taken through how the process of reforms post-1991 impelled media, technology and governance dynamics. The module examines how the radically altered policy framework of 1991, operationalised through a triptych of liberalisation, privatisation and deregulation, came to orchestrate the workings of the media industries. The impact of these changes on public service broadcasting and the trends driving the dynamics of digitisation and convergence are also explored in this module.

Module 2: Engaging with Interests Groups

This module begins by reflecting on the key terms and ideas that have gained currency in the discussions on governance. Students build on their grasp of the emergent media milieu and understand how the changes have provoked a rethinking of the relationships between various actors—that is, between the state and the citizens, media outlets and consumers and among several types of media outlets and trade bodies. This helps reflect on the rationale of regulation, the principles of underlying models of governance and the efficacy of institutional arrangements of regulatory governance in India.

Module 3: Grappling with Re-Regulation

This module is delivered in a hands-on *workshop mode*. It is taught by taking up the most effervescent sectors, that is, sectors that are witnessing increased regulatory activity in the media industry as case examples. It builds on the familiarity with policy arrangements in various media sectors and institutional structures of media regulation. It delves deeper into concerns of access, equity and the public good which stand central as much to debates on governance as to approaches to policy analysis. In doing so, it is recognised that unravelling successive policy arrangements requires drawing on multiple sources and not just reading into explicit 'Policy' announcements. The module aims to help students have a thorough understanding of Re-regulation.

Course Concept Map

Figure 7.1: Concept Map of the Course: Regulation in Theory and Practice

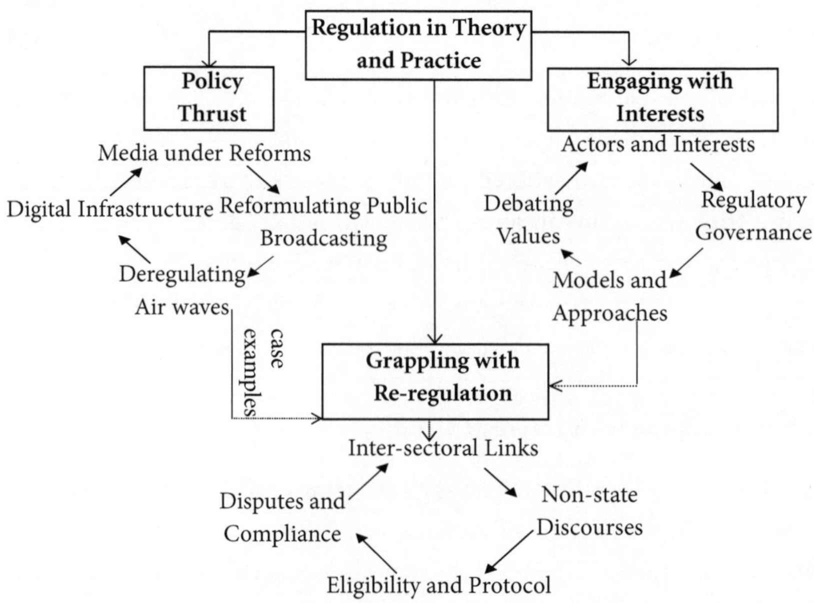

Source: Authors

Course Instructional Objectives

The course aims at building a larger understanding of the existing media environment in India. Enumerated below are the larger instructional goals of this paper, which the teacher should try to do:

- Inculcate among students an understanding of why and how a policy is made.
- Enable students to identify actors involved in the field of policymaking.
- Through theoretical and practical training, equip the students with the ability to examine policy arrangements post-deregulation.
- Demonstrate to the students how reforms in the media sector post-1990s have provoked a rethinking in the relationships between various actors in policymaking.
- Appraise the students on issues of access, equity and public good in the field of policy formulation.

Course Learning Outcomes

After completing this course, the students will be able to:

- analyse the concept and process of regulation in the field of media post-1991 reform process.
- analyse why and how a policy is made and how changes in the commercial, technological and institutional framework of media industries have changed the dynamics between various actors in policymaking.
- extract relevant information from primary and secondary writings generated from the government, industry and academic quarters in media policy.
- relate the process of policy formulations with the larger media environment and multi-institutional trends in various segments of the media industry.
- assess and appraise issues of access, equity and public good in the policy formation process and its outcome.

Introduction to the Hands-on Project

The first two modules of the course address the post reforms (i.e., the 1990s) media policy environment in which students simultaneously study in the class. Through these modules, they are familiarised with building instruments of media policy in India over the last twenty years. They are also required to examine post-liberalisation policy arrangements and see how reforms have changed the commercial, technological and institutional frameworks of media industries. After they have empirically grasped the multifaceted institutional trends in various segments of media policy, the final module—Grappling with Re-Regulation—is taught in a hands-on workshop format to empower the students with an informed vantage point to examine specific experiences of policymaking.

The hands-on project workshop allows you to examine various facets of the policymaking process by analysing a range of documents and understanding the relationships between different actors in policymaking. This enables students to develop the skill to identify relevant documents and actors that influence the policymaking process and exposes them to the pulls and pressures of a complex policymaking process. It will enable you to see how institutional changes taking place in the field have provoked a rethinking in the relationship between those involved in the policy process.

The idea of this exercise is to go beyond theoretical teaching of policy in the classroom and to equip you with the ability to identify for yourself what feeds into (or influences) the policymaking process and map the shifts taking place therein. It further asks you to analyse this change and, through this exercise, understand the context and background of a policy and see the policy as a product of the territory from which it emerges.

Project Concept Map

The relationship among various themes and sub-themes involved in the hands-on project workshop module is given in Figure 7.2.

The concept map largely brings out different layers and processes involved in the workshop and its links. The main aim of the hands-on workshop is to help unravel and analyse media policy; any policy can be seen as presented/reflected through key policy documents. All policies ostensibly aim to address the underlying objectives of the assessment, equity and public good. Key documents are finalised and arrived at based on the policy framework—that is, the latter feeds the former.

Figure 7.2: Concept Map for the Project: Mapping Policy Shifts

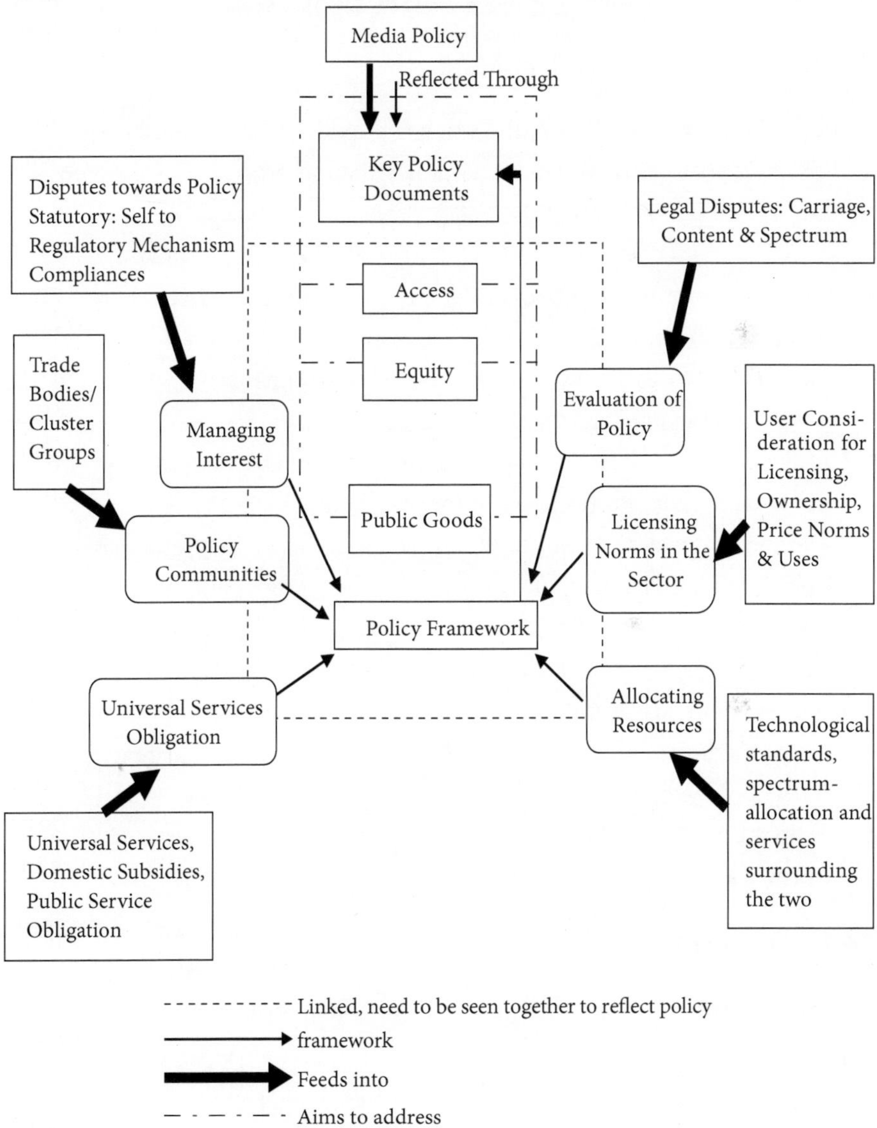

Source: Authors

A policy framework can be seen to have six main components/verticals (Figure 7.2): evolution of policy, licensing norms in the sector, allocation of resources, universal service obligations, policy communities and managing of interests post-policy through regulatory mechanisms. Further, there is an apparatus/ question that helps unravel and feed into each of these.

Project Instructional Objectives

Through the project workshop, the teacher provides a hands-on, practical and in-depth understanding of the media policymaking process. Enumerated here are the larger learning goals of the policy project.

- Inculcate among students an understanding of the context and background of a policy document.
- Help students to identify what feeds into (influences) and impacts the policymaking process.
- Make students see a policy as a product of the territory (prevailing environment: institutions and interests) from which it emerges.
- Demonstrate to students how key concepts used in the classroom are operationalised in the real world during the study of policy.
- Show how changes in the environment are bringing about policy shifts.
- Empower the students to identify relevant documents and experts in the sector, which are examined to help them in the process of policy analysis.
- Help students to see how values of access, equity and public good play out in the policy formation process.
- Help students uncover the interests and compulsions underlying policy options exercised by the government.

Project Learning Outcomes

At the end of the hands-on policy project workshop, the students will be able to:

- bring out the context and background of a policy document and examine a policy as a product of the territory (i.e., prevailing environment: institutions and interests) from which it emerges.
- make connections between theoretical concepts used in the study of policy and how they are used/translated in the policymaking process, that is, operationalise key concepts explored during classroom instruction.
- identify and analyse a range of documents (e.g., laws, statutes, judgements, recommendations, etc.) and key issues within these documents that feed into policy.

- identify key people working in relevant policy sectors and interview them to understand the policymaking process better.
- analyse and review area-related policy literature.
- identify key shifts in policy frameworks within a sector.
- examine how access, equity and public good are reflected and linked in the policymaking process and subsequently in various policy arrangements.
- conceive and structure a report on policy analysis.

Key Concepts

We have briefly enumerated eleven key concepts further. An understanding of these will be helpful and required in undertaking this hands-on workshop. These concepts shall often be used at various stages of this exercise. Some other key concepts or terms that do not find mentioned here but are used during the course of the exercise can be found in the Glossary section at the end part of this book.

Policy arrangements

This is defined as the way in which the components of a policy are arranged vis-à-vis each other—that is, how they are placed in relation to the other. There can be changes in how they are placed and how they interact with each other. For example, we see licensing norms and allocation of resources as two components or even merged as one component. Similarly, the stakeholders in a policy can be brought together under one umbrella or divided into trade bodies and civil society organisations.

Policy shifts

This suggests a substantial change in the relationship between different policy components or in one component itself. For example, if spectrum usage is made open/free, then spectrum allocation as a component will be dropped, reflecting a major policy shift.

Policy output

These are things that the policy process produces, such as laws, regulations, rules, et cetera. These emerge out of the policy formulation process itself.

For example, if there is a demand for larger bandwidth and faster download speed to be incorporated in the broadband policy and finds a place in the same, the new bandwidth and speed should be seen as an output.

Policy outcome

These are the results of policy implementation. Outcomes can be intended or unintended, positive or negative. These can be arrived at only after a policy has been evaluated. If we take bandwidth and speed as mentioned in the 'output' example, it will have to be analysed for the outcome if the changed and improved parameters have brought about the required benefits. So, here one needs to go beyond what is contained in a policy to be able to analyse the policy for its desired outcome.

Regulatory models

These are models (rules, regulations, guidelines) to regulate any industry. Models are outlined through regulatory policy.

Regulatory policy

This is defined as a policy that poses limitations, restrictions, restraints or mandates on persons, groups and businesses, thus reducing their discretion to act.

Regulation brought about through policy can be of many different types. Enumerated here are three main types of regulatory models.

1. *Statutory regulation*: The process of setting up rules by the government to oversee the functioning of an industry/business (in our case, the media industry) and to check compliance for these given set of rules.
2. *Self-regulation/self-regulatory policy*: Self-regulation is when an industry/business regulates itself, that is, when non-state actors in a given sector come up with a set of rules and claim to adhere to it. Thus, a self-regulatory policy is when those that are ostensibly being regulated have much influence over what can and cannot be done by them and others in their sector.
3. *Co-regulation*: This happens when both government and industry/business (to be regulated) come together to evolve a set of rules that need to be followed and also check for compliance together.

Universal service protocol/obligation
The obligation to provide access to basic telegraph services to people in rural and remote areas at affordable and reasonable prices, diversifying network participation.

Access
The ability to use, as opposed to merely reach. Very simply, access can be seen as the ability to make contact or reach. More specifically, in terms of communication, it should be seen not merely as the reach of a particular service in an area but also the ability of the citizens to use the given infrastructure/product/service.

Equity (in terms of benefits)
In politics and public policy, equity is generally thought of as the practice of treating people the same way, regardless of their race, ethnicity, gender and so on. In communication, we can see it as equal, uniform access in terms of infrastructure/products/services for divergent groups/preferences in the population.

Arbitration
Settlement of disputes.

Technological standards
Standards set by the government that must be met while granting licenses. They are set in order to bring in the best (intended) technology to a given sector in order to cut down costs as well as to enhance benefits to the consumers and better utilisation of resources (efficiently, economically, rationally and optimally).

Setting up the Hands-on Project

The students are introduced to the project workshop after they have been acquainted with the course Regulation and Theory in Practice. This module—Grappling with Re-Regulation—is essentially an exercise to familiarise students with the skills and practice of policy analysis.

Through this hands-on project, the students are familiarised with policy dynamics of institutions, organisations and practices, and interventions by various stakeholders in the media milieu. The efforts in the workshop will be to translate this theoretical understanding into a practical approach, in which students will be asked to look at both primary and secondary documents while navigating the policy environment.

From the theoretical modules, the students will be able to relate to how the process of re-regulation is leading to policy shifts in the field of media regulation. They will also be able to explore the relevance and functioning of new institutional structures and the interface between them. The industry and the citizens are introduced in the other modules.

While policy analysis, in general, can include looking at both policy output and policy outcome, this hands-on workshop exercise primarily focuses on policy outputs and not outcomes. Policy outputs are what becomes visible at the end of the policy formulation process: laws, rules, regulations, et cetera. This forms the first stage of policy analysis, where the aim is to understand the context and environment from which a policy emerges. Policy outcomes can be reached only after evaluating the effectiveness of different policy parameters once the policy is in operation. This is the second stage of analysis. In the hands-on workshop, we are concerned only with the first stage, which focuses on outputs that can be unravelled through a range of documents and interviews and not outcomes that require the gathering of data for the field.

This mapping exercise is planned to help students understand that *policy* is largely a product of the context and the environment in which it is produced, nurtured or re-evaluated. Through this process, they will come to realise that since policy addresses the needs of a range of stakeholders, studying the background and the context will provide cues about the need of the policy itself.

This will lead to an understanding and unravelling of the policy itself—that is, it will help uncover the interests and compulsions underlying policy options exercised by the government.

The students undertaking this hands-on activity come with a grounding in media policy in twentieth-century India (theoretical) and document analysis (practical), which are covered in the earlier semesters of the master's programme. The hands-on workshop is conducted over a semester and includes sixteen classes of ninety minutes each.

Project Instructional Design

The hands-on workshop, like all others, needs to be planned and organised before being executed. A detailed description of the instructors is given on the following pages. For the students, some tips, which they should be mindful of before undertaking an extensive and detailed exercise such as this, are spelt out subsequently. The planning has to keep in mind that policymaking is a dynamic exercise and merely examining the final policy document does not lead to a complete understanding of the context. Thus, the students will need to examine a range of documents and conduct expert interviews for this purpose in order to explore the context and background of a given policy document and come up with a better analysis of a policy shift. The instructors will have to ensure that students are made aware of this database and help them in the recovery of documents. The discussion further spells out what and how the teacher needs to do to prepare and set up this hands-on policy workshop.

Planning the Project Workshop

This covers the work to be done by the instructor before the hands-on workshop can be introduced to the students. All the information that the instructors gather and put together while planning this need not be shared fully with the students but must be available with the teachers should the need arise. The teachers/instructors need to:

- make a list of possible policy sectors they may want students to map.
- aggregate known sources/lists of policy documents for each sector.
- chalk out the universe that will throw up secondary documents to be examined by the students.
- come up with a list of probes in the field of policy studies along which the workshop can be designed.
- list a series of questions within each vector/section, which can help students in unravelling the policy mapping process.

- know that probes can be clustered into sections, each representing a policy issue.
- select secondary readings for each group (based on policy sector/vertical they are mapping).
- divide the students into groups (with a judicious mix of fast-moving and slow-moving students).
- list four to five experts within the policy sectors being examined; students should be able to interview these experts.
- call in sector experts to talk to the students or to conduct an exercise with them in order to familiarise them with the area being studied.
- think of a pre-workshop exercise (which will help the students in approaching the workshop).
- come up with and use step-wise (incremental) exercises in the workshop in order to help the students systematically do their work.
- familiarise yourself with the issues and debates in the policy sectors being mapped.

Conducting the Project Workshop

This part deals with classroom instructions of students by an instructor. It should be done in stages as students need to be prepared before they undertake an exercise of this kind. First, the idea behind the hands-on workshop and its mandate needs to be spelt out for the students. Then, they should be familiarised with the issue of policy analysis by reading relevant literature. Then they should be told in detail what each of them needs to do in the hands-on workshop and how they can go about doing it most systematically. Student work should be reviewed at regular intervals to see that they are on the right track.

- Devote the first few (two) classes for introducing the workshop to the students. Discuss the aims of the hands-on workshop and its relevance (policy analysis, the context of policy and its relevance).
- Conduct classes on hands-on workshop design: How is the workshop designed and why is it designed in a particular way (its spread and components, documents, interviews, news reports, academic articles etc.)?

- How will the project workshop be conducted (group/individual; work to be done in the classroom/outside of the classroom)?
- Explain the evaluation criteria. Students should not only be made aware of what form of output is expected (PPTs, narratives, etc.) but also about the basis for assessment.
- Provide a detailed explanation of the substantive parts of this exercise. Maximum time is needed to be devoted for this as these constitute the axis along which the exercise will be conducted.
- Along with each probe parameter, discuss suitable concepts, key terms, relevant theories and models (if required), secondary and primary sources of data, et cetera. Also, discuss ways in which these can be obtained by the students.
- Students should be made aware that data for mapping can be collected from common access information, restricted access information and how even lack of information/data can be used and plotted.
- Remind the students that policy being a product of historical context the mapping exercise should be done keeping this in mind.
- Instruct students on how they will do the mapping exercise: chronologically, keeping the policy at the centre of the web and then plotting changes and influences.
- Review project workshop exercises, assess interim mapping work done by students, pinpoint the gaps and address their queries.
- Finally, ask them to arrange individual exercises together and come up with a broader narrative for the policy being studied.
- Other than the sixteen workshop classes, three more classes should be assigned for students' interim presentations (two classes) and a final presentation (one class).

Pre-Project Workshop Exercises

Before starting planning for the hands-on workshop, given in the following box is an exercise to be undertaken, which will help get an idea about the subject—media policy analysis—which is explored in the hands-on workshop. Doing this exercise will help make sense of and connect to the larger idea of media policy in key deliberations in the field.

Literature Review of Policy Analysis Readings
Thoroughly go through the readings listed below. Try to unpack and asses the article to pin-point what it is saying on the larger question of media policy analysis.

1. van Cuilenburg, J. and McQuail, D. (2003) 'Media Policy Paradigm Shifts: Towards a New Communications Policy Paradigm.' *European Journal of Communication*, 18(2): 181–207.
2. Freedman, D. (2010) 'Media Policy Silences: The Hidden Face of Communications Decision Making.' *The International Journal of Press/ Politics*, 15(3): 344–361.

Key: Look at the evidence the author is using and the structure of the arguments made. Identify the range of evidence used in the article. Assess how the author presents their arguments in relation to alternative perspectives in the field being addressed. Locate any gaps or inconsistencies in the argument being presented.

Assessment criterion: When you have completed literature review as an exercise, your teacher will assess you on: the ability to clearly identify the voices, perspectives and arguments put forth in each of the articles; ability to extract five main points that the article is trying to make and see how they all link to the larger theme of policy analysis. Reviews should be well structured and succinctly written, highlighting the issues in order of importance.

Please note:

- This exercise is compulsory for all students as it will be assessed and graded.
- For doing this, you will be using up to 500 words for each of the two readings.
- Readings will be provided by the instructors in the classroom.
- You will be given two weeks to carry out this exercise.

Hands-on Project Workshop Design

This section spells out both the nuts and bolts of the hands-on project workshop (that is, how this is to be conducted and what resources are to be used during this exercise) as well as the substantive part of the exercise. It illustrates how the larger sphere of analysis can be broken down into smaller doable parts for the students and then tied back into a larger sector-wise narrative. It also spells out the documents and resources (both to be given by the instructors and those that the student need to mind) to be used for undertaking this policy mapping exercise.

Templates: The Constituted Context of Policy

In Box 7.1, twelve templates are presented. These templates are the defining points around which the policy workshop is conducted. The first six templates, 1–6, bring out the bases of this exercise (i.e., why we should do it and its context) and what all will be required to get the exercise done like documents and interviews then how the nut and bolts of the exercise can be disaggregated and aggregated (breaking down of exercise).

The next six templates, seven to twelve, form the substantive part of the policy workshop. They are components/verticals, as shown in the concept map, which is reflected in the policy framework (Box 7.1):

Box 7.1: Policy Framework

1. Why study media policy analysis?

   It is important to address this question as it will not just help in justifying the workshop but
   emphasise the importance of undertaking an exercise like this. Studying policy analysis
   helps to:

   - understand the policymaking environment in the media sector in India.
   - uncover the interests and compulsions underlying policy options exercised by the government.
   - operationalise key concepts explored during classroom instruction.
   - identify key shifts in policy frameworks within a sector.
   - examine how values of access, equity and public good are addressed in different policy arrangements within a sector.

2. The context of policy:

   - Policy is largely a product of the context and the environment in which it is produced, nurtured or re-evaluated.
   - Since all policy addresses the needs of a range of stakeholders, studying the background and the context provides cues about the need itself.
   - This in turn helps in understanding and unravelling the policy itself.

3. Documents to be studied:

    - Primary documents: These will include key policy documents of the sector being examined.
    - Secondary documents: Government documents (acts, bills, proposed bills, annual reports of relevant ministries); industry documents, court cases/orders, citizens' charters/CSO reports.
    - Other resources: Academic books and articles, interviews with persons working in related fields.

4. Why use a range of documents?

    - Policymaking is a dynamic exercise. Looking at the end result—the final policy document—often does not lead to a full understanding of the context.
    - Examining documents like consultation papers, recommendations, comments or even tribunal cases help in better comprehending the need and the process.
    - Wider study of the process helps to explore the context and background of policy documents and also helps in better analysing the outcomes.

5. Interview as a resource

    - Interviews with area-specific experts can provide subjective insights.
    - Experts can be crucial to the policy mapping process as they can help fill the information gaps.
    - They can help in corroborating information from other sources.
    - Interviews can be done with people in the industry, government and/or advocacy groups.

6. Breaking down exercise

    - The larger exercises can be broken down into smaller parts and divided among students.
    - List probes in the field of policy studies along which to design the workshop.
    - These can be core policy issues along which the territory to be mapped can be sliced.

- Within each of these probes/verticals, a series of questions have to be devised, which can help the students in unravelling the policy mapping process.

The next six templates, as aforementioned, can be seen as probes/verticals. These form the key axis of the workshop around which the analysis will be conducted. Each of them also has a set of questions or parameters that need to be explored and answered to come up with the components of each of the verticals. Answering these and bringing out the shifts in each of the verticals is key to the mapping exercise.

7. Evolution/content

   - How do we locate this segment in the wider context of media reform since 1991? Is there an identifiable trajectory of (legal) disputes that led to a formal policy framework?
   - How are carriage and content separated in the administration of this segment?
   - What are the aspects of content that have attracted regulation? If a new platform/medium, how have the existing frameworks been modified to suit this?

8. Licensing norms

   - What are the criteria for applying for a license? Are there stipulations for M&A and/or reselling of licenses?
   - What are the norms for ownership (including foreign investment & cross-media)? Are there clauses safeguarding concentration?
   - Are there norms to regulate pricing of and taxes on products/services?

9. Allocating resources

   - Is one technological standard specified in a policy or not? What are the debates about the adoption of technical standards for the platform concerned?
   - How is spectrum allocated in this segment?
   - What have been the controversies in spectrum allocation in this segment?

10. Universal service

- What is the framework for universal service protocols for government entities? Have these been amended over the years?
- Are there subsidies for those who cannot afford hardware/services? How well have these schemes been implemented?
- What public service obligations exist for private firms? What have been the arguments to expand/remove these?

11. Policy communities

- What kinds of knowledge have trade bodies produced to shape policy?
- Have citizen groups been consulted or been otherwise involved in decision-making processes?
- What kinds of knowledge have civil society organisations (CSOs) produced in trying to shape policy? What are the key differences between knowledge produced by CSOs and trade bodies?

12. Managing interests

- What disputes emerged in courts/tribunals following (each) policy announcements? Did these lead to (further) amendments?
- Are there mechanisms of statutory, self- or co-regulation in this segment? Have fresh ones been proposed?
- Have trade bodies or citizen groups conducted initiatives to check compliance with or measure the impact of specific policy protocols?

How to Analyse the Parameters of the Templates

The key questions provided in the verticals (discussed earlier) assigned to individual students are the key to undertaking the analysis as they provide cues for what to look for under each section. Answering these adequately will help students in identifying points/issues around which the mapping exercise can be carried out. However, before starting the exercise and even while it is on, students must refer to related concepts and issues that were discussed in class in theoretical modules. Even though processes such as liberalisation, privatisation and governance may be discussed in class in the context of other sectors, students need to relate them to the sector they are mapping while they undertake the exercise. Further, mapping exercises should be undertaken keeping in view key policy documents as well as secondary documents; these documents should be based on cues mentioned in an earlier subsection. The effort should be to pinpoint the shifts, unearth when and why these shifts took place and finally what was fed into the policy and what was filtered out.

For each vertical, arguments have to be made based on the evidence collected: from the pre-policy arguments/discussions, what concrete points went through the funnel. If any specific event or situation points towards why a particular point found a place in policy or was omitted, it should be clearly stated.

Let us look at one specific illustration to elaborate on this point (see Figure 7.2). One of the six verticals enumerated in the previous section is used here to see how and what feeds into the policy documents. Licensing norms is one of the components of the policy framework that finally leads to a policy document. Components of licensing include ownership norms, licensing criteria and pricing and taxing norms (see Figure 7.3). The effort should be to highlight these points, map changes in them, if any, over the years, and then finally see what makes it to key policy documents and what gets filtered out and why.

Figure 7.3: Licensing Norms as an Example

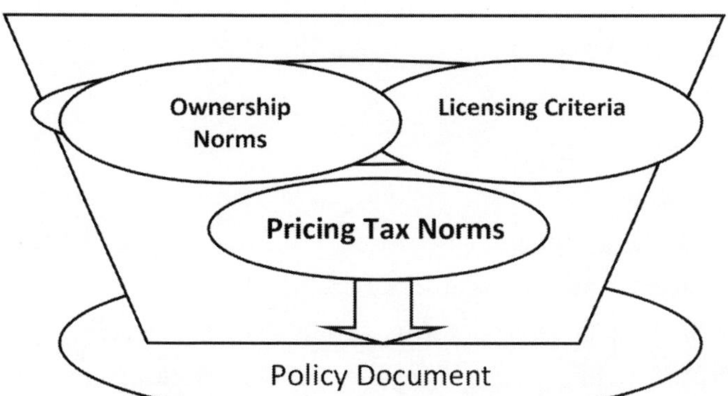

This exercise should be done for each of the verticals separately before trying to put it together for the larger policy sector being studied and analysed. The resulting work has to be stitched together at the end of the mapping exercise and aggregated to form a larger narrative and presentation on each of the specific policy sectors. A conclusion should be made after collating and assessing the outcomes for each of the verticals.

How to Do the Policy Project Workshop

The exercise will require the students to look at, examine and select relevant information from a wide range of material. For undertaking an exercise like this, it is important that the students not only understand why and to what end is this being done but also to have some sense as to how the work should be planned and undertaken for the best results. The following approach and steps will help in doing the work in a planned manner and will assist in reaching the required output.

- Use the pre-project workshop readings on policy (both general and sector/vertical specific) to familiarise yourself with the idea of policy analysis.
- Understand that policy is a product of historical contexts and situations; therefore, a mapping exercise should be done in its historical context.
- Remember to keep the policy at the centre of the web and then attempt to plot how ideas, people, institutions and events influenced the space of policy and the policy document itself.
- Read the policy documents carefully.
- Cull out the important points.

Once this is successfully done, and before one proceeds to the next stage, one needs to look for documents other than the primary policy document given to you, which are relevant to the sector and vertical that you are probing. This mining of documents is part of the hands-on workshop exercise and should be done with utmost diligence; it forms the backbone of the exercise as it throws up data and other related information. The following box gives the details of this exercise.

Hands-on Workshop Exercise: Listing Relevant Secondary Documents
Mine for secondary documents from the large universe of resources and come up with a list of documents. Explain why each document has been selected and what parts/sections from the document are more relevant to the sector and vertical being mapped by you. This is to be brought to class and to be discussed with the instructor and/or with fellow students.

Key: Make sure you have scanned through all of the categories for possible documents before finalising the list.
Assessment criteria: This exercise is crucial to the mapping. It will impact the overall work being done by you. You will be judged by the instructor on your ability to identify relevant documents based on the sector and vertical being mapped and also on your capability to comprehend, cull and use appropriate parts of the document directly linked to your work.

Note:
- This exercise is compulsory for all students as it will be assessed and graded.
- Instructors will only guide on the relevance of documents; the mining exercise will have to do by the student.
- You will be given two weeks to carry out this exercise.
- Map chronologically—a timeline based on all the documents you are able to access.
- Plot the contingencies that led to the documents and specific points within the document and where their genesis lies.

On completing this work, one is about half way through the policy workshop. The box below gives some hints on how self assessment can be done. It is important to incorporate this step in the conducting the hands-on workshop as it guards against last minute discovery of omissions or mistakes.

Mid-Project Workshop: Self-Assessment of Work
After undertaking the mapping exercise, the student is expected to look at the material collected and assess if it is relevant and adequate for undertaking the analysis. Answering the following questions will help in this exercise.

- What and where are the information gaps?
- Why are they there? Is it the lack of documents/material referred to? Or has the material not been used effectively?

- Have you been able to address all the questions listed under your vertical?
- What is not been done? How do you plan to address that?
- Do you need to interview someone to get more details? If yes, then whom?
- Are you able to make sense of the material collected? What is it leading to/indicating? If not, how will you address it? Do you plan to interview any expert for this? If yes, whom?
- How does your vertical lend to the larger idea of policymaking?
- Conduct an extensive search for information that supports the evolution of this contingency (through secondary documents and other resources like interviews).

  Once the self-assessment exercise is done and the gaps identified by the students, they need to explore additional material as well as identify and interview people to help them fill the information gaps.
- Identify experts in the field and conduct interviews (see the next box on this exercise).
- Use information and source triangulation—i.e., use more than one source or piece of information to cross-check facts and information.
- List the information/data sources referred to in the documents.
- Finally, use all the data gathered from documents (primary and secondary) and other resources like interviews and articles, and plot it chronologically to reflect the shifts in policy. Build a narrative based on this.
- Bring together the narratives of all the verticals under the same sector. Cull out important aspects from each to conclude on the larger policy shifts in the sector.

Project Workshop Exercise: List of Experts to Interview

Identify experts within the sector being mapped. These can be from the industry, government or advocacy groups in the area being mapped. The vertical being mapped should also be kept in mind while identifying experts.

They should be able to address/explain gaps in the mapping exercise. The names should be shared, discussed and finalised in consultation with other students covering the same sector but different verticals.

Key: Let the mid-workshop assessments and the gaps recorded therein be the main criteria for identifying interviewees.

Assessment criterion: The ability to identify relevant people for the interviews and to frame appropriate questions that will help fill the gaps or bring additional information for the exercise.

Time assigned: one week for identifying interviewees; two weeks for conducting interviews.

Timeline
16 weeks – Total hands-on workshop time
1 week – Introduction
2 weeks – General literature review + sector-specific literature review
1 week – Peer review of the literature review
2 weeks – Searching for secondary documents and aggregating them
1 week – Mapping the material from the secondary documents
1 week – Looking for gaps
1 week – Identifying people for interview
2 weeks – Doing interviews
2 weeks – Collating material
1 week – Writing individual narrative
2 weeks – Aggregating and assessing sector-wise material

(Bringing the verticals together)
1 week – group (sector-wise) PPT preparation.

How Will Students Be Evaluated

Student evaluation for the hands-on workshop will be done based on three outputs:

- Literature review of policy analysis as well as a sector- and vertical-specific readings.
- Interim presentation: Individual narrative (on the vertical covered).
- Final outcome (on the sector covered): this will have two components.

    - Group narrative
    - Group PowerPoint presentation.

Assessment: 25 per cent weightage
At an overall level, the students may be tested for their ability to grasp the idea of policy analysis and to be able to locate the policy in its larger environment.

Specifically, they can be assessed for their ability to:

- identify and study a range of documents (laws, statutes, judgements and recommendations) that feed into policy.
- identify key/relevant issues from within the documents and be able to map them chronologically (identifying areas that have impacted policy formation).
- review literature on the positives and negatives of policy (i.e., understanding evaluation of policy).
- identify key people working in relevant policy sectors to be interviewed to get a better understanding of the policymaking process.

Key Things to Focus On

An exercise like mapping policy shifts is an extensive and rigorous exercise. One needs to be well-prepared for this and needs to brush up on some of the theoretical knowledge acquired in the earlier courses of the master's programme and also connect with the earlier hands-on policy workshops, particularly the one on document analysis.

Planning the Hands-on Workshop

One should not jump into the thick of things; rather, plan a systematic way of thinking about approaching and conducting the exercise.

- One needs to equip oneself with the details of the hands-on workshop provided by the instructor in the class and understand the purpose of this exercise and its relevance in the larger course structure.
- Return/refer to some of the concepts taught and issues discussed in other modules of the paper (e.g., privatisation of services post-1990s, emergence of new actors, institutions and models in the mediascape and their relationship with each other).
- One needs to understand, through classroom instruction and policy readings, that the final policy document often does not lead to a full understanding of the context of the policy. Therefore, it is important to identify secondary documents for the sector and the vertical to be probed/mapped.

- Realise that examining documents like consultation papers, recommendations, judgements, reports, et cetera are required to better map and understand the policy process and shifts.
- One needs to identify people from the industry, government, advocacy groups in the area being mapped in order to fill the gaps and corroborate information from other sources and gain insights into the policy being analysed.
- And finally, this being a group exercise, the students should understand the structure of the hands-on workshop, its requirements and assessment criteria in order to deliver the project in the required format.

Students in the Classroom

Students should try to understand and act upon the following key issues during classroom teaching:

- Policies are context- and environment-dependent.
- Policies are meant to address the needs of a range of stakeholders.
- Policymaking/policy shift takes place under a variety of pulls and pressures.
- Studying the background of a policy or mapping policy shifts provides cues to these needs as also the pulls and pressures.
- Try and understand the keywords and concepts and see how they are operationalised during the workshop/practical policymaking process.
- Raise questions whenever unable to understand the instructions and the concepts being discussed in class.
- Bring your findings to the class and discuss their relevance and placement in the mapping exercise with your co-students and instructor.

Students' Self-Evaluation

Before writing out and submitting the final work, students should try to assess their own work. The following are some boxes to check before finalising the hands-on project workshop exercise.

- Is the format for the narrative/PPT correct?
- Introduction: What should come here?

- Under what headings/sections should the article/narrative/PPT be written? Put down pointers to what you will write under each section; what material will be used for this.
- Conclusion: Based on the shifts, what should you be aiming to conclude? This should strictly be based on the evidence found and mapped by you during this exercise
- References and bibliography: Ensure that all the substantive information/data used by you in the output has been referenced. At the end of the narrative, have a bibliography section that records all primary and secondary documents as well as interviews from where the information has been used.

Illustrative Case Study

List of media sectors

This exercise of mapping media-policy shifts can be undertaken in any of the media sectors that have seen movement after the liberalisation process kicked off in the 1990s. The following is a list of possible sectors for which this exercise can be undertaken:

- Broadcasting sector
- FM radio
- Community radio
- Broadband
- Telecom

The case

Through examples in the telecom and broadband sectors, let's examine how this policy workshop can be designed. Presented here is an illustrative case of a past hands-on workshop organised as a group exercise.

- The class was divided into two groups of seven students each.
- Each group was to analyse policy frameworks in a particular media segment over a period of time.
- The two student groups looked at:

   - Broadband policy
   - Telecom policy

- Each of the two areas of study was subdivided into six investigative/analytical verticals.
- Each student in the group was assigned one vertical and was responsible for examining this area with reference to the larger policy sphere of the specified field.
- Other than the documents provided, students were expected to locate related documents, review relevant literature and conduct interviews.

Principal/primary documents

These were identified by the teacher and given to the students. So, primary documents, irrespective of the sector chosen for analysis, have to be identified and sourced by the teacher. For this specific exercise, the primary documents for the two sectors identified for the analysis were:

- *Telecom*

   - *New Telecom Policy, 1999.* Department of Telecom, Ministry of Communications and Information Technology, Government of India.
   - *National Telecom Policy, 1994.* Department of Telecom, Ministry of Communications and Information Technology, Government of India.

- *Broadband*

   - *National Broadband Action Plan, 2010.* Department of Telecom, Ministry of Communications and Information Technology, Government of India.
   - *Broadband Policy, 2004.* Department of Telecom, Ministry of Communications and Information Technology, Government of India.

Secondary documents

Policy analysis cannot be limited to merely looking at and analysing policy documents. Examining documents like consultation papers, recommendations, judgements, et cetera helps in better understanding the policy process and shifts.

Secondary documents were mined and identified by the students from a suggested (by the instructor) but large and open-ended database. The following are the spheres from which the documents needed to be selected for the given exercise:

- *Telecom*
    - Telecom Regulatory Authority of India (TRAI) consultation papers, recommendations and stakeholder comments in relevant areas.
    - TDSAT: Relevant judgements.
- *Broadband*
    - Telecom Regulatory Authority of India (TRAI) consultation papers, recommendations and stakeholder comments in relevant areas.

Students made use of a range of documents available in the government, industry and civil society arena in order to make their mapping exercise rich. A large canvas was mined for the sector- and vertical-specific material. These included:

- Government documents (acts, bills, proposed bills, annual reports of relevant ministries).
- Industry documents.
- Court cases/orders.
- Citizens' charters/CSO reports.

Other resources

Other than the aforementioned documents, students used the following:

- Articles in newspapers and magazines.
- Academic books and articles.
- Interviews with persons working in a related field.

Illustrative student outputs

Figures 7.4 and 7.5 are slides from the PowerPoint presentations made by the students on these two policies (i.e., telecom and broadband). This exercise was also organised based on templates elaborated earlier. Individual students, as pointed out in the previous section, were assigned one vertical each to map. The analysis of the verticals was done through both a narrative report and a PowerPoint presentation. Figures 7.4 and 7.5 show one such PowerPoint slide from the presentation.

Telecom policy

The slide-shot in Figure 7.4 is from the vertical Allocating Resources and brings out what technological standards were employed and what were the debates going on regarding which technologies should be endorsed in the policy to make the services most cost-effective and give them a wide reach.

Figure 7.4: Example of Telecom Policy

Technological Standard

- **Technological Standard Adopted**

I. National Telecom Policy 1994- To make the country a manufacturing base & exporter of telecom equipment.

II. New Telecom Policy 1999- Allowed Fixed Service license holders to use variety of technologies to serve subscribers including WLL (Wirelss in Local Loop).

- **Debates on Adoptions of Technical Standards**

I. 4-wire or 6-wire analogue trunks along with Fixed Division Multiplexers (FDM) used in Indian long distance telephone network until 80s.

II. Debate around the goal to acquire design capability & reduce cost capitalizing on the software expertise in India

Broadband policy

The slide-shot in Figure 7.5 is from the vertical Allocating Resources. Here the student has tried to bring out who allocates resources, why the resource should be allocated and how and through what components the process of allocation plays out.

Figure 7.5: Example of Broadband Policy

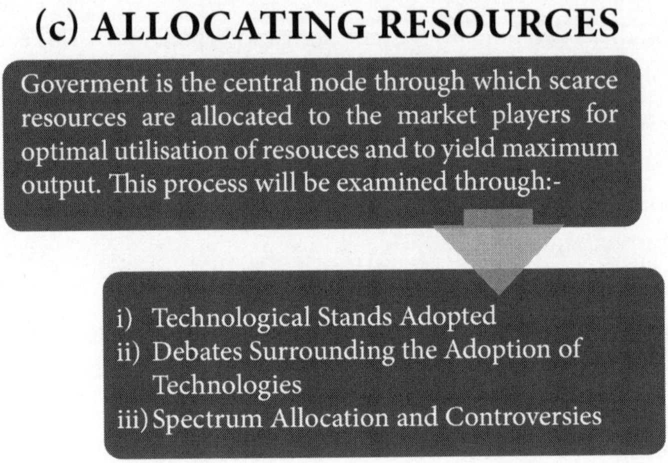

Questions on Presentation

Questions (based on the templates)

The following questions are indicative only:

- What is the aim of this exercise? What is it that you have set out to do?
- What is the time span you have covered for the mapping exercise? Is it relevant to the primary documents allotted to you?
- How did you go about selecting the secondary documents and identifying the key parts relevant to your work?
- On what basis were the people for the interviews selected? What are some of the questions you asked them and why?
- What are the most relevant policy shifts that you have identified in the sector being mapped by your group?

Questions (based on specific verticals in the template)

These questions are indicative only:

- List out some of the examples of legal disputes in the sector allocated to you during the specified timeframe.

- How are carriage and content separated in the administration of the sector being studied by you?
- How are norms of concentration addressed in the sector being mapped by you?
- What are the debates around the adoption of technological standards in the specified sector?
- What is a USO fund? What are the main arguments for expanding or removing subsidies in the sector being examined?
- List the main trade bodies and CSOs in the sector being examined by you.
- Make explicit the changes found in policy statutes triggered by disputes.

Further Exercises

This book illustrates a significant outline of how a policy mapping exercise can be carried out in order to map policy shifts in any given media sector that has seen movement post the reforms process in the 1990s. The instructors or students can pick any of the sectors for the mapping exercise. However, students attempting to do the exercise individually should pick specific verticals for an additional exercise of this kind.

Exercise: Take the *Draft Broadcast Bill, 2007*, as the primary document. Map the policy shifts in the licensing norms for the broadcasting sector.

Key: Identify key secondary documents for the sector and relevant papers from other resources. Try to address the components of licensing norms. Get down to the mapping exercise based on the steps given in the workbook.

Length: Do a 2,000-word write-up bringing out changes in the licensing norms in the broadcasting sector.

Time to be taken: Since this exercise is done using only secondary documents and no interviews, it should be done in five weeks,

Alternate exercises: A similar exercise can be done for the broadcasting sector from any of the six verticals—evolution, licensing norms, allocating resources, universal service, policy communities and managing interests—based on the mapping outline elaborated in the earlier sections of this workbook.

Evaluation and Assessment

In any academic exercise, as in this hands-on policy workshop, the evaluation and assessment criteria have been both explicit and transparent. Evaluation is done based on the performance of students in the course and hands-on workshop.

Skills learnt

- Ability to identify a range of documents that feed into the policy process and are produced by various stakeholders.
- Ability to identify key issues within each document, especially those that have impacted the final policy.
- Ability to identify and use relevant quantitative data from a range of documents.
- Ability to review academic literature to evaluate policies and/or policy shifts.
- Ability to identify and interview relevant people to fill information gaps.
- Ability to conceive and structure a report on policy analysis.

Assessment (components)

Student evaluation is an ongoing exercise throughout the duration of the hands-on workshop. It has three components.

Literature review
Apart from individual reviews of literature, which is to be consulted and examined, each review exercise also included a peer review. This could be within a group or across the group and within the same vertical. The readings and instructions on this were provided by the instructor.

Individual write-up (2,000 words)
An individual student's write up on a specific area (vertical).

Group write-up (13,000 words)
One group reports on a specific sector. For this, individual narratives on all the six verticals/components covered by different students were put together. This write-up also included a sector-specific introduction and conclusion (to be

deduced from the six individual write-ups) as well as references for the larger mapping exercise for each of the sectors.

Group PowerPoint presentation
Here, each group (sector-wise) presented the mapping exercise for their sector using a PowerPoint.

Assessment (content)

This section elaborates on why certain evaluation criteria were used and on what basis the contents produced by the students were assessed.

Literature review
Peer review has been introduced in order to widen the canvass of mandatory reading followed by an analysis of the same by the students. This exercise, besides enhancing the capacity of students to review primary literature, also aims to empower them with the ability to pinpoint gaps and problems in another person's assessment of the literature. From an assessment point of view, we shall examine if a student has been able to identify and understand the main points/issues being addressed in an article. And, at the level of peer review, if they are able to locate the points missed out by others and suggest ways to incorporate them.

Narrative
Students have to always keep in mind that mapping is an evidence-based exercise. So they have to invest a substantial amount of time and energy in looking at primary documents, seeking information in secondary documents and through interviews. The students were assessed based on the number of documents consulted, not just quantitatively but also qualitatively, and in terms of their skills to extract and use relevant information at the correct juncture. Similarly, how the interview component is reflected in the narrative was also assessed. At a broader level, the students were examined for their ability to answer effectively, coherently and clearly all the questions posed within their verticals based on the earlier two components.

Group narrative
Under this exercise, the students were made to collate into one comprehensive report all the work done individually under each vertical. This entailed

putting together all the verticals and assessing them to come up with a common introduction and conclusion for the analysis of the given sector. Assessment will be based on how well the verticals have been represented and integrated into the final exercise.

Assessment (presentation)

The content aspect of the PowerPoint presentation was based on a group narrative. Here, both the presentations and the students were evaluated on the basis of the following skills:

Content

Have all the issues/questions raised been addressed? Is the presentation clear and coherent? Is appropriate evidence employed? Is there a clear introduction, a main body that maps the shifts in policy and a clear conclusion? Evidence of research and reading, appropriateness of sources, correct grammar, punctuation and spelling are required.

Coherence

The following shall be examined: clarity in speech, a connection between PPT slides and what is being said by the presenter, connection between previous and next slides and, of course, their relevance to the larger question/point being addressed.

Argument

The following are important: the ability to explain shifts or mapping arguments based on concrete data/information (not hypothetical generalisations) culled during the exercises.

Creativity

How well are the linkages made between different parts of the presentation and how are they brought out?

Organisation

How well is the material mined, organised and displayed?

Criteria for Grading

Grades criteria Exercises	**A (Excellent)**	**B (Good)**	**C (Average)**	**D (Poor)**
Literature review	Not simply a summary of the articles but a critical evaluation of the same in the context of policy analysis.	A summary and an evaluation but missing some of the points.	Merely a summary of the article.	Incorrect or incoherent summary.
Interview	At least two interviews done with relevant people to fill the information gap in the mapping exercise with correct inputs.	Just one interview but still leading to reducing the information gap.	Interview/s done but with wrong people, or relevant people but not posing relevant questions, therefore, not getting relevant answers.	No interviews done.
Narrative	Clearly and coherently presented report, employing appropriate evidence. Has a clear introduction, the main body that maps the shifts in policy over the years and a clear conclusion. Evidence of research and reading; appropriateness of sources used. Correct grammar, punctuation and spelling.	Clear report with appropriate use of evidence but format not very tightly knit. Evidence and research good but could be more expansive. Appropriate use of resources. Correct grammar, punctuation and spelling.	Clear report but fewer resources used and not evidenced clearly, thus mapping exercise not robust and rich. Format not tightly bound. Language and grammar average.	Confused report without proper mapping of shifts in policy and thus unsound conclusion. Inadequate research and reading. Poor language.

Grades criteria Exercises	**A (Excellent)**	**B (Good)**	**C (Average)**	**D (Poor)**
Presentation	Clarity in speech; clarity in connection between ppt. slide and what is being said by the presenter; connection with previous and next slides; linkages between different parts of the presentation; succinct and appealing organisation and display of material.	Clarity in speech and connections between ppt. slides and presenter; links between slides; organisation and display of material average.	Clarity in speech; connections between slides missing at some junctures; presenter unable to fully explain the gaps; display and organisation of material average.	Connections between slides weak; presenter unable to explain links and gaps; display and organisation of material poor.

Additional Readings

Ahluwalia, Montek S. 'Economic Reforms in India Since 1991: Has Gradualism Worked?' *Journal of Economic* Perspectives 16, no. 3 (2002): 67–88.

Arun, T.G. 'Regulation and Competition: Emerging Issues in an Indian Perspective.' *WP Series* no. 39. Centre on Regulation and Competition, University of Manchester, 2003.

Athreya, M.B. 'India's Telecommunications Policy: A Paradigm Shift.' *Telecommunications Policy* 20, no. 1 (1996): 11–22.

Baxi, C.V. 'The Current Context of Corporate Governance in India.' *Global Business Review* 6, no. 2 (2005): 303–314.

Farmer, Victoria L. 'Nation, State, and Democracy in India: Media Regulation and Government Monopoly.' Paper presented at International Communications Association Preconference on India and Communications Studies. Chicago, 2009.

Jordana, Jacint and David Levi-Faur. 'The Politics of Regulation in the Age of Governance.' In *The Politics of Regulation: Institutions and Regulatory Reforms for the Age of Governance*, edited by Jacint Jordana and David Levifaur, 1–28. Jerusalem: Esward Elgar, 2004.

Price, M.E. and S. Verhulst. 'Riddles of Media Governance: Multiple Stakeholders, Multiple Objectives, Multiple Perspectives.' Public Lecture by M.E. Price at Contours of Media Governance, International Seminar by Centre for Culture, Media and Governance with IDRC, CCMG, Jamia Millia Islamia, New Delhi, 8–10 December 2008.

Singh, Rahul. 'The Teeter-totter of Regulation and Competition: Balancing the Indian Competition Commission with Sectoral Regulators.' *Washington University Global Studies Law Review* 8 (2007): 71. (A study commissioned by Competition Commission of India at Indian Institute of Management, Bangalore.)

Thussu, Daya Kishan. 'Privatizing the Airwaves: The Impact of Globalization on Broadcasting in India.' *Media, Culture & Society* 21, no. 1 (1999): 125–131.

Vagliasindi, Maria and Pietro A. Vagliasindi. 'The Economics of Auctioning and Related Regulatory Issues: The Economic Viability of the Auction Provision of the Bill and Alternatives for Direct-to-Home Licenses.' *Cardozo Journal of International and Comparative Law* 5 (1998): 467.

Virmani, Arvind. 'A Communications Policy for the 21st Century.' *Economic and Political Weekly* 35, no. 23 (2000): 1907–1910.

Section 3

Professional Development and the Future

8

Professional Development of Media Educators

Santosh Panda

Introduction

In this chapter, we analyse further the case for pedagogy in media education and media educators, focusing primarily on project-based learning (PBL) to implement theoretical discourses on media policy and governance in a classroom context. Media literacy competencies have been discussed in relation to pedagogic interventions that can be made to teach various stages of media literacy competencies. Various aspects of PBL have been analysed from the viewpoint of media educators' interventions in relation to the broader framework of scholarship of teaching and learning, which stresses the pedagogy of the discipline and researching discipline pedagogy. In this analysis, 'professional learning' comes to the fore of continuing professional development; therefore, the professional development of media educators has been located within a professional learning continuum in the entire professional career, in place of a one-shot orientation or refresher course as practised in the university human resource development centres (HRDCs), earlier known as Academic Staff Colleges.

Pedagogy and Media Education

Education, in a broader sense, is concerned with learning throughout life, formal and informal, and with a purpose ingrained in values and purpose of life and in the socio-cultural context in which living is situated. While education encompasses the entirety of learning experiences, including curriculum, content, processes, experiences, reflections, assimilation and transformation of the being, pedagogy within this is more concerned with how that takes place and how that is taught as also facilitated. In the context of formal education, the connection of education is to learning and students, while the connection of pedagogy is to training and teachers (Kansanen 2003). Learning, which can be both formal and informal, is more connected to guided processes and practices relating to aims and goals, to curriculum and content and to the context. Pedagogy within this process becomes more normative and deals with the most appropriate processes and strategies of teaching and facilitating learning. In other words, the instrumentality of learning is dealt with by pedagogy while learning itself is open, broad and can take place for itself without any involvement of pedagogy (or, for that matter, andragogy). Hinchliffe (2001) writes, 'Pedagogy views learning instrumentally whereas education views learning for its own sake' (35). Insofar as formal teaching-learning is concerned, pedagogy assumes the centre stage towards how learning should be directed and facilitated. So, it is a conscious effort by the teacher to enhance the learning of the students.

Both 'didactics' and 'pedagogy' have been used interchangeably by scholars. However, there are cultural differences in how teaching-learning is viewed. While the European tradition is generally concerned with didactics or pedagogy, the Anglo-American tradition is more concerned with curricular exercises (rather than pedagogy). Therefore, it is not surprising that the British influence on Indian educational practices emphasises more on curriculum (and not on pedagogy—which is visible in the curricular practices in higher education in which pedagogic discourses are almost non-existent).

In media education/media studies, as in other disciplines, the emphasis has often been more on curriculum rather than pedagogy. While media studies is more concerned with the selection, integration and transaction of the curriculum on media education/studies, this book focuses and showcases pedagogy, media pedagogy and pedagogy-in-practice, especially in relation to the constructivist and inquiry-based theoretical tradition of PBL. When we move towards more of open education (i.e., removal of restrictions to educational opportunities), open learning (i.e., addressing individual autonomy and pathways of learning), open educational resources (i.e., use of teaching-learning resources declared as open under Creative Commons), open pedagogy (i.e., use of OER as also co-creation of knowledge by teachers and students) and open educational practices (i.e., flexible but integrated use of all the above in the educational practices), the constructivist pedagogic method of PBL assumes the centre stage of teaching-learning (besides other constructivist and experiential learning methods). Further, in the context of connectivist teaching-learning, PBL gets more space and leverage for application in experiential and inquiry-based collaborative learning through social media networks and social technologies.

It may be underlined that teaching-learning in media studies/education needs to go beyond media literacy learning to more of engagement in technology–pedagogy discourse so as to enhance the quality of teaching-learning. Two of the media-based pedagogic interventions are of importance: project-based online learning and e-portfolio. Media literacy education deals more with reading, writing, speaking, listening and viewing with specific learning outcomes relating to aligning media constructions with languages, social reality, commercial and political implications, audience negotiation and ideology and values (Westbrook 2011). The author argues for teachers to go beyond media literacy to media literacy pedagogy, which informs teachers' teaching styles and establishes connections with issues such as gender, culture, power, ideology and social justice (i.e., critical media literacy). Also, teachers need to engage with digital media that challenges multiple literacies such as print, audio, video, et cetera. Such an engagement with pedagogy and constructivist teaching deals with teachers' beliefs, critical reflection and praxis (both theory and practice).

Media educators and teachers of media studies generally engage in a variety of ways in classroom teaching, media analysis, media production, policy analysis and media relating to development. The engagement involves inquiry, analysis, communication, evaluation, reflection, among others. Besides, as underlined by Friesem (2019), 'We should consider how our students can reflect on their media use as part of their identity' (3). Based on experiences in teaching a course for media professionals, the author argues for access, reflection, civic engagement and ethical standards as part of professional practice. As part of five PBL stages, five digital and media literacy competencies were developed based on engagement in pedagogic activities:

Stage 1: Exploring perspectives/media literacy of 'access'/pedagogic activity of triangulation and synthesis

Stage 2: Critical review of examples/media literacy of 'analyse and evaluate'/ pedagogic activity of examination of data reliability

Stage 3: Production of research-based output/media literacy of 'create'/ pedagogic activity of writing and presenting a research paper
Stage 4: Review and feedback/media literacy of 'reflect'/pedagogic activity of documentation and critical review for the future
Stage 5: Disseminating research-based output/media literacy of 'act'/pedagogic activity of building ethical codes and accurate representation

The author followed the 'personal digital inquiry' approach given by Coiro et al. (2016) to address the research question through PBL, which involved collaboration, group discussion, exploration and reflection across a variety of PBL activities. This process may be compared with the PBL processes followed in media policy analysis in the four case studies presented in Chapters 4 to 7.

Project-Based Learning

It is essential to develop skills and competencies that can facilitate students and teachers to see beyond the classroom discourse (theory and application) and relate to and apply in the larger local and global contexts. An array of skills and competencies join together to be classified as twenty-first–century skills (P21 2007; 2011):

- Twenty-first–century subject skills
- Learning and innovation skills (critical thinking, communication, collaboration, creativity)
- Information, media and technology skills
- Life and career skills

In a brief but succinct articulation, Geisinger (2016) categorised the skills into four sets: cognitive skills, intrapersonal skills, interpersonal skills and technical skills, which are cast against three dimensions of information, communication, ethics and social impact. A comprehensive listing of twenty-one skills, along with student activities and cases, given by Kaufman (2013), shall be handy to the media educators. In the P21 framework, all of these skills are organised across curriculum and instruction, learning environments, standards and assessment, and professional development (Panda 2021). A constructivist, inquiry-based, project- and portfolio-based learning encompasses all these four organisational dimensions, and, therefore, professional development of media educators needs to be grounded across these four dimensions insofar as professionalism is concerned, though continuous professionalisation through professional learning takes place across a variety of professional sites, processes, products and reflections.

As has been discussed in the second chapter, PBL is a method of teaching-learning based on the constructivist formulation of learning theories and addresses more of contextual, inquiry-based and reflective learning. For the effectiveness of PBL, it should be integrated with the curriculum, the transaction of which facilitates students to apply knowledge into practical contexts to develop deeper and meaningful learning. Mergendoller et al. (2006) underline three theoretical roots for PBL: (i) the articulation by the American educator John Dewey on the constructivist use of intellectual and practical problems towards inquiry-based and problem-solving teaching-learning, (ii) the cognitivist-constructivist learning theory tradition, which emphasises on concrete (rather than abstract) learning through existing practical problems and/or anticipated future problems for deeper and sustainable learning and (iii) the teaching-learning tradition of medical education (e.g., McMaster University in Canada and Maastricht University in the Netherlands), which extensively uses problem-based and project-based learning for real-world health education. The origin of PBL is traced to the American teacher Killpatrick, who emphasised whole-hearted learning by doing based on individual choice (Graff and Kolmos 2007). PBL includes both cooperative learning (motivation and organisation) and collaborative learning (cognitive processes).

PBL as a method may include research surveys, discussions, community surveys, brainstorming, policy analyses and analysis of relevant related literature. Teachers and students may engage in an individual or collaborative setting, charged with professional learning tasks and environments (tech4learning.com). There is a stress on student-focused learning environments; engaging in group dynamics across peer diversity and peer coaching; engaging in collaborative learning with individual control over their learning and undertaking a variety of assessment tasks to ensure higher-order reflective learning. While the learning outcomes define what needs to be achieved, the project tasks demonstrate the process of engagement and achievement of the learning objectives/outcomes. Authentic tasks and authentic assessment ensure the development of competencies of collaboration, problem-solving, creativity and innovation. Examples of learning outcomes, learning processes, performances and assessment rubric for media policy and governance are explained in detail in the four case studies presented in Chapters 4 to 7.

PBL, which involves real-world contexts, multiple perspectives, complex tasks, collaborative engagement in authentic tasks, interdisciplinary knowledge, authentic assessment and multi-outcomes, does have a significant impact on student learning in terms of increase in the understanding of real-world contexts and problems, analytical and critical thinking abilities, and graduate professionalism and professional practice (in terms of enhancement in research, problem-solving, teamwork, responsibility and allied competencies). Extending this formulation, Sindre et al. (2018) paraphrased effective PBL characteristics in terms of effective: context of teaching, range of implementation, context of learning, institutional context, personnel involvement and assessment rubric, which teachers and educators need to design and develop competencies for. In a recent review of research, Guo et al. (2020) reported a significant positive impact of PBL on higher education students in respect of cognitive outcomes (cognitive strategies), affective outcomes, behavioural outcomes (skills) and artefact performance (creation of tangible artefacts), and that PBL engages students in the active construction of knowledge while developing real-world products (Krajcik and Shin 2014).

Scholarship of Teaching and Learning

In pursuance of quality in teaching and learning in our professional practice, we the teachers have generally stressed curriculum design, rather than on pedagogy, across disciplines. During the early present century, two dominant considerations have emerged—one concerns learners in the term of 'twenty-first–century learning' and the other concerns teachers in the term of 'scholarly teaching'. These are also globally visible in colleges and universities in media studies education. Scholarly teaching, which also guides how professional development and professional learning will take place, involves the practices of the discipline as well as the knowledge base and research in teaching-learning in the discipline. Invariably, there is stress on discipline research over discipline teaching. Of late, it has been articulated by scholars that discipline teaching and researching discipline pedagogy is as valuable as discipline research. The pedagogic practise, therefore, has moved from stressing 'teaching' to stressing 'learning', and pursuing discipline pedagogy research is as essential as pursuing discipline research.

Any professional development formulation must consider professional reflective practice in discipline pedagogy and research in discipline teaching across a lifelong 'professional learning' trajectory. In the teaching profession, professionalism is as important as professionalisation in the field. Strong professionalism (through initial training and professional development) is limited in vision and operation unless it is taken forward through the professional learning pathways towards strong professionalisation. Professional learning, and therefore professionalisation, ensures effective engagement in professional practice, which is contextualised, based on innovative practices and outcomes and related to professional standards of a professional organisation(s) and concerned discipline regulator(s). Elsewhere, the author writes, 'While a formal professional development provision may ensure mundane and essential innovations in curriculum design and teaching-learning (including assessment), a wider professional learning formulation attempts to bridge research-policy-practice gap' (Panda 2018, 133). Therefore, any professional development formulation needs to go beyond the one-shot provisions such as 'orientation programmes', 'refresher courses' of university human resource development centres and university ARPIT programmes to a wider, flexible and lifelong formulation to consider a variety of scholarships happening at various levels, as also to contribute to sustained professional growth.

Continuing Professional Development

So far, professional training and professional development have been the forte of the university staff colleges/human resource development centres, with occasional interventions and contributions from concerned professional organisations. In the field of media studies and media education, the same provision exists, with little intervention from professional organisations that have come up very recently; for instance, International Telecommunications Union and All India Communication and Media Association (AICMA).

Continuing professional development needs to be viewed as a personal process of development and growth in a personal development trajectory and, therefore, must provide for diversity, flexibility, personal choice and personalisation. It could be credit-based and resource-based pursuance of professional growth and development (Figure 8.1).

Figure 8.1: A Generic CPD Framework for Higher Education

Source: Author

The formulation derives largely from the historical phases of teacher professionalism articulated by Hargreaves (2000): pre-professional, autonomous professional, collegial professional and post-professional. The last two phases are critical in a professional learning formulation. In the case of collegial professionalism, there is a prevalence of a culture of collaboration, and the teacher responds positively to changes and reforms that are complex and uncertain. In the case of post-professionalism, the teacher undertakes conflict resolution between de-professionalising and redefining professional learning in a flexible, diverse and inclusive manner.

The ASCs and HRDCs have been successful insofar as the initial intervention of professional training is concerned, though the programmes have been generic, non-continuous and have not delved deep into discipline pedagogy and researching discipline pedagogy. Moreover, the academic performance indicator (API) system also does not recognise such a formulation. There is also a need to situate theory in praxis, based on individual needs and choices (though within a professional learning boundary with possibilities of cross-discipline dialogue). Lack of self-engagement in practice also leads to the absence of practical engagement of students in context. The formulation of a long-term professional learning trajectory as outlined in Figure 8.1 requires at its foundation the belief and commitment of an institution as a lifelong learning organisation.

The professional development trajectory is based on certain premises:

- Professional development needs to be viewed within a larger formulation of 'professional learning'.
- A teacher's workload needs to be balanced between teaching and research, and therefore discipline pedagogy and research in discipline pedagogy.
- Insofaras teaching is concerned, there should be a prevalence of, and it should be based on, the 'scholarship of teaching and learning'.
- Research and publications relating to discipline pedagogy should be equally viewed with discipline research and publications, including considerations/weightage in the API.
- The CPD pathway needs to be viewed within a need-based, flexible and modular trajectory. It should be credit-based, resource-based, blended, flexible, interdisciplinary and grounded in practice. The formulation must address the need-competency-identity triad.
- There should be a balance between individual scholarship, professional ethics and institutional and social action.
- Any CPD formulation and intervention needs to be linked (besides personal growth) to evidence-based teaching-learning, institutional quality assurance and accreditation.
- Such a formulation can work better when there are both national and institutional policies on continuing professional learning in the teaching profession.

The implementation of such professional learning/development programmes needs to recognise complex pathways towards experiential, transparent and evidence-based individual and collaborative engagement of teachers in teaching, learning, research and community development. This, though, does not preclude the existing orientation and refresher training; it rather builds on them to a larger formulation of self-learning, institutional intervention and collaborative engagement. This requires a professional learning network, professional development of credit-based resources (offline as well as digital/online), professional development centres (extending the existing Human Resource Development Centres and Teaching-Learning Centres), comprehensive database (needs, competencies, specialisations, achievements, scholarship of teaching-learning, research, among others) and professional learning bank of credits (PLBC) and credit accumulation and accreditation. This needs to be linked to evidence-based teaching, teaching-learning portfolios, and discipline research and publications within the institutional internal quality assurance database.

In media education and media studies, continuing professional development of educators could be contextualised within a professional learning formulation as outlined here, which is blended, and provides for individual choice-based CPD pathway. Pedagogy is the heart of such an exercise, and PBL subsumes such pedagogic professional learning. In this context, the engagement of professional associations like AICMA assumes significance.

References

Coiro, J., J. Castele, and D. Quinn. 'Personal Inquiry and Online Research.' *The Reading Teacher* 69 (2016): 483–492.

Friesem, Y. 'Teaching Truth, Lies, and Accuracy in the Digital Age: Media Literacy as Project-based Learning.' *Journalism & Mass Communication Educator* 74, no. 2 (2019): 1–14

Geisinger, K.F. '21st Century Skills: What Are They and How Do We Assess Them?' *Applied Measurement in Education* 29, no. 4 (2016): 245–249.

Graff, E.D. and A. Kolmos. 'History of Problem-based and Project-based Learning.' In *Management of Change*, edited by Erik Graff and Anette Kolmos, 1–8. Rotterdam: Sense Publishers, 2007.

Guo, P., et al. 'A Review of Project-based Learning in Higher Education: Student Outcomes and Measures.' *International Journal of Educational Research* 102 (2020): 1–13.

Hargreaves, A. 'Four Ages of Professionalism and Professional Learning.' *Teachers and Teaching: History and Practice* 6, no. 2 (2000): 151–182.

Hinchliffe, H. 'Education or Pedagogy?' *Journal of Philosophy of Education* 35 (2001): 31–45.

Kansanen, P.J. 'Studying the Realistic Bridge between Instruction and Learning: An Attempt to a Conceptual Whole of the Teaching-Studying-Learning Process.' *Educational Studies* 29, no. 2/3 (2003): 221–232.

Kaufman, K.J. '21 Ways to 21st Century Skills: Why Students Need Them and Ideas for Practical Implementation.' *Kappa Delta Pi Record*, April–June (2013): 78–83.

Krajcik, J.S. and N. Shin. 'Project-based Learning.' In *The Cambridge Handbook of the Learning Sciences*, edited by R.K. Sawyer, 275–297. New York: Cambridge University Press, 2014.

Lou, Y. and S.K. MacGregor. 'Enhancing Project-based Learning through Online Between-Group Collaboration.' *Educational Research and Evaluation* 10, no. 4–6 (2004): 419–440.

Mergendoller, J., et al. 'Pervasive Management of Project-based Learning: Teachers as Guides and Facilitators.' In *Handbook of Classroom Management: Research, Practical and Contemporary Issues*, edited by C.M. Evertson and C.S. Weinstein. London: Routledge, 2006.

P21. *Framework for 21st Century Learning*. Washington, DC: Partnership for 21st Century Learning, 2007; 2011.

Panda, S. 'NEP 2020 and Reflections on Curriculum and Pedagogy in Higher Education.' In *National Education Policy 2020: Issues, Challenges, and Reflections*, edited by R.P. Das and S. Panda, 102–127. New Delhi: Indira Gandhi National Open University, 2021.

Panda, S. 'Professional Development of Teachers in Higher Education.' In *India Higher Education Report 2017: Teaching, Learning and Quality in Higher Education*, edited by N.V. Varghese, A. Pachauri and S. Mandal, 132–164. New Delhi and London: SAGE, 2018.

Sindre, G., et al. 'Project-based Learning in IT Education: Definitions and Qualities.' *Uniped* 41 (2018): 147–163.

Westbrook, N. 'Media Literacy Pedagogy: Critical and New Twenty-First–Century Literacies Instruction.' *E-Learning and Digital Media* 9, no. 2 (2011): 154–164.

9

The Future of Pedagogy and Technology in Media Education

Biswajit Das

Introduction

In the earlier chapters, we discussed media policy and governance, including the curriculum and learning design issues (Chapter 1). The second chapter exclusively dealt with the discourses and pedagogical practices and their implications on teaching-learning strategies regarding project-based learning (PBL). It also highlighted the emerging issues, challenges and need for learning in the twenty-first century. It was followed by a discussion on learning design and curriculum for media policy and governance. Moving forward, we discussed institutionalisation and disciplinary contours and the educational implications of media studies in Indian academia (Chapter 3). The next four chapters (Chapters 4 to 7) demonstrated PBL on various media policy and governance themes. And Chapter 8 provided a formulation on continuing professional learning and professional development of media educators.

This concluding chapter highlights the future of media education in India with specific reference to pedagogy and changing forms of technologies in education in contemporary times. It may be addressed in two contrasting scenarios of growth and trajectory of higher education in India. The first refers to the growing enthusiasm among Indian policymakers to initiate innovations in pedagogy and learning to meet the challenges of internationalising higher education and ensure standard and compatibility globally. The second stems from the lack of resources, skilled human power and relevant infrastructure in Indian institutions of higher learning. Astute policymakers have realised that technology can triumph over the present malaise by catalysing innovative pedagogy and curricular exercises through flexible learning and addressing the crisis in trained workforce and infrastructure. While acknowledging such potential technologies in higher education, policymakers have not adequately provided a pathway to integrate and blend innovations with the existing institutionalised forms of pedagogy and conventional learning environments. Before any suggestive measures could be taken in this regard, the pandemic outbreak in 2020 added to the anxieties already prevalent in teaching and learning of higher education in India.

Technology and Media

Since the start of the Covid-19 pandemic, educational institutions have witnessed a shift from conventional classroom teaching to online teaching with the help of technology. The Indian academia got caught in panic and chaos during the shift from the physical to the virtual mode of learning. While policymakers were unclear amid copious committee reports that provided mixed reactions to online teaching and learning, the problem accentuated further. The question was how to replicate the interactive classroom experience of teaching and learning online? As Bagga-Gupta et al. (2019) point out, this distinction as 'physical-virtual, digital-analogue, online-offline and the myriad other ways of describing contemporary lives need to be recognized. It is not one or the other—there is a continuum and permeability between these (apparent) dichotomies, in and across spaces and arenas.' Buckingham (2007) highlights that digital technology offers significant challenges and opportunities for media educators. The past decades have witnessed massive investment in information and communication technology in the education sector (Buckingham 2007, 111). Various kinds of new technologies have made entry into the classroom with a new 'smart look' to the earlier classroom space where the remnants of old and hazy blackboards are languishing and awaiting repair and treatment. But the recent entry of technology has converted these spaces to 'smart classrooms'. While it may have been an administrative requirement to justify the number of smart rooms in educational institutions, it is too early to judge and make a correlation between access and use of these technologies and the purpose for which these are used and the outcome of such use. Throughout these discussions, the role of the teacher is conspicuously silent, which has made technology the prime mover of transformation in the education sector. This view presents a deterministic outlook, and its failure has been well documented (Cuban 1986). However, one needs to move ahead with the constructive potential of these technologies. As Buckingham (2007) highlights:

> Media education offers a clear and rigorous conceptual framework that can be extended across the range of media and that goes well beyond the instrumental approach of ICT training. Best practice in media education involves a combination of "hands-on" creative production and critical reflection which seeks to build on students' existing pleasures and experiences of media. (2007, 112)

The recognition of ICT opens up various queries and implications for our engagement with future modes of learning in the twenty-first century. Bagga-Gupta et al. (2019) highlight the nature of technologically infused contemporary human existence that may be marked with distinct phases such as connectivity, access to information, internet-enabled technologies to create content and, finally, AI-supported technologies. This shift may be framed as 'web of things' to 'web of thoughts', dealing with the dimensional aspect of learnings such as what, where, when, why and how. Online education offers promise but not without problems. These problems are structural, cultural and technological. Besides, Miège (2008) says,

> Communication science researchers have confined themselves to applying analytical frameworks borrowed from the study of the mass media, in that they focus their research on the relationship with the means of communication in what amounts therefore to a media-centred approach. The fact that ICT is more interactive than the 'traditional' media has not altered this perspective, which we deem to be media-centric. (118)

Before we engage with these contested issues, let us glance at the status of media education in India. As discussed in Chapter 3, we realise that questions on teaching and learning have been largely neglected, which resulted in a state of confusion and misunderstanding between theory and practice in media education. This structural tension has been held together by the persistent belief that media education is a core institution of democracy. Even though it is taught in a vocational manner, it constitutes a relevant field of study at the university level. This distinction is blurred, and it adds confusion to the ongoing difference between media education and educational media. As educational media has a variegated history starting from audiovisual aids to the use of ICT in the curriculum of media education, these aids remained as peripheral and, at best, tools for media education. These tools may help in increasing efficiency. However, its monolithic, bureaucratic and therapeutic imperatives may not be undermined. It may address the problems but certainly not the roots, which are social and related to the lived experiences of teachers and students (Selwyn 2011, 33). Technology enthusiasts highlight the possibility of cognitivist, constructivist and socio-cultural theories of learning and technology in media education. Still, these claims are based on supposition, beliefs and conjecture due to a lack of conclusive evidence based on credible empirical reasoning and research (Selwyn 2011, 86). Students in the classroom space are continuously texting, sending emails, checking Facebook, verifying the sources and references provided by the teachers. The internet and the web have made them accessible to specialised knowledge that would not have been possible by print and face-to-face interaction. The information through the internet and web no doubt created a precondition of knowledge, but not knowledge per se. The language, vocabularies, discourse and means of expression acquired through these technologies enable certain meanings at the cost of excluding ideas acquired through socialisation and collective cultural expression (Schmidt 2008, 101).

The past decades have witnessed the gradual entry of 'instructional media', 'multimedia' and 'smart classroom' into the existing classroom space to encourage teachers to use these technologies for instructional purposes. It also includes the use of e-courses, MOOCs, simulation games and computer-supported presentation in the classroom. Teachers are in a quandary about whether and how to move from their traditional role to embrace technology in multiple ways for educational purposes. Before this dilemma is resolved, already, media ecologists across the world have started inaugurating the success of media technology's inroads into the citadels of education with a commentary on school as a custodian of print culture (McLuhan 1962, 215). Postman (1982, 42) goes one step ahead by sealing the school's fate based on dependence on the printed word as he views school as an invention of the printing press. Changes occurred along with the introduction of radio, television and, finally, new media technology. McLuhan terms it as 'baffling' with customs and values for a child between two worlds (McLuhan 1995, 222). Lynch (2002) views it as the end of school as an institution. Scholars (Kellner and Share 2005, 2007; Kellner 2001) defensive of the school project opine that it is not the demise of school; instead, it is the proliferation of technologies by form and culture that initiates a kind of media literacy in the school. They plead for multiple literacies, assuming that new technologies are changing every aspect of our society and culture; hence, the need to comprehend and use them to transform the world.

Further, they argue that the changing global economy requires different skill sets. It may not be achieved within the existing arrangements for technology in education. As highlighted, the current system takes recourse to submission to authority, rote memorisation and the banking concept of education as propounded by Freire (1970). As Kellner (2004) says, 'Intense pressures for change now come directly from technology and the economy and not ideology or educational reformist ideas, with a new global economy and new technologies demanding new skills, competencies, literacies, and practices' (11). Although change is highlighted, one is not clear about its outcome and purpose. Thus, media literacy has become a saleable proposition over the past decades by scholars as a new paradigm extended to study visuals, multimedia and digital technology, et cetera (Burn and Durran 2007; Elkins 2008; Hobbs 1998; Hobbs and Jensen 2009; Jewitt 2008; Kist 2005; Potter 2011; Rivoltella 2008; Tyner 2010; Williams and Zenger 2012). Despite an emerging consensus on literacy in media, the potential of literacy is not much explored. For instance, Graff (1987) critiques in his 'myth of literacy' that it is more than a set of skills and orientation, and he delinked from

> the constellation of social, political and economic practices precisely because, when reduced to a set of skills, it is something that can be affected by the school system, one of the most powerful and far-reaching social institutions of modern societies. Outcomes can be measured and a wide array of objectives sought after, if never actually met. (Druick 2016, 1127)

Moreover, such arguments register the use of media in education and maintain a conspicuous silence about how can 'pedagogy work with the media'.

Pedagogy and Media

Any discussion on pedagogy and media ensures that it needs to be engaged with media education from an educational perspective. By 'educational perspective' we are referring to teaching and learning about media education. However, this may not be dissociated from questions about knowledge in media education in India. As a field of inquiry, media education is a relatively young field in India. The potential is immense and it allows us to empower students by inculcating critical faculty and the ability to think, decode and analyse. Besides, the dominant models before us are mostly Western, especially from English-speaking countries (Cheung 2009). On the contrary, the issues of teaching and learning have been largely neglected and have perhaps resulted in confusion and misunderstanding between theory and practice in media education in India.

In contemporary times, media schools do more than train students for the media industry workforce. There are layers of media schools with different purposes and interests depending upon the nature of funding of these institutions. Invariably, the pedagogical philosophy of the majority of these institutions has been 'learning by doing' and the standards employed have been those of the mainstream media industry's. However, not all media schools have engaged with similar practices, nor do they care about the social need of media for a vibrant democratic society. Before we settle this unresolved issue in media education, our experiences about literature on pedagogy reveal that it has different connotations and purposes, subject to use. It has received equally critical scrutiny due to its political and liberating potential in society, hence in the academic institutions (Freire 1970; Illich 1971). Even though much discussion is in the air in social sciences and education curriculum about engaging with various models of pedagogies and alternative pedagogies, critical pedagogies and radical pedagogies, these are confined to individual teachers' effort to engage with the mode of delivery within the subject. These efforts have not made much headway in the overall teaching and learning system in Indian higher education. These institutions are focused on a subject-centred curriculum devoid of any progressive education to bridge the gap in social inequality, both within the society and the classroom.

Our concern is not to explore and identify the reasons. The scope of our work does not address these concerns. Our concern in this volume is to address what we teach, how we teach, how we connect with the curriculum and, finally, how educational media tool is used judiciously for engagements and for executing hands-on assignments creatively. Pedagogy is the root where design is experimented with and practised. The recent 'National Education Policy 2020'

(Panda 2021) emphasises evidence-based teaching. It has created bewilderment and anxiety in academia. Conventionally, academia was focused on curriculum, and the teachers had the freedom to choose the mode of delivery to attain the goal of the curriculum. Rarely did anyone question the means and methods used to reach the goal of the curriculum. The idea of evidence-based teaching emphasises documentation of various pedagogies used in teaching and learning. We have, in this book, showcased the application of evidence-based teaching and learning strategies in media and communication studies. It has translated theoretical and abstract ideas and knowledge in light of new academic developments and effective learning and teaching designs that can be taken up in any classroom setting and applied to any curriculum in higher and further education.

Practising educators of media education and new media studies in Chapters 4 to 7 have authentically reported on work-based projects as pedagogy as well as teaching and learning practice for transacting curriculum at the master's level. They have demonstrated how pedagogic interventions could ease out learners and instructors to make teaching and learning handy and engaging. The present work (see Chapters 4 to 7) underlines PBL as good practices in teaching media policy and delivering practical experiences to students in discerning policy formulations, their foundations, shifts and challenges.

We realise that the discussion on media and pedagogy must engage critically with (a) educational media, (b) the theory of media education and (c) media socialisation (Qvortrop 2007). As Qvortrop (2007) highlights, three things may happen when we combine media with pedagogy. It may connote a particular kind of teaching and learning like in other allied disciplines; another possibility is a type of educational theory related to socialisation; and finally, the use and role of media in education (Qvortrop 2007, 2). These three factors may not be exclusive but overlapping, which constitutes media pedagogy.

As we discussed earlier, media education has double disadvantages. It makes the teachers teach and encourage the students to learn about media while at the same time discouraging them from being vulnerable to influences of media-related messages. Conventional media-education courses comprise critical analysis, aesthetics and mastering the tools of media in producing statements. As Qvortrop (2007) notes,

> Media pedagogy includes three basic elements: First, it includes a theory of media education, i.e., a theory of the way in which one can teach the pupils

> and students to use media, and how one can teach them about media as a phenomenon in society. Second, it includes a theory of education within the context of "media-socialisation", i.e., within the context that mass media represent a special aspect of socialisation in relation to the pupils. Third, it includes a theory of educational media. (17)

However, the discussion on media education underscores the role of the teacher and teaching as communicative. All teaching is mediated. This mediation occurs not only between teachers and students but also between students and the subject and teachers and the subject. When teachers teach in the classroom, they use various skills such as language and kinesthetics that deal with bodily signs to express ideas. These ideas are very much commonly agreed upon and encoded in society. The teachers are not only making an effort to share ideas; they are equally watching other people's expressions and convictions through the same set of signs. These signs are based on mutual agreement on certain codes in society, which are specific to class and the culture of upbringing and socialisation. Luhmann (1986) says, 'Teaching is a specialized expression of the general improbability that systems understand system' (48). Here Luhman refers to both teachers and students as two separate and distinct closed systems operating in the classroom. Due to their distinctiveness, most of the interactions between teachers and students may not be uniform, subject to what the students see and understand. Still, the teacher cannot understand what the student sees and why he or she reacts in a particular manner. No matter how the teacher teaches and demonstrates with all available gestures to convince the students, it is difficult to know whether the student understands or not. Here, media or communication is used to make the improbable as probable with the help of mediated effect. Hence, all communication is mediated. Finally, since all teaching is reflexive, both teachers and students observe each other, and their actions are governed by 'instructions'. Qvortrop (2008) calls it the dramaturgic media, where teaching becomes acting with the help of blackboard, chalk/marker, podium and overhead projector, et cetera.

Conclusion

Media Policy and Governance is an interdisciplinary curriculum that is geared towards a critical intervention in problem-posing, which opens up a space for discussion and development of experiential learning through projects that encourages students to blend theory and practice in media education. This approach is antithetical to conventional teaching practices that view students as empty vessels waiting to be filled with information by a teacher. It encouraged students to relate to their histories, experiences, perspectives, ideas and critiques, thereby creating a diversity from which educators could learn and become empowered. It has helped in the capacity of learning as well as the ability to refine learning. Our experiences with such an exercise show that it helps in bridging the hierarchy between teachers and students. The templates provided by the teacher, both tangible and intangible for students, help students in learning and developing critical thinking, research, writing and life skills. They help in demystifying alien theoretical repositories and exploring a praxis-oriented understanding where both theory and practice converge. Thus, the classroom practice may be extremely enlightening to engage with new theoretical insights and challenges.

Media education has tremendous potential, but this potential may not be confined to the mere acquisition of technology in the classroom. Instead, the classroom space has to be reinvigorated as an important and differentiated form of knowledge collectively owned by students and teachers.

References

Bagga-Gupta, Sangeeta, Giulia Messina Dahlberg, and Ylva Lindberg, eds. *Virtual Sites as Learning Spaces: Critical Issues on Languaging Research in Changing Eduscapes.* Switzerland: Springer Nature, 2019.

Buckingham, David. 'Media Education Goes Digital: An Introduction.' *Learning, Media and Technology* 32, no. 2 (2007): 111–119.

———. *Media Education Literacy: Learning and Contemporary Culture.* London: Polity Press, 2003.

Burn, Andrew and James Durran. *Media Literacy in Schools: Practice, Production and Progression.* London: SAGE, 2007.

Cheung, Chi-Kim, ed. *Media Education in Asia.* Singapore: Springer Science & Business Media, 2009.

Cuban, Larry. *Teachers and Machines: The Classroom Use of Technology since 1920.* Colombia: Teachers College Press, 1986.

Druick, Zoë. 'The Myth of Media Literacy.' *International Journal of Communication*, 10 (2016): 1125–1144.

Elkins, James, ed. *Visual Literacy.* London: Routledge, 2008.

Freire, Paulo. *Pedagogy of the Oppressed.* New York: The Continuum International Publishing Group, 1970.

Graff, Harvey J. *The Labyrinths of Literacy: Reflections on Literacy Past and Present.* London: Psychology Press, 1987.

Hobbs, R. 'The Seven Great Debates in Media Literacy Movement.' *Journal of Communication* 48, no. 1 (1998): 16–32.

Hobbs, R. and A. Jensen. 'The Past, Present and Future of Media Literacy Education.' *Journal of Media Literacy Education* 1 (2009): 1–11.

Hrachovec, Herbert and Alois Pichler. *Philosophy of the Information Society.* Frankfurt: Ontos Verlag, 2008.

Illich, Ivan. *Deschooling Society.* New York: Harper & Row, 1971.

Jewitt, C. 'Multimodality and Literacy in School Classroom.' *Review of Research in Education* 32 (2008): 241–267.

Kellner, D. and J. Share. 'Critical Media Literacy and the Reconstruction of Education.' In *Media Literacy: A Reader*, edited by D. Macedo and S.R. Steinberg, 3–23. New York: Peter Lang, 2007.

———. 'Toward Critical Media Literacy: Core Concepts, Debates, Organizations, and Policy.' *Discourse: Studies in the Cultural Politics of Education* 26, no. 3 (2005): 369–386.

Kellner, D. 'Technological Transformation, Multiple Literacies, and the Re-Visioning of Education.' *E-learning and Digital Media* 1, no. 1 (2004): 9–37.

———. 'New Technologies/New Literacies: Reconstructing Education for the New Millennium.' *International Journal of Technology and Design Education* 11, no. 1 (2001): 67–81.

Kist, William. *New Literacies in Action: Teaching and Learning in Multiple Media*, vol. 75. New York: Teachers College Press, 2005.

Luhmann, Niklas. 'Systeme Verstehen Systeme.' *Zwischen Intransparenz und Verstehen. Fragen an die Pädagogik* (1986): 72–117.

Lynch, Julianne. 'What Can We Learn from McLuhan? Electronic Communication Technologies and the Future of Schooling.' In *AARE 2002: Problematic Futures: Educational Research in an Era of Uncertainty*. AARE 2002 Conference Papers, 1–16. Australian Association for Research in Education, 2002.

McLuhan, Eric and Frank Zingrone. *Essential McLuhan*. London: Routledge, 1997.

McLuhan, Marshall. 'Address at Vision 65'. In *The Essential McLuhan*, edited by F. Zingrone and E. McLuhan. New York: Basic Books, 1995.

———. *The Gutenberg Galaxy: The Making of Typographic Man*. Toronto: University of Toronto Press, 1962

Miège, Bernard. 'For a Communications Approach to the Use of ICT in Education.' *Convergence and Fragmentation: Media Technology and the Information Society* 5 (2008): 117–130.

Panda, S. 'Indian National Education Policy 2020: Teacher Education as Part of University System and Stand-alone Institutions.' *Journal of Indian Institute of Public Administration* (Odisha) 27 (2021): 306–323.

Postman, N. *The Disappearance of Childhood*. New York: Random House, 1982.

Potter, W.J. *Media Literacy*. Los Angeles, CA: SAGE, 2011.

Qvortrop, L. 'E-learning: A Knowledge Theoretical Approach.' In *Convergence and Fragmentation: Media Technology and the Information Society*, edited by Peter Ludes, 131–151. London: Intellect Books, 2008.

———. 'Media Pedagogy: Media Education, Media Socialisation and Educational Media.' *Seminar.net* 3, no. 2 (2007).

Rivoltella, Pier Cesare, ed. *Digital Literacy: Tools and Methodologies for Information Society*. Hershey, PA: IGI Global, 2008.

Rotella, C. 'No Child Left Untableted.' *New York Times Magazine*, 26 (2013).

Schmidt, S.J. and Münster. 'Media Philosophy: A Reasonable Programme?' In *Philosophy of the Information Society*, edited by H. Hrachovec and A. Pichler, 89–105. Frankfurt:

Ontos Verlag, 2008. (Proceedings of the 30th International Ludwig Wittgenstein Symposium, Kirchberg am Wechsel, Austria, 2007.)

Selwyn, N. *Education and Technology: Key Issues and Debates*. London and New York: The Continuum International Publishing Group, 2011.

Tyner, Kathleen, ed. *Media Literacy: New Agendas in Communication*. New York: Routledge, 2010.

Williams, Bronwyn and Amy A. Zenger, eds. *New Media Literacies and Participatory Popular Culture Across Borders*. New York: Routledge, 2012.

Glossary

Jesna Jayachandran

Conditional access (CA)

Protection of content by encryption. CA is part of the subscriber management system (SMS) to block usage by non-subscribers. It is used in both analogue and digital systems and on all three platforms (cable, satellite and terrestrial).

Convergence

Coming together or interlocking of information technology (computing) companies, telecommunication networks and content providers (publishing, newspapers, magazines, music, radio, television, films and entertainment software). Media convergence brings together computing, communications and content.

Digital dividend

Radio-frequency spectrum freed by the digital switchover.

Digital media

Media that communicate audio, video or text information in a digitised (instead of the traditional analogue) format. They include traditional analogue media outlets that have 'gone digital', e.g., TV and radio stations or newspaper web portals. Or they may be outlets that only exist on the internet, e.g., news websites, blogging sites, social media.

Digital multiplex (MUX)

The technical infrastructure for the terrestrial dissemination and bundling of digital programmes and additional services contained in a digital data stream. Access conditions to MUX for content providers, and also the regulation of MUX, vary widely from country to country.

Digital switchover

The process of upgrading broadcasting transmission infrastructure to carry digital rather than analogue signals. For the purposes of this project, digital switchover is considered to have commenced in June 2006, when the ITU's Regional Radiocommunications Conference (RRC-06) reached Regional Agreement GE06, establishing frequency plans for terrestrial digital broadcasting in the principal spectrum bands across Europe, Africa, the Middle East and Iran. Switchover is to be completed by 2015. In Africa, the digital switchover is planned to be completed in two phases, by 2020. However, so far only six African nations have completed the switchover process from analogue to digital. There is no firmly-agreed deadline for digital switchover in other parts of the world. This process refers to terrestrial infrastructure. In parallel, a process of digital switchover takes place in cable and satellite platforms.

Digital television broadcast standards

Technical specifications for broadcasting in a specific country. These include settings for various processes such as multiplexing, conditional access, audio, video and transmission channel coding, et cetera.

The list of such standards includes the DVB family (Europe), the ATSC family (North America), the ISDB family (Japan and parts of South America), the DMB family (Korean), and the Chinese digital video broadcasting standard family.

Digitalisation

The technological, regulatory and market changes that come about with the shift from analogue to digital media, including the internet. This shift takes place in three areas:

- The production of programmes/content where all production equipment (e.g., cameras, recorders, editing suites and archives) becomes digital, i.e., both hardware and software. This leads to a complete restructuring of the working processes of programme makers, e.g., journalists in newsrooms.
- The transmission systems (terrestrial, satellite and cable) delivering content to households. The term 'digital switchover' (DSO) has specifically to do with changing the terrestrial broadcast net from analogue to digital technology.
- The household equipment (radio, television, PCs, mobile devises, etc.) used by listeners, viewers and internet users, et cetera.

Although digitisation is basically a shift from analogue to digital technology, it has huge influence on the whole value chain, the media market, media policy and regulation, and on the way media are used by citizens.

Earnings per share (EPS)
Earnings per share or EPS are the amount that a shareholder obtains from the ownership of a firm's/company's share. More precisely, it is returns on per share that a shareholder receives for possessing or bearing a company's share.

Electronic programming guide (EPG)
A menu of programmes continuously updated to give users information about the programming schedules. It is usually associated with television.

Employee share ownership plan (ESOP)
An employee share ownership plan (ESOP) is the practice by which companies provide shares in their company as part of the salary to staff members. ESOP therefore permits employees to become owners in the shares of the company. Employee ownership in the company appears to increase production and profitability and also improve employees' dedication and sense of ownership.

Gatekeeping
Gatekeepers in the digital broadcast chain are those companies/entities in a position to control the 'admission' of consumers to specific programming. This important type of control over new functions in the chain (such as digital multiplexes, electronic programming guides, conditional access and subscriber management systems) will also determine the flow of funding.

Initial public offering (IPO)
An IPO, or initial public offering, is the sale of shares by a company to the public for the first time. Technically, it is when a company is 'going public'. Investors can apply in upcoming IPOs by filling an IPO application form. These forms are usually available with stock brokers for free. Investor can also apply in IPOs online through online stock brokers like ICICI Bank, Share Khan, et cetera.

Internet Protocol Television (IPTV)

Television services delivered by broadband internet instead of traditional terrestrial frequencies, satellite signal or cable television.

Licensing

Licensing is required for using resources and performing telecommunication activities, which includes providing services with certain guidelines that the licensees have to abide by, failing which they will not be eligible to get a license.

License defines the scope and limitations for using technologies and providing services, and typically requires payments to governments for the privileges associated with the license.

Mobile device

A handheld computing device with touch input or small keyboard and a display screen. Mobile devices include:

- Communication devices (mobile phones, pagers and cordless phones)
- Mobile computers (smartbooks, tablet PCs, handheld PCs, etc.)
- Media recorders (digital camcorders, cameras and audio recorders)
- Media players (e-book readers, portable DVD players, etc.)
- Personal navigation devices
- Handheld game consoles

Mobile platform

A mobile operating system controlling a mobile device. They are similar to the operating systems used on desktop computers and notebooks. Mobile platforms include iPhone OS, RIM's BlackBerry, Symbian OS, Palm WebOS, et cetera. This project will not analyse these systems, but it will look at news content carried by mobile devices.

New media

Electronic communication enabled by computer technology that is characterised by non-linearity (interactivity). These include websites, audio- and video-streaming, email, 'social media' (information-sharing, interactive/participatory websites, including blogs and wikis).

Platform

A platform is a system that delivers media contents. The main media platforms are: broadcasting, internet, mobile telephony. In television, 'platform' is used to describe the means of transmission (e.g., cable, satellite, terrestrial).

Profit after tax (PAT)

Profit after tax is obtained by deducting all the expenses (i.e., interest, salary, depreciation and tax, etc.) from the total revenue. PAT is also known as net profit of a firm/company.

$\pi = TR$ – all expenses
where π = profit of the firm, TR = total revenue

PAT can be fully retained by a firm/company for used in its business. However, dividend is paid to the shareholders from this residue.

Promoters and non-promoters groups

A promoter is one who has an overall control over the company and is authorised to take all decisions that could benefit the company in terms of increase in profit and future growth of the company. A promoter can be one person or more than one. For example, Anil Ambani and Mukesh Ambani are the main promoters of Reliance Group.

A group of promoters includes the immediate relatives of the promoters, for example, Tina Ambani, Nita Ambani and other relatives within the Ambani family hold Reliance Group shares.

1. **Classification of promoter(s)**

   Promoters are classified into two categories:

   (i) Indian Promoter(s)

   An Indian promoter is any individual or a company or companies who own the shares of the company and participate in the decision mechanism of the company actively. For example, RRPR is an Indian promoter of NDTV Ltd.

(ii) Foreign Promoter(s)

A foreign promoter includes any individual or a company or companies who own the shares of the company and participate in the decision mechanism of the company actively.

2. **Classification of non-promoter(s)**

Like promoter(s), non-promoter(s) also categorised into two categories:

(i) Institutional non-promoter(s)

Institutional non-promoter(s) includes all financial institutes that act as a financial resource to the company. The primary work of this institutional non-promoter(s) is to provide financial assistance to the company.

(ii) Non-institutional non-promoter(s)

This category includes all non-financial institutes. Like institutional non-promoter(s), they invest their money in the company but they do come under the financial institutions. For example, Ambience Advertising Ltd. is a non-institutional non-promoter of NDTV Ltd.

Subscription management system (SMS)

A combination of software and hardware aimed at organising and operating the operator's business. The system contains all relevant information about clients and keeps track of orders, credits, invoicing and payments.

Subsidy

'Unearned savings to offset production costs' are one of the oldest forms of financial tool through which governments pay companies, organisations or individuals to do (or not to do) some (un)desired form of activity.

User-generated content (UGC)

Various sorts of media content produced by users. UGC includes blogs, wikis, social networking sites, trip planners, customer review sites, photo and video sharing websites, discussion boards, et cetera.

White spaces

The unused electromagnetic spectrum between frequencies, usually used as protection bands against interference.

About the Editors and Contributors

Editors

Biswajit Das is a professor and founding director of the Centre for Culture, Media and Governance, Jamia Millia Islamia, New Delhi. He has over four decades of teaching and research experience in the field of theory, method and history of communication in India. Professor Das has been a visiting professor at York University (Toronto) and Kyung Hee University (South Korea) and a fellow at the University of Windsor (Canada), Maison des Sciences de l'Homme (Paris), Inalco (Paris), Charles Wallace Trust (London) and the Indian Institute of Advanced Studies (Shimla). His publications include *Media and Mediation* (2005), *The Social and the Symbolic* (2007), *Communication, Culture and Confrontation* (2010), *Media Pedagogy in Commonwealth Asia* (2016), *Gandhian Thought and Communication* (2020) and *Caste, Communication and Power* (2021). His latest book, *Seeing South Asia: Visuals beyond Borders* (2022), is being published by Routledge, London. Professor Das has published in and is an advisory board member of several national and international journals. He is also a member of the National Repository of Open Educational Resources, MHRD, and the coordinator of Centre with Potential for Excellence in Media and Communication Studies (2016–2021), Special Assistance Programme, UGC (2014–2019), SPARC (2020–2022) and headed UGC's MOOCs programme in media and communication studies as its project investigator (2016–2017), coordinating three hundred sixty modules and authoring thirty modules uploaded on UGC-INFLIBNET for postgraduate programme in media and communication studies. Currently, Professor Das is the president of All India Communication and Media Association. His email id is biswas.das@gmail.com.

Santosh Panda is a professor of distance education and a director at the Staff Training and Research Institute, Indira Gandhi National Open University (IGNOU), New Delhi. Besides PhD, he has a certificate in education television from the BBC, UK, and a certificate in online teaching from the University of Maryland, USA. He started teaching in 1984 at Kurukshetra University, and to date he has thirty-seven years of teaching, research and administrative experience at universities. In the past, he has been the chairperson of the National Council for Teacher Education, a statutory national regulator of the Government of India; a Fulbright senior scholar at the University of New Mexico, Albuquerque, USA; the director of Association of Indian Universities (AIU), Delhi, and Centre for Flexible and Distance Learning, University of South Pacific, Fiji; the founding director of Inter-University Consortium for ICT, IGNOU, New Delhi, India. He was a visiting professor at the University of London, UK; Manchester Metropolitan University, UK; University of New Mexico, USA; Beijing Normal University, China, and University of Guadalajara, Mexico, and an adjunct professor at the University of Maryland, USA. Dr Panda has presented keynote addresses and conference papers, as well as conducted pre-conference and conference workshops, in more than twenty-five countries; he has also presented convocation addresses at five universities. He has published forty-eight papers in refereed international journals, forty-four book chapters, nineteen books and thirty-four conference papers. His latest books include *Technology-Enabled Learning: Policy, Pedagogy and Practice* (2020), *Planning and Management in Distance Education* (2017), *Economics of Distance and Online Learning* (2008). His email id is spanda.ignou@gmail.com

Vibodh Parthasarathi maintains a multidisciplinary interest in media policy/business/history. Associate professor at the Centre for Culture, Media and Governance, Jamia Millia Islamia, New Delhi, he has held visiting positions at the University of Queensland, KU Leuven, University of Helsinki and Indian Institute of Technology Bombay. He has also been an affiliate researcher at SASNET (Lund University) and non-resident fellow at the Centre for Media, Data and Society (Central European University). Parthasarathi has been at the forefront of media policy research in India and a winner of numerous grants from leading international bodies, including the Ford Foundation, Canada's IDRC, Hivos and Social Science Research Council, besides India New Zealand Education Council steered by UGC. Within and beyond his varied scholarly collaborations, he is fascinated by questions of media regulation in the longue durée, experiences of digital transitions and media policy as a knowledge enterprise. Widely published in journals in his field, including *Digital Journalism, Media, Culture and Society* and *Journal of Digital Media and Policy*, he has also curated special issues on themes ranging from media modernity to the public sphere. Parthasarathi's co-edited books include *Media and Mediation* (2005), *The Social and the Symbolic* (2007) and *Communication, Culture and Confrontation* (2010), which were part of a triptych from SAGE; the critically acclaimed double-volume *The Indian Media Economy* (OUP, 2018) and *Platform Capitalism in India* (Palgrave/IAMCR, 2020). He has been invited to be the editor and advisor in book series at MIT Press and Oxford University Press and to the international editorial boards of journals such as the *Journal of Communication* (Oxford) and *Global Media and Communication* (SAGE). He is currently the associate editor of *Journal of Digital Media and Policy* (Intellect). His email id is vibodhp@yahoo.com.

Contributors

Nabeela Inayati is an independent researcher and former project staff at the Centre for Culture, Media and Governance, Jamia Millia Islamia, New Delhi.
Email: nabeelainayati@gmail.com

Jesna Jayachandran is an assistant professor of sociology at Guru Nanak Dev University, Amritsar, Punjab.
Email: jesna.sociology@gndu.ac.in

Athikho Kaisii is an assistant professor at the Centre for Culture, Media and Governance, Jamia Millia Islamia, New Delhi.
Email: akasmao@gmail.com

Prashant Kumar is a professor of economics at Satyawati Evening College, University of Delhi, New Delhi.
Email: prashant@satyawatie.du.ac.in

Pradosh Nath is the director of Centre for Knowledge, Ideas and Development Studies, Kolkata. He was formerly the chief scientist of NISTADS, New Delhi, and an ICSSR fellow at the Centre for Culture, Media and Governance, Jamia Millia Islamia, New Delhi.
Email: pradoshnath@gmail.com

Aradhana Sharma is an independent researcher and former project fellow at the Centre for Culture, Media and Governance, Jamia Millia Islamia, New Delhi.
Email: sharma.aradhana@gmail.com

Ritu Sinha is an assistant professor of sociology at Ambedkar University, Delhi, and a former visiting/adjunct faculty at the Centre for Culture, Media and Governance, Jamia Millia Islamia, New Delhi.
Email: ritusinha2000@gmail.com

Index